1/18/93

Happy BIRTHDAY!

May you CONTINUE
to go in wisdom, health &
Happiness wherever you
travel!

Real & I had several
WILD nights in Moscow —
he's NOT IN NY now to
sign it, so I will

Love

(friend of the Author)

GORBACHEV, YELTSIN

AND THE LAST DAYS
OF THE SOVIET EMPIRE

GORBACHEV, YELTSIN

AND THE LAST DAYS
OF THE SOVIET EMPIRE

•

BY
NEIL FELSHMAN

ST. MARTIN'S PRESS
NEW YORK

Design by Robert Bull

Library of Congress Cataloging-in-Publication Data
Felshman, Neil.
    Gorbachev, Yeltsin and the last days of the Soviet Empire / Neil Felshman.
        p. cm.
    "A Thomas Dunne book."
    ISBN 0-312-08200-2
    1. Soviet Union—Politics and government—1985-1991. 2. Gorbachev, Mikhail Sergeevich, 1931-   .
3. Yeltsin, Boris Nikolayevich, 1931-   . I. Title.
DK288.F446   1992
947'.085—dc20   92-24154
                                        CIP

First edition: October 1992

10 9 8 7 6 5 4 3 2 1

TO JOSLEEN WILSON,
MY FAVORITE WRITER

ACKNOWLEDGMENTS

Many thanks to friends and associates in the former Soviet Union who helped, particularly: Henry Borovik, Rama Vernon, Max Lafser, Eremy Parnov, Felix Burtashov, Yevgeny Simonov, Ludmilla Saraskina, Mikhail Roshchin, Sergei Serebriany, Mikhail Chiguir, Nora Grinberg, Edward Shornik, Sergei Barantsev, Joan Reed, Georgi Andjuparidze, Nika Shcherbakova, Lyudmila Teplovodskaya, Olga Skorobogatova, Anatoly Belyayev, Mark Minkov, Alexander Blokhin, Susan Hartman and, most important to this project, my friend and interpreter, Irina Bazhenova.

In the United States, I have had help from a number of people to whom I am ever grateful. For editorial and research assistance I owe a great deal to Cynthia Carpathios, Warren Liebesman, and Lynne Rogers, who did yeoman work.

I want to thank Tom Dunne, Reagan Arthur, and Patty Rosati at St. Martin's Press, and my agents Barbara Lowenstein and Madeleine Morel, who first suggested I undertake this book and encouraged me to keep going even as the world changed.

•

I owe a special debt of gratitude to Janet and Isaac Asimov who lent friendship, support, and encouragement throughout. I also want to thank my family—my mother, Jeff, Harriet and Dave Weistrop, and Susan and Paul Houtkooper.

Finally, thanks to supportive friends and colleagues: Stuart Geminder, Lorraine Melina, Donna Rama, Debra Sherline, Frank Pelly, Ed Chalfin, Stewart Halpern, Dan Hedges, Joe Doyle, Perry Bernstein, and Heather Sacco. And to intrepid companions in the Steppes, Ray Errol Fox and Lisa Sonne, *spacebo bolshoi*.

CONTENTS

GORBACHEV, YELTSIN

AND THE LAST DAYS
OF THE SOVIET EMPIRE

FOREWORD

•

THE POWER SHIFTS

•

Before we can begin to live in the present we must
atone for our past; we must break with it.
But such atonement can only be achieved by suffering,
only by tremendous, unremitting effort.
—Anton Chekhov, *The Cherry Orchard*

I'm one of the millions of people who owe a debt of gratitude
to Mikhail Gorbachev. The climate created by his policy of
glasnost (openness) in the late 1980s made it possible for me
to become a frequent and working visitor on cultural exchange projects in what was the Soviet Union.

In my travels to and around that fascinating country,
I've been lucky enough to meet and become good friends
with a number of people who have given me some insight
into their lives and the changes taking place in their land.

"Do you feel it?" a friend asked.

"What?"

"How it has changed since you were here last, six
months ago."

I had returned to the United States in July of 1990 after

1

about two months in the Soviet Union. Now, in February 1991, at the beginning of another two-month stay, friends asked if I could feel a new level of tension in the street. I felt little of it.

On a sunny early March Sunday morning I plunged into a huge crowd (the participants' estimate: 500,000; *New York Times* estimate: 100,000) gathered to cheer for Boris Yeltsin and boo Gorbachev in Manezh Square just outside the Kremlin wall. It was a pleasant day, warm in the sun, although the air was cool. The crowd was constantly shifting as people sidled and pushed their way around. But there was no pushing back, just good-humored courtesy (rare in Moscow queues), shouting support for Yeltsin; a carnival atmosphere.

Late the next evening, my friend and I were walking along downtown Hertzen Street behind three shuffling babushkas. One of the old ladies turned to the window of a grocery store, where a dim light shone from the back. She shook her fist and shouted at the store, "You rascals! You've got food in there and you're keeping it for yourselves!" She walked on a little with her friends and then stopped again and turned, saying to no one in particular, "Rascals!"

"See?" my friend remarked.

A few days later we were waiting on line at McDonald's on Tverskoi Boulevard, when a young man broke into the line. Another man pushed him and the two squared off momentarily. After some heated words (and no real punches) the offender went to the back of the line.

"See?"

Being born, raised, and living in New York City, I frankly thought the level of tension was not that great, but things had clearly been getting worse. Everything cost almost twice what it had six months earlier, and there were greater price increases in store. Little was generally available, although many Muscovites had the connections they needed to get food and other necessities (if they had the money). A city Communist party official in his mid-forties said he had never seen things so bad.

A year earlier, Gorbachev's popularity had begun to erode, but there was little talk about a Soviet government without him. Now, many liberals and intellectuals in and out of government circles were saying that Gorbachev's historical mission was past and he was becoming irrelevant.

Gorbachev had made mistakes. His moves to mollify conservatives had cost him much support among his former allies, the liberals, and had failed to win him much affection with the right wing or the party faithful. The liberals feared further crackdowns on civil liberties.

On March 27, I was warned by a friend, Alexander Blokhin—a deputy in the Supreme Soviet of the Russian Federation—that there were tanks on the outskirts of the city and that Gorbachev had refused to allow a demonstration in the city by the Yeltsin democrats. He said that a confrontation might take place and I should be careful. He added that Thursday, March 28, would be an important day and things would start in the late afternoon.

It wasn't only his warning that put us on guard. The Moscow Hotel is where the congressional deputies from outside Moscow ordinarily stay. At the hotel, security is always present but not strict. On Wednesday the usual old men in hotel uniforms who cursorily glanced at guests' hotel cards as they came and went were replaced with a crew of young colorless men wearing gray suits and sour expressions. These KGB *apparatchiki* read each card avidly and looked at its owner with permanently narrowed eyes before allowing anyone to pass.

A friend in New York got through on the phone at

three-thirty A.M. Moscow time on the 28th to tell me that
the Wednesday *Times* had front-page pictures of the tanks,
along with a news story that a confrontation might occur.
No such news was available from any source in Moscow
except rumor.

I made myself a pot of tea and worked all morning. Irina
Bazhenova, the translator from the Moscow theater that
produces my work, called at around noon. She was free-
lancing for the day, interpreting for her American friend,
Susan Hartman, executive director of Connect US/USSR.
Irina said that troops were everywhere on the streets. I was
going to try going out with my camera to take some pictures
and see what would happen. I said I'd walk to the theater
offices in Hertzen Street, then to the theater on Tverskoi
Boulevard and back to the hotel. We planned to keep in
touch by phone during this short foray.

There were more KGB in the cavernous hotel lobby
than had been there the day before, but none commented on
the camera slung over my shoulder as I left. The Moscow
Hotel takes up a full square block. On one end is the huge
Manezh Square, which lets into Red Square. It was here
that supporters of Yeltsin had demonstrated peacefully two
weeks earlier. Now Manezh Square was empty. Pedestrians
are not permitted to cross above ground the wide intersec-
tion here where Marx Prospect meets Tverskaya Street.
(This, Moscow's main drag, was called Gorky Street from
the thirties until just a few months before, when the City
Council restored the prerevolutionary name—Tverskaya.)
The underground tunnels crisscross the area. Fourteen
lanes of traffic were moving freely on Marx Prospect (now
Hunter's Lane) and on Tverskaya Street, but the entrances
to the tunnels were guarded by soldiers who kept out everyone but those with special passes or a Moscow Hotel guest

•

identity card. Crowds had gathered on the two corners facing Manezh Square. They were just waiting.

Although Manezh Square was empty, Red Square was
packed with military vehicles. Backed up against the
Kremlin wall that guards the entrance to Red Square was
a line of ambulances. It was gray and cold and there was an
air of ominous expectation. After taking some pictures of
Red Square with the military vehicles, I pointed the camera
around just to see if the soldiers would react. They didn't.

My hotel card got me through the tunnels and up to
Tverskaya Street; I walked along one side up to Ogarev (the
name of a Decembrist, and friend of Pushkin) Street, where
I turned to go to the theater office. Ogarev Street was lined
with long flatbed military trucks. I took pictures and again
no one objected. As I turned up the alley that led past the
Composer's Union, I saw a young Russian also photograph-
ing the military vehicles. He had a good camera, and I
asked him if he thought there would be any trouble taking
pictures during the afternoon's demonstration. He said he
didn't know, but he was going to try.

I took some pictures of troops along the way to Hertzen
Street, but in a couple of instances thought better of it. I
stopped and had a cup of tea with some friends at the
theater office. Everyone was leaving for the day at three
P.M. Some were frightened and were going directly home,
others were going to the meeting.

I swung past the big new theater on Tverskoi Boulevard
and walked up toward Tverskaya Street. The line at Mc-
Donald's was as long as ever. Things seemed normal away
from Red Square and the Kremlin. I walked back down
Tverskaya toward Red Square and my hotel.

I passed a cul-de-sac about fifty yards up Tverskaya
from Marx Prospect. It was entered through a high, or-

nately decorated arch. The entire space was teeming with troops just waiting for something to start.

I returned to my hotel and had lunch sent up (not as easy as it sounds). After lunch I began to look for a vantage point in my hotel to observe and photograph what would happen in the late afternoon. My apartment windows faced a quiet interior courtyard at the end of the hotel away from Manezh Square. At the far end of a block-long corridor were windows that overlooked the square from six flights up, but you could not see Tverskaya Street, down which there was a planned route of march from Pushkin Square to Red Square. I asked the woman on the floor, the *dyezhurnaya,* if I should take my camera out with me on the street during the demonstration. She said I should not. I asked if I could take pictures from the hall window. She said yes.

I went back to my room and Irina called to say that the view was good from Susan's twentieth floor room in the Intourist Hotel, half a block away. She said you could see Tverskaya Street, Manezh Square, Red Square, and even New Arbat Street, down which there was to be another contingent of marchers. (Recently returned to its prerevolutionary name, New Arbat Street had been Kalinin Prospect, named after one of Stalin's more vicious henchmen. When I expressed satisfaction that the street had been renamed, Irina said, "Oh, Kalinin wasn't so bad. After he sent his wife to prison he continued to write to her for years.") I packed my camera in my shoulder bag along with a couple of rolls of film and went to Susan's room at the Intourist.

It was about four-thirty P.M. when I arrived. In the short walk some of the dread that I had felt earlier was dispelled by a brief appearance of the sun from behind the clouds. But even as there was sun and blue sky on one side of the street, it snowed lightly in the sunlight for a short time on the other.

The twentieth floor offered good views of the places for potential action, but I felt too far removed. I wanted to know what it was like in the street. Irina said she wanted to come with me, but Susan, promising friends that she'd steer clear of any possible difficulty, stayed behind and gave Irina her hotel card so that Irina could get in and out of the Intourist Hotel. Through the window we saw that the police had stopped traffic on Marx Prospect and allowed the crowds on the corners to swarm across the street into Manezh Square, where they gathered around a waving Russian Federation flag and a sign on a stick that said "Gorbachev Must Go." I loaded the camera with extra-fast film that would give me good depth-of-field even in fading light, and headed, a little nervously, for the street.

In front of the Intourist Hotel the street was empty of its usual traffic. The Gypsy kids who swarm over the raised area in front of the hotel, incessantly pestering and begging, were gone. No cars moved on Tverskaya. The street was clear of traffic from Marx Prospect up the wide sloping street almost to Pushkin Square, about five blocks distant.

We walked into the street and then we saw movement on Tverskaya. Out of Ogarev Street, where earlier I'd seen the flatbed trucks, and from other side streets further up Tverskaya, came the trucks. They moved like olive drab elephants nose-to-tail across Tverskaya, effectively blocking the street at three places along the proposed route of march. A babushka came down the street. She called to me as I took pictures: "Show the world," she said. "Show the world how our leaders behave."

Soviet Army troops poured out of the cul-de-sac near the end of Tverskaya, forming a tight line across the street between Marx Prospect and the trucks. From Red Square, a line of buses was accompanied by troops from the Ministry of the Interior wearing green combat fatigues and high-domed green helmets, carrying long metal shields and clutching wooden batons. The troops and buses swept Manezh Square clean and moved the group clustered around the Russian Federation flag out of the square and up into Tverskaya Street. For a while the troops stood blocking the square, and the demonstrators milled about in the street.

Standing in front of the Intourist Hotel, I was taking pictures in both directions, particularly of the troops. One man standing nearby said, "We are witnessing an important moment in history." Irina was close to tears. "I can't believe it. How could they, to their own people?"

With a microphone and recording backpack a man came over to me and asked, "Are you an American?"

"Yes," I replied.

"Could I interview about this? I am from Radio Estonia."

"Yes."

"What do you think of this event?"

"I think it doesn't make much sense."

Before he could ask his next question, the troops had moved across the entire street, from building-edge to building-edge, sweeping aside everyone in their path. It happened so suddenly, and while they didn't seem to be moving quickly, in a remarkably short time they were upon us, banging the batons against the shields they used to push us away, but otherwise making no sound and looking empty-eyed right through the people they were herding before them. I stumbled a little, but stayed up and half-walked, half-ran before them. I was shocked and scared, my heart beating fast as I was quickly pushed towards the windows in front of the Intourist Hotel, then moved further up the street.

Irina, right next to me, reached into the pocket of her coat and fished out Susan's hotel card. "Your hotel card," she shouted. "Show them your hotel card!" I got out the card that showed I was a resident of the Moscow Hotel and held it in front of the face of the soldier who was pushing me. The pressure immediately let up and he allowed me to slip around between him and the man next to him as they went by.

Both Irina and I were behind them. I was breathing hard. The air was very cold, but my face was hot and flushed. As the fear drained away, I felt exhilarated. Irina was angry. "Who pays them enough to do that?" she cried.

I looked toward the square. Another line of troops had formed and was sweeping stragglers and those missed by the first rank up Tverskaya. These were not Ministry of the Interior troops in their green uniforms. These were KGB, wearing white helmets and gray jackets. They also carried batons and shields, but the shields were not long, they were small and transparent, made of Plexiglas, and were more mobile than the shields the others carried. There was a crush of people trying to get into the Intourist Hotel, behind the plate-glass front windows, where they could still see what was happening but keep warm and out of the way of the troops' sweep. Irina showed the Intourist Hotel card, I showed my U.S. passport, and we pushed our way inside just ahead of the new wave.

Once they had passed we went back outside. It was very quiet and was getting bitterly cold. A few stray snowflakes fell. Trucks and troops lined Tverskaya Street. Between two of the ranks, a small band of people trapped by the sweeps continued to wave the Russian Federation flag. Down Tverskaya, where it emptied into Marx Prospect, a long line of police blocked the entrance to Manezh Square and Red Square. A small crowd had gathered there, milling about. An old man yelled at the police, "I hope you get enough food for protecting them!"

Nothing further happened as it began to get colder and darker. We could not quite see up Tverskaya as far as Pushkin Square, so we didn't know if the meeting went on. We went back inside and up to the twentieth floor.

From her vantage point upstairs, Susan said she couldn't help but admire the military precision with which the troops had cleared the area. I took a couple of pictures of an eerily empty Manezh Square and Red Square before a heavy snow began to fall.

When the snow stopped, it was dark and we decided to go to Pushkin Square to see what was happening. It was warmer now and the street glistened, black and wet. Tverskaya was blocked to traffic, so we walked up the middle of the broad avenue toward Pushkin Square to see if the meeting had taken place. We heard that the Metro had stopped running. There was a feeling that something important had happened, but it had not disturbed the line of people in front of the Estée Lauder shop, still waiting for entry to buy an eighty-ruble bottle of eau de cologne.

The troops were strung across the avenue. These were the troops of crack Soviet Army divisions, not the KGB and riot troops with their hard faces and shields, helmets and batons. They were young men in soft Army hats who joked with the people who passed through their ranks. I took a picture of Susan with one of them, and he gave her an address where she could send a copy.

A speaker was exhorting the crowd at Pushkin Square, but we couldn't make out what he was saying because of overamplification. We walked rapidly toward the crowd, until we spotted Blokhin, who had warned us about what was going to happen today. We had seen him speaking on television at the Supreme Soviet in the early afternoon. He

•

was euphoric about the day's events and wanted to tell us the inside story. We collared him and took him into the hard-currency section of Pizza Hut on Tverskaya. (The for-rubles section, where a slice of pizza cost five rubles, was closed and without its usual line down the street; at the hard-currency section, pizza and beer for four cost more than sixty dollars.) The lights were half-out, but we were shown to a table, where Blokhin began his story.

He had risen early that morning to drive from his suburban apartment to a meeting of democratic deputies, and then to the Russian Federation Congress at the Hall of Congresses in the Kremlin. By arriving early, the democrats planned to get a jump on their Communist rivals.

The Russian Federation Congress was split about evenly between Communist and non-Communist deputies. In order to control the day's debate, the democrats grabbed the floor immediately. Their advantage lay in the presence at the podium of their leader, Boris Yeltsin, then chairman of the Supreme Soviet of the Russian Federation.

They held the floor from the opening of the debate, seeking a censuring vote against what they considered Gorbachev's unconstitutional ban on their meeting planned for the afternoon.

They all knew that troops had entered the city with the purpose of stopping the meeting. They wanted it to go on record that Gorbachev was exceeding his power by trying to stop the meeting, by force if necessary, but they would give Gorbachev a chance to call off the troops. The vice-chairman of the Russian Federation Supreme Soviet, Ruslan Khazbulatov, was asked to call Gorbachev with the request. He did, but Gorbachev reiterated his opinion that the meeting was contrary to the public welfare and that he had a right and an obligation to protect the public welfare.

•

Finally, in the afternoon session, they gathered enough votes to pass a censuring statement, 532 votes to 286.

At about five P.M., many of the democratic deputies walked from the vast hall where they had met, inside the Kremlin walls, out into Manezh Square. They were going to march together to the meeting place at Pushkin Square, and they were prepared to meet resistance.

"I was frightened, but excited also," said Blokhin. I understood exactly what he meant. I, too, had been both frightened and excited by the afternoon's activity.

"When we began to walk up Tverskaya Street and there were troops ahead of us blocking the way, my heart started to pound loudly. Most of those in the front rank with me had their deputy's pins on the lapels of their jackets, under their coats. I pinned mine outside on my coat so they would know exactly who I was. Look, it has left a hole in the coat. We shouted to the troops to join us or let us pass. They let us pass. There was no confrontation and I breathed a sigh of relief.

"When we got to Pushkin Square, many of those waiting wanted to march back down Tverskaya to the Kremlin, but we dissuaded them. We didn't want to push the situation to a confrontation that could turn ugly. We held our meeting without violence—we won. It has been an important day in the history of Russia."

Blokhin was right. March 28, 1991, was an important day in the history of Russia and the Soviet Union. The president of this vast nation—one of the most powerful men on earth—had brought fifty thousand troops into the capital to stop a small rally for his rival, and he had failed completely.

According to presidential advisor Alexander Yakovlev, Gorbachev was counseled by Yakovlev against interfering with the demonstration. "I said to Mikhail Sergeyevich, 'If

•

just one soldier slips and accidentally kills one of the demonstrators, there will be the biggest funeral Moscow has ever seen. And dozens of speakers will accuse you of murder and whip the crowd into a frenzy, calling for your resignation.' He still thought he should not permit the demonstration, but agreed finally that he would not urge the troop leaders to actively oppose it."

Gorbachev himself agreed that his opposition to the demonstration was a mistake. By ordering fifty thousand troops into Moscow, it seemed that he was using a cannon to swat a fly.

On Tuesday, April 2, the prices of most products in the Soviet Union went up again. This time prices were doubled, trebled, even quadrupled, and with much fanfare. Stores still had little to sell, although the weekend's bread panic when there was nothing on the shelves of the bread stores was alleviated. The price of a crusty medium loaf went from an average of twenty-two kopeks to forty-four, still less than it cost to produce. Many stores closed, since the employees didn't know how much to charge for products.

People in the street seemed a little grimmer. There was a Gypsy woman begging in her usual spot on Tverskaya Street alongside the telegraph office, her child in her lap, her hand extended upward for coins, her head bowed. A man came along and kicked her hard from behind, kicked her again as she tried to squirm away. He shouted down at her as she sprawled on the sidewalk. Her child jumped to the wall of the building and cowered there. She got to her feet and screamed and spit at the man as he walked away. Then she hit him in the back with a canvas shoulder bag she was carrying. He turned and threatened her and then smacked her on the head with his hand. She spat at him and cursed again as he turned and walked up the street. A minute later she was in her usual position, but nearer the wall so she could not be attacked from behind.

By the end of April, Muscovites had adjusted to the new prices and daily life went on much as it had before. Increased prices at McDonald's meant shorter lines for a time, but eventually they reached the same lengths as before the price rise. In a society undergoing change, eruptions take place and then things continue as before, with small changes to adjust to.

But on March 28, the balance of power changed in the Soviet Union. It swung overwhelmingly over to Yeltsin and was from then on irreversible. For Gorbachev, the events of March 28 were his most serious mistake, because they exposed his vulnerability. It was a clear lesson about the bankruptcy of Soviet power at the top. The democrats understood it. Unfortunately, others in the Communist party hierarchy failed to understand.

CHAPTER ONE

•

THE OLD GUARD'S
LAST STAND

•

I T seemed as though everyone in Moscow on the morning of August 19, 1991, was awakened by the telephone ringing.

"Turn on the television," a friend would say.

A nervous announcer, barely able to look directly at the camera, reported that President Mikhail Gorbachev was ill and that a state-of-emergency committee was assuming the powers of government. "There is mortal danger for our motherland," read the announcer. "The country has become ungovernable."

After the announcement on all television channels (four in Moscow), a film of the ballet *Swan Lake* was run. The significance of the music was not lost on most Russians. Whenever a leader died in the Soviet Union, Tchaikovsky was played on radio and television. Many citizens of the Soviet Union believed their president was dead.

People who lived along broad Kutuzov Avenue, which runs downtown into New Arbat Street past the wedding-cake office building known as the Russian Republic's White House, heard the early morning rumble of tanks moving into positions downtown to keep the peace.

15

Before the weekend that presaged the coup began, former presidential advisor Alexander Yakovlev publicly resigned with melodramatic fanfare from the Communist party, warning of a planned coup by Party reactionaries. In a report on the front page of the August 17 *New York Times*, Yakovlev was quoted as saying that the Communist party leadership was "making preparations for social revenge, a party and state coup."

While many had been warning of a right-wing coup for months, the timing of Yakovlev's prediction couldn't have been better. By resigning, Yakovlev was merely beating the leadership to the punch, since the Party hierarchy had called for his expulsion on the previous day. Saying that "the revolution in society has not led to a revolution in the Party," Yakovlev turned in his Party card complaining about a "smear committee, masterminded and orchestrated by the Central Committee."

Right from the start, the plotters of the coup sought legitimacy. Tass, the official Soviet news agency, carried to the West a statement by Gennady Yanayev, Gorbachev's vice-president, who was the spokesman for the emergency committee:

At the instruction of the Soviet leadership I hereby notify that a state of emergency is introduced in individual localities of the Union of Soviet Socialist Republics for a period of six months from August 19, 1991, in keeping with the Constitution and laws of the U.S.S.R.

All power in the country is transferred for this period to the State Committee for the State of Emergency in the U.S.S.R.

The measures that are being adopted are temporary. They in no way mean renunciation of the course toward profound reforms in all spheres of life of the state and society.

These are forced measures, dictated by the vital need to save the economy from ruin and the country from hunger, to prevent the escalation of the threat of a large-scale civil conflict with unpredictable consequences for the peoples of the USSR and the entire international community.

His statement continued at length in an effort to reassure nations that the "emergency" would by no means affect the Soviet Union's international commitments, and concluded with this faint hope: "The leadership of the USSR hopes that the temporary emergency measures will find proper understanding on the part of the peoples and governments, and the United National Organization."

The officials behind the putsch owed their jobs to the man they betrayed.

Spokesman Gennady Yanayev, fifty-four, was a Party hack that Gorbachev appointed his vice-president over much objection from the Supreme Soviet in December 1990. Yanayev, like Gorbachev, had studied law, and the coup plotters used his position as Gorbachev's possible replacement as another stab at legitimacy.

Vladimir Kryuchkov, sixty-seven, headed the KGB. A protégé, like Gorbachev, of former general secretary Yuri Andropov, he had been an outspoken critic of *perestroika* since his appointment to his post by Gorbachev in 1988. He had been warning Gorbachev about Western influence on Soviet policy and calling for an increasingly hard line.

Dimitri Yazov, the sixty-seven-year-old defense minister who controlled the vast Soviet Army, was appointed to his position by Gorbachev in 1987. He had taken a reformist

approach to a top-heavy defense establishment, but saw a
sharp drop coming in both the size and influence of the
Soviet Army.

Boris Pugo, a Latvian and former head of the Latvian
KGB, fifty-four, had been one of Gorbachev's concessions
to the right wing when he appointed him to succeed the
liberal Vadim Bakatin as minister of the interior in 1990.
Pugo was a brutal hard-liner whose ministry had used
troops to control crowds and demonstrations within the
borders of the Soviet Union. Troops from his ministry had
killed civilians in Lithuania in January 1991, and were used
to control the demonstrators in Moscow in March.

Valentin Pavlov was the fifty-three-year-old prime minister of the Soviet Union, appointed by Gorbachev in January 1991. Pavlov opposed the moves toward economic
reform advocated by Yeltsin and the democrats in the Supreme Soviet. Just weeks before the coup, Pavlov had un-
successfully attempted to constitutionally usurp many of
Gorbachev's powers as president, but the Supreme Soviet
refused to go along.

These men were the leaders of what became known as
the "Gang That Couldn't Shoot Straight." Other members
of the gang were conservative Communist party officials
Oleg Baklanov, Vasily Starodubtsev, and Alexander Tizya-
kov.

In a litany of things left undone by those who planned
to seize the stewardship of the Soviet Union was putting
Boris Yeltsin under arrest or simply making sure that the
populist president of the Russian Republic was silenced. On
Sunday, August 18, Yeltsin was not at his home in Moscow.

Konstantin Kobets, a former high-ranking officer in the
Soviet Army recruited by Boris Yeltsin as head of the Russian Republic's Committee on Defense Issues, was spending
the weekend at a dacha in a compound just outside the

•

capital. When at six A.M. on Monday morning he heard on the radio about Gorbachev's illness, he knew a coup was taking place. He went immediately to the dacha being used by Boris Yeltsin. The leadership of Yeltsin's government arrived also, and they met with Yeltsin for almost an hour, approving a statement that condemned the coup leaders as criminals and called on the police and soldiers to disobey any orders from them.

At about seven-thirty A.M., Yeltsin and the leaders left the compound to go to the White House. They took a different route than usual and arrived at the White House about eight A.M. A tank company was already there and had set up positions around the center of the government of the Russian Republic, but the soldiers did not interfere with Yeltsin or his people.

A few years before, Boris Yeltsin had learned the value of dramatizing. As Communist party head of Moscow, he occasionally rode the bus or stood on line (always with cameras trained on him) to show his solidarity with the people.

Now, Yeltsin aides convinced the crew of at least one tank to come over to the side of the Russian president. This was part of the bulwark of Yeltsin's defense against the coup.

Around noon on Monday, Yeltsin jumped up on the tank in front of the Russian White House. The picture was compelling. Yeltsin read a statement condemning the coup, calling it illegal and calling for the arrest of the plotters. He also called for a general strike against the "Emergency Committee."

It was a masterstroke. While critics might question Yeltsin's commitment to democracy, no one could question his courage. And courage was a good quality to possess in the ensuing days.

•

Though the makers of the coup controlled television, most radio and the press, Yeltsin and the leaders of the Russian Republic—barricaded in the White House—found ways to get the message out. By telephone, fax, photocopying and satellite transmission to Western radio and television, they called for resistance to the coup, and the Russian White House became the center of that resistance.

The BBC, Radio Liberty, and the Voice of America have been telling Soviet citizens something other than the official line for years; now the people in Moscow and St. Petersburg and throughout the Soviet Union tuned in and heard of the resistance to the takeover, resistance to the loss of the freedoms they had achieved during the *glasnost* of the past six years.

In the West, the story on the streets of Moscow was played out, blow-by-blow, on television. That story got back to Moscow and affected the events there. The communications technology that was only beginning to be available in the Soviet Union—plus the continuous twenty-four-hour-a-day, seven-days-a-week coverage of news events throughout a global communications community—made a control of information needed for a successful takeover of government impossible.

At seven A.M. on Monday morning in New York City (two P.M. in Moscow) I felt sick when I saw the screaming headline across the front page of *The New York Times:* "GORBACHEV IS OUSTED IN AN APPARENT COUP BY SOVIET ARMED FORCES AND HARD-LINERS . . ." I was preparing for an October return to the USSR, which dimmed in significance as I thought about my friends in Moscow. I turned on the television and dialed the overseas operator. I asked if lines were open to the Soviet Union and if I could still direct-dial to Moscow. "Of course," was the response. As if there were nothing of importance happening.

It took longer than usual to get through, since the lines were continually busy. But after about half an hour I reached the offices of the theater I worked with in Moscow. My associates were excited to hear from me. Everyone was at work, but a contingent was planning to go to the White House.

"There are tanks in the street, right in front of your door," Irina told me. "But they're very friendly to the people," she continued. "They don't look as if they're going to shoot anybody."

I had been worried about troops in the streets of Moscow. In the conscript Soviet Army a large percentage of draftees were from other republics. They might not consider Russians as their own people and, consequently, might have little compunction about shooting them. Friends in Vilnius, Lithuania, said that the troops that sprayed their capital with bullets were high on a combination of tranquilizers and vodka fed to them by their officers—a claim that might possibly be true, and was worrying, true or not.

Irina said that she was going to the White House, but had promised her mother that she wouldn't stay all night or put herself in danger. I got a time schedule from her so I would be able to keep in contact during the next few days.

"One thing is a little strange," Irina said finally. "The feeling in Moscow streets is very much business-as-usual—as if nothing extraordinary was happening. Everybody is going to work as always, and little is being made of tanks in the street or a coup going on."

People in Moscow who worked in places where there was television hooked into CNN did what many Americans did that day and watched the coup being played out on television.

At five P.M. in Moscow, the coup leaders held a televised news conference. The gray men sat somberly as their spokesman, Gennady Yanayev, insisted that Gorbachev was ill and warned against Yeltsin's provocation.

"I knew we were finished then," Minister of Defense Dimitri Yazov said after he was arrested. "I looked at Yanayev's shaking hands and I knew. I was used to Gorbachev—always so confident and smooth."

Right from the start, things did not go their way. A carefully negotiated Union Treaty, which would transform the Soviet Union, was to be signed on August 20. The treaty moved power from the center and handed it to the republics. On August 17, three days before the document was to be signed, Soviet prime minister Valentin Pavlov called a meeting of his cabinet to discuss the treaty. The prime minister was very critical. "I don't care what they say," he told his deputies. "That treaty won't work. They're playing political games. These games will lead to trouble."

Word of the meeting reached Gorbachev at his vacation home in the Crimea. He immediately called his deputy prime minister, Vladimir Shcherbakov, in Moscow.

"I was driving home," Shcherbakov remembered. "Gorbachev called me in my car. I couldn't get a word in. He was swearing his head off. I said, 'Please, Mikhail Sergeyevich.' He said, 'Don't interrupt me.' He said, 'Don't you understand? If there's no treaty, there will be civil war. The state is falling apart.' "

Even as they spoke, Prime Minister Pavlov made his way to a KGB compound south of Moscow. There he joined KGB chief Kryuchkov, Gorbachev's chief of staff Valeri Boldin, and Defense Minister Yazov.

Dimitri Yazov claimed they had no plan to overthrow the government. "There never was a conspiracy. Nothing had been worked out. Nothing. We just met the day before, on the 17th."

The leaders were convinced that the treaty would spell

•

the end of the Soviet Union. In an interview after the coup collapsed, Pavlov said they were acting from the purest intentions. "We decided we needed a state of emergency. The economy was disintegrating. We had to avert famine and the collapse of the state."

Yazov said that they agreed that Gorbachev could no longer cope with the foundering ship of state. "It had become increasingly apparent that he had lost control or that he was simply burnt out. Then we decided to send a team to see him."

The men later insisted that all they wanted to do was explain their views, and get the president's opinion. According to Vladimir Kryuchkov, "We wanted to say to him, we have to take steps to stabilize the situation. Those steps may be unpopular, but we have no alternative. In any case, we believe the people will back our actions."

The conspirators selected a delegation to fly to see Gorbachev in the Crimea the next day. Gorbachev's large summer home faces the Crimean Sea, surrounded by miles of empty beach, dunes, and trees. A single long dock stretches out from the beach towards the open sea.

When the conspirators arrived, having traveled first by plane and then by limousine to the compound, they marched directly into the house and into Gorbachev's office. Gorbachev was shocked at their behavior. "Before I could invite them in, they had already gone into my office. I wasn't used to such conduct, such familiarity. They were led by the head of my presidential staff, Valeri Boldin."

The group had deliberately selected Boldin because he was trusted by Gorbachev; they felt he would be able to persuade the president to go along with their plan. Instead, Gorbachev and his wife were shocked by Boldin's involvement. The studious, calm Boldin had been a close family friend, as well as a colleague, since the Gorbachevs first came to Moscow in 1978.

Gorbachev refused to agree to the group's demand for a state of emergency: "I said I wouldn't resign or put my name on their decree. I said, 'Who sent you here? I'm not a fool.' They said, 'We've set up a committee.' I asked, 'What committee? Who were the members?' As they listed the names, I began writing down their names on a scrap of paper on my desk."

The members of the delegation left suddenly, but they first placed extra guards around the house and cut the telephone lines, completely isolating the president and leaving him a prisoner in his own compound. They only did it, Kryuchkov would say later, in order to have "a few clear days to impose order."

After the conspirators left, Gorbachev, shaken, held the piece of paper in his hand. The last name on the list was Anatoly Lukyanov, the speaker of the Supreme Soviet, and the second most powerful man in the Soviet hierarchy.

Gorbachev had written his name in small letters and placed a question mark next to it. He couldn't be certain that Lukyanov was part of the plot and hoped that he was not. The two men had known each other since their college days, more than forty years. Lukyanov had the power—the success of the coup depended on his support. Without his participation, Gorbachev believed, the coup would immediately collapse.

"I could see they were scared," Gorbachev recalled. "I don't think they expected my reaction. They thought I could be removed quietly like Khrushchev. There was no question of my agreeing with them. They could not just remove me."

Gorbachev tried each of the ten telephones in the house one by one, but they were all dead. Even the military hot line. "We have a military hot line in each of our homes," Raisa said. "That phone was kept under a cover. No one is allowed to touch it, even to dust it. He took off the cover, lifted the handset, and it went dead. Then we knew. That was that. When we realized we were under arrest, and when we discovered who the conspirators were, we were terribly hurt. We felt bitterly betrayed."

On Sunday afternoon, at his dacha, Foreign Minister Alexander Bessmertnykh was out for a drive in the woods. Suddenly, out of the dark forest, a snow white car appeared and cut off his automobile. A man got out and told Bessmertnykh he was wanted on the phone. On the other end of the line KGB chief Kryuchkov told him that he had to talk; he had a plane waiting to bring him to Moscow. Kryuchkov said nothing further.

It was late when Bessmertnykh arrived at the Kremlin. The foreign minister walked into Pavlov's office to find the coup leaders: Kryuchkov, Yazov, Pavlov, and Yanayev, the men who organized the trip to the Crimea. The speaker of the Supreme Soviet, Anatoly Lukyanov, the last name on the list, also had been called back from his vacation.

"All the top leaders were there," Bessmertnykh recalled, "except Gorbachev. No one took the lead. They were sitting at the long table, or milling around. The chairman's desk was not occupied."

The delegation that had visited Gorbachev said the president had dismissed them; but they claimed he said, "Do it, you'll see what happens."

Pavlov claimed that most of the people at this meeting, even members of the "committee," had no idea what was going on. Lukyanov asked for their plan, but the plotters said they had none.

Kryuchkov took Bessmertnykh next door and told him they were forming an emergency committee to govern the country in this state of emergency. He took it for granted that Bessmertnykh would join the committee.

Bessmertnykh asked, "Is this Gorbachev's idea? Is this his solution to the crisis?"

Kryuchkov hesitated, then replied, "No, Gorbachev is seriously ill."

Bessmertnykh said, "No, I won't be a member of that committee."

After the coup, Lukyanov gave the Soviet Parliament his version of his own reaction. "I told the plotters, that as chairman of the Supreme Soviet I had no intention of taking part in the work of that emergency committee. I said, 'I'm not going to sign any of your documents.'"

Lukyanov had not told the full story. According to one of the coup leaders, Lukyanov agreed to publish a statement in the name of the Supreme Soviet saying that the Union Treaty, to be signed on the 20th, was unconstitutional.

If Lukyanov, the guardian of the Soviet Constitution, said the Union Treaty was illegal, then, the conspirators reasoned, the coup was justified. In addition to this legal maneuvering, the conspirators also needed a public reason for unseating Gorbachev.

Since Gorbachev had refused to sign their decree setting aside the treaty, someone else would have to. They needed to name a new president quickly. According to the Constitution, Vice-President Yanayev would take over if the president was ill. Although Gorbachev wasn't sick at all, they had to make it look as if he were.

The plotters drew up a statement saying Vice-President Yanayev was assuming power because of Gorbachev's ill health. They told Yanayev, "You have to sign. There's no going back now." The statement began making the rounds of the leaders, bouncing from one desk to another. No one wanted to actually put his name on it. Finally, at four o'clock in the morning, they all signed the statement so that all would be equally responsible.

The coup leaders had seized control of all broadcasting. They repeatedly broadcast their own statement by Speaker Lukyanov attacking the Union Treaty. Lukyanov later claimed that although he agreed to the statement denouncing the treaty, he had refused to join the coup.

Only the Supreme Soviet could declare the new regime illegal. And Speaker Lukyanov was the only person with the authority to recall that ruling body. He chose not to assemble it for a full seven days, claiming it was impossible to set up a session any faster.

In contrast, Yeltsin ordered his Russian legislature to start in two days. People quickly identified the Soviet White House as the seat of resistance to the coup.

Back at the compound in the Crimea, Gorbachev and Raisa followed the news on a small Sony radio. Anatoly Chernayev, Gorbachev's aide, recalled that they all three sat in a circle on the floor, turning around the radio, which had run-down batteries, trying to pick up the news. Gorbachev's staff had also managed to fix up a primitive antenna for the television. The deposed president also watched the trembling Yanayev, the new "president" and spokesman for the coup, hold his press conference. He claimed that the coup leaders had the support of the "absolute majority" of the republican leaders. He said further that their intention was to restore order and save the country. "We will do everything to ensure that force isn't used against civilians," Yanayev promised. "We must do everything to prevent excesses."

After watching Yanayev's broadcast, Gorbachev recorded a message to the world on the family video recorder.

Sitting in front of the camera in his shirtsleeves, looking wan and disheveled, Gorbachev said: "Everything that Yanayev said, and the arguments which the committee have used, are outrageous lies. This is treason. An anti-state crime. The decision to make Yanayev president and all subsequent decisions are illegal."

Inside the Kremlin, Gorbachev supporters were desperate to find out what had happened to him. Information was scant and rumors were thick. Yanayev, questioned by everyone, was incoherent. "Gorbachev's sick. He's incapacitated. He's had it. We had to do this. It was for the best."

Across the hall from the offices of the coup leaders, Gorbachev loyalists—Vadim Bakatin, the liberal former minister of the interior, and Yevgeny Primakov and Alexander Yakovlev, both former presidential advisors—began to plan their opposition.

They first tracked down the foreign minister, Alexander Bessmertnykh, and asked him to join their statement condemning the coup. He refused, saying that it would be up to him to explain the takeover abroad and that he would have to remain on his post to do so.

Russian poet and sometime politician Yevgeny Yevtushenko was jogging in the village of Peredelkino, a sylvan suburb of Moscow where noted Soviet writers have dachas, when a neighbor called to him: "See you at the White House." Realizing that that was where he wanted to be, Yevtushenko left immediately and drove downtown. He entered the White House and stood beside Yeltsin in a window facing the crowd below.

Around the world, Russian writers, musicians and just plain people tried to get back to Moscow. Russian Republic

•

deputy Alexander Blokhin was himself in the Crimea on vacation. A series of machinations got him to the White House. By Tuesday afternoon, Elena Bonner, widow of Andrei Sakharov, was at the White House, where she spoke to the crowd, saying that the coup would fail because the people of the Soviet Union were no longer cattle. Mstislav Rostropovich, the famed cellist who emigrated to the United States years ago, found his way to the White House without a visa.

The White House was now surrounded by a human shield of thousands, waving flags like a heaving sea. Inside, thanks to an oversight by the coup leaders, the telephones still worked. Yeltsin was able to speak to political leaders and reporters all over the world. Through Yeltsin, the Western leaders affirmed their support of the deposed government.

Yazov would say later, "We didn't think of cutting off the phones inside the White House. We thought we just had to make a declaration and the people would say, get on with it."

The coup leaders made the next move, declaring a curfew for Tuesday evening. Rumors spread that the White House would be stormed that night.

Yeltsin didn't believe the army would attack, but he was worried about KGB groups. KGB deserters had informed Yeltsin that the KGB had a detailed plan to seize the White House. "An elite group of the KGB, called Alpha Group, specializes in such things," Yeltsin said. "Their orders were to destroy the first two floors of the building. Machine-gun everything. Their main task was to seize me, and if I tried to escape, they were to shoot me."

Late that night, phalanxes of tanks rolled through the dark streets. A shout went up from the crowd in front of the White House. "Sheverdnadze's coming!" In the center of the huge square packed with people, the white hair of former foreign minister Eduard Sheverdnadze appeared.

Speaking from the middle of the crowd, the democratic leader said: "The fate of our nation is being decided. The future of democracy and freedom is being decided. Long live the people. To our youth, who make up the majority here, I salute you all."

The crowd cheered and swelled. The threat appeared to be averted, although out on the Garden Ring Road, soon after midnight on Tuesday, three young men clashed with moving tanks and the only life's blood of the coup was spilled.

There was a construction project near the White House, and it was plundered by the crowd who sought to protect Yeltsin from government troops. Everything that could be used was piled upon the barricades. A theater advertising kiosk from the theater I am associated with, constructed from a junked nuclear missile, was piled on.

Inside the White House, masked men planned retreat routes and set up their defenses. Clearly, the army was not anxious to attack Yeltsin, who had been vigorously supported in his presidential campaign by the younger officers.

Shots were fired and a half-hearted attempt to get past the barricades was easily turned aside with no injuries or bloodletting on either side. As the third day of the coup dawned, news filtered back to the Russian Parliament that coup leaders Kryuchkov and Yazov, along with Lukyanov, were headed for the airport to fly to the Crimea and make a deal with Gorbachev.

Inside the White House, the assembly reacted in confusion. Yeltsin was worried because he had no idea what the plotters were up to. They had taken two planes. The coup leaders flew in one plane and the presidential plane was empty except for its pilots. The Russians felt they were planning to secretly move Gorbachev to another location.

A delegation appointed by the Russian Parliament rushed to the airport. They were one hour behind in the race to get to Gorbachev. All was chaos at the airport. One member of the delegation spoke to the press: "The plotters of the coup have flown secretly to Gorbachev. They've misled us. They've tricked us all. We're afraid of what might happen to Gorbachev."

Vadim Bakatin was at a press conference when he was informed that the plotters had gone. He raced to the airport and saw the plane ready to taxi out onto the runway. "The aircraft steps had been removed, and the engines were running. I grabbed a microphone from a technician and shouted over the noise of the engines, 'Tell them Bakatin is here. Stop the engines and bring back the steps.' Finally, they got the message. The engines were turned off and the stairs put back."

Bakatin's late arrival delayed the plane by twenty minutes, minutes that were to prove vital.

On board were Russian vice-president Colonel Alexander Rutskoi and twenty-eight armed men. Their purpose was to bring Gorbachev back, whatever condition they found him in.

Gorbachev's allies were flying into territory still controlled by the coup leaders. They could have been rushing headfirst into a trap. In fact, they learned later that the marines guarding the Crimean airport had been ordered to attack their plane when it landed. The late arrival of the plane confused the troops, and they failed to attack when the plane finally set down.

The coup leaders were still an hour ahead of their pursuers. After landing, they filed into a long line of limousines and headed for the compound. In the driveway, they got out of the cars, one after another and stood looking up at the second-floor balcony where Gorbachev's office was. Looking down on them was Anatoly Chernayev, the Gorbachev aide who had remained under arrest with him. "I stood there above them," Chernayev said. "I can see it now. We sized each other up. Then they started bowing to me."

At this moment, the coup collapsed. Three days earlier, the conspirators had demanded Gorbachev's resignation. Now they came to capitulate.

Later, at his interrogation, Defense Minister Yazov said, "I wanted to sink into the ground. I felt eternally guilty for what we'd done to Gorbachev and Raisa. I felt guilty in front of the people and the Party."

Back at the airport, the Russian delegation prepared to drive to the compound. They decided the politicians would go first. If they didn't return within three hours, the armed men would follow them.

Inside his office, Gorbachev and Chernayev heard more cars pull up and more car doors slamming. They went into the dining room and found their friends had arrived to rescue them—Rutskoi, Primakov, Bakatin, and six Russian deputies. Chernayev recalled the moment: "Gorbachev went in first. They simply dived on him. They started hugging him and kissing him on the cheek, especially Rutskoi."

Rutskoi said he had expected Gorbachev to look ill. "But he came in, cheerful, smiling, and swearing his head off. He didn't mince words. He called a spade a spade. It was a coup, it was treachery."

Gorbachev refused to speak with the waiting conspirators, but agreed to talk to Lukyanov alone. Primakov and Rutskoi remained in the room as witnesses.

Lukyanov tried to justify his actions. Gorbachev responded with a stream of four-letter words. "You're the top

•

lawyer of our whole country," he said. "Why didn't you uphold the law? You're the president of the Supreme Soviet. Yeltsin called his legislature. Why didn't you call ours? You should have thrown yourself at the tanks to defend that constitution you always wave around."

Lukyanov said, "There was nothing I could do."

Gorbachev said, "Why didn't you stand with Yeltsin? Why didn't you support Yeltsin?"

Then Gorbachev said, "Get out. Wait out there."

The delegation wanted to move quickly to take Gorbachev back to Moscow. Colonel Rutskoi took the president in his plane, together with the armed guards. He also took the KGB chief on board as a hostage, as a precaution. In those hours, anything could have happened.

To get Kryuchkov aboard the plane, Rutskoi promised him a private talk with Gorbachev. Once on board, Primakov arrested him.

As the delegation plane landed in Moscow with Gorbachev on board, the passengers and crew were unsure who was in control of Vnukovo Airport. Rutskoi told the crew to keep the engines turning. If the plane was fired on, his security chief had orders to jump out of the plane with his machine gun blasting. He would fight to the end while the plane took off again.

The plane set down without incident. As Gorbachev walked down the steps, he was met by several officious representatives of the Soviet Parliament, who sheepishly and formally shook his hand. Even those who had betrayed Gorbachev were there to meet him. "You could sense their hypocrisy and treachery," said Colonel Rutskoi. "How low can you stoop—to betray a man and then go to meet him at the airport?"

The next morning, the Russian legislature met, triumphant, and Yeltsin announced the arrest of the coup leaders. One conspirator was missing, the minister of the interior, Pugo. He was later found, a suicide, in his home by the KGB. He had shot himself in the mouth. His wife lay on the floor beside him, covered in blood, with two gunshot wounds.

The Russian and then Soviet empires have always been particularly susceptible to a coup. The field of conflict could be contained and controlled by even a small force with the will to succeed. The people have always just gone along.

In the October Revolution of 1917, the field of conflict remained in St. Petersburg, where the government was then centered. The Bolsheviks were a small force, but they managed to gain control of St. Petersburg and eventually the entire empire. In the August 1991 coup attempt it was obvious early that events would be played out in the streets of Moscow.

"How could it fail?" Vladimir Posner, American born former Soviet journalist, apologist, and television personality, now living in New York City, queried sometime later. "We had always done what those in power told us to do. These people who headed the coup headed the army, the Interior Ministry, and the KGB. How could they possibly fail?"

While there was clear dissatisfaction with Gorbachev's running of the country, a spring survey among representative Soviet cities by the Soviet Center for Public Opinion and Market Research showed that fewer than 10 percent of the people would support a military takeover.

In the end, it was only a small percentage of Soviet citizens—a handful of Muscovites—who made the difference. But it was enough. Six years of *glasnost* had proved too difficult to roll back.

CHAPTER TWO

·

BUILDING AN EMPIRE

·

NORTH of what is today Turkey and Iran, between the Black and Caspian seas in the southern Steppes, is the cradle of Russian civilization. Here, along the northern shores of the Black Sea almost three thousand years ago, were outposts of Greek civilization farming the fertile land. The Hellenic colonists grew wheat, barley, and oats, which were sent back to Greece in sailing ships. They also spread the Greek language and customs and traded the crafts of the brilliant Greek artisans. But by the time of Jesus Christ's birth, little was left of either the outposts or Greek influence.

Six hundred years after the birth of Christ, the area was dominated by the Khazars, a Turkish nomad tribe that settled in the region and developed trade between Byzantium in the east, the land of the Arabian caliphs in the south, and the Slavic tribes. They had enough skill in the art of war to keep their domain secure, but they were primarily traders rather than raiders and warriors and they ruled the region with a gentle hand. They linked the trade routes of the various peoples of the Caucasus, bringing fur,

·

wax, and honey from the north, exchanging these for textiles, spices, and gold from the south.

The Khazars brought to the Slavic tribes the influence of
the most civilized cultures of Europe and Asia. From the
strategic advantage of their lavish walled cities, they kept
peaceful trade moving along the Dnieper and Volga river
routes. It was said of the Khazars that they treated all men
fairly. When the Jews were expelled from Constantinople,
the capital of the Byzantine Empire, they were welcomed in
the Khazar capital city of Itil. The Khazars listened to
religious argument on behalf of the Muslim religion, Christianity, and Judaism, and the Khazar leadership converted
to Judaism in 746, although they said each person was free
to follow his own conscience in worship. Historians think
today that some Russian Jews are descendants of the Khazar people. The influence of the Khazars ended in 969, when
their cities were attacked and defeated by Prince Svyatoslav of Kiev, grandson of the leader acknowledged to be the
founder of the Russian nation—Rurik.

In the year 862 a settlement was founded in the north
near the Baltic Sea at Novgorod. The people of this settlement, led by Rurik, were the small beginnings of the Russian Empire. They were of Varangian (from a Norse word
that means "sworn men") descent, one of the Scandinavian
tribes that roamed south to attack and pillage settlements
in the Steppe. Far to the south, these early Russians made
their capital. There had been a town here called Metropolis
as early as the second century, but in the tenth century
Rurik's son Igor and grandson Svyatoslav occupied and
expanded Kiev, which is called The Mother of Cities. For
the next seven hundred years, during the age of the great
empire of Kiev and after, all Russian rulers traditionally
claimed direct descent from the Varangian Rurik.

Rurik's great-grandson, Vladimir, was the leader who

•

made Kiev a center of civilization. As a young man, Vladimir had a zest for living. He acquired more than eight hundred wives, often by force. He also hunted—men as well as animals—and feasted with barbarian gusto. But as Vladimir grew older, he came under the influence of the culture of Byzantium and of its religion, Greek Orthodox Christianity. Vladimir made this religion, which developed into Russian Orthodoxy, the official religion of his realm, and he forced all of Russia to accept it.

In the golden age of the city-state of Kiev, which lasted until the thirteenth century, free peasants farmed their land and free merchants traded goods with East and West. Kiev was ideally situated along established trade routes, and it became a wealthy, peaceful state. In the East or in western Europe, no state was so large or influential, no city was so grand or splendid as Kiev.

This was the beginning of a Russian culture, a Russian people. Kiev was centrally situated, accessible to Asia, the Middle East and western Europe. It absorbed culture from all of these, as the princes of Kiev married with the daughters of leaders of states in all domains to solidify alliances and guarantee trade routes. While initially Kiev was as liberal and free as any state created upon the ideals of Greek and Roman thought and law, it also gradually absorbed a more autocratic tradition. From the Byzantine culture was created a Russian political ideal—the unified state headed by a powerful absolute ruler supported by a loyal bureaucracy. It became the way Russia would be ruled for a thousand years. Yet the culture and traditions of the West have also played their part, making Russian culture as schizophrenic as the two-headed eagle of the Romanov coat-of-arms.

The uneasy Russian princes sent out their armies to bring to heel all of the free peasants within range and enslave them in serfdom (a system of slavery in which the slaves were "permitted" to pay taxes and serve in the army), where they owed life and wealth to the princes. The princes learned their political lessons and consolidated their power by using more repressive procedures of governing. This meant increasing resistance from the people being ruled and made for greater and greater difficulties in trade and passage between states. While in the year 1000 Russia was at the center of a great artery of commerce vital to western Europe, by 1200, according to British historian John Lawrence, "she had become a distant land, hard of access and leading to nowhere."

Genghis Khan was probably the most successful conqueror who ever lived. The son of a Mongol chief, raw and untutored, he built an army of devoted fierce fighters on Mongol ponies that defeated any army it faced, even if that army was twice its size. During a long lifetime, Genghis's empire extended north to the Arctic, south into India, east to Korea and the Pacific Ocean and west to the river Dnieper. When he died in 1227, he had already planned with his sons to expand the Mongol empire even further.

In 1237, not long after the signing of the Magna Charta in England, hordes of Mongol horsemen led by Genghis Khan's grandson, Batu, swept westward across the Steppe and subjugated all in their path. In Europe, these Mongols were called Tartars, supposedly because they came from Tartarus—Hell. Russia now came under the Tartar yoke and an even crueler concept of government than was known before.

The Tartar overlords exacted their yearly tribute from the Russian land, and the people sank into generations of poverty and vicious squabbling among themselves. It was a time of stagnation of a subjugated people while western Europe laid the foundations for the modern world. Now

•

Russia was even more remote from its European neighbors, and this remoteness guaranteed that the country would be a latecomer to new developments.

For more than two hundred years the Tartar yoke held. At first, representatives of the Tartars remained in every city and village. But gradually they relaxed their grip, depending on their reputation for cruel revenge to keep the Russians in line. The boyish Prince of Novgorod, Alexander Nevsky (the name Nevsky commemorating the young leader's defeat of his enemies at the Neva River), commanding a small army, defeated much larger forces of Swedes and Lithuanians, but he was not foolish enough to challenge the Tartars. They made him Grand Prince of Vladimir, and he kept the peace for them in their captured lands to the end of his life. Russian princes ruled under a Mongol flag. When one of the Russian princes died, his heir was required to travel to the Mongol capital and pay dear tribute for the right to rule in Tartar lands.

Russia expanded out of Kiev to the north and now grew rapidly in the principality of Muscovy, the capital of which was Moscow. Moscow extended its influence, at first through the statemanship of its princes, and then with the support of the Russian Orthodox Church. This period is known as the Age of Muscovy, when Russia turned in on itself, resenting and fearing foreigners from the West. But there was an intense curiosity about the Europeans as well as a strong desire to impress them.

The expansiveness, affection, and hospitality that is a natural part of the Russian character led Russians to welcome Western visitors and emissaries, but fear, contempt, and a sense of inferiority that has lasted to this day made them hold back from lasting associations and alliances with the West.

Westerners, while they were attracted to Russia by the

•

vastness of the land and the friendliness of the people, were also afraid of the developing Russian power and Russian barbarism learned from Byzantium and the Tartars.

By 1480, the Tartars had little of their power or reputation remaining. So Ivan III, "the Great," neglected to send his tribute. Ivan, a descendant of Rurik, was both cruel and cowardly. He knew that the present Tartars possessed only a shadow of their former strength, so Ivan was surprised to see a Tartar army advance to the banks of the Oka River, threatening him. He sent a counterforce of Russian soldiers to face them across the river. The opposing troops shouted curses at each other, but neither side moved for days. Too frightened to attack, Ivan finally ordered his soldiers to retreat. As the Russians prepared to fall back, the Tartars also decided to retreat. Thus ended the Tartar yoke.

Ivan the Great ruled for forty-three years. He believed that national unity was the goal that would secure Russia as a nation, and so he sent his armies to seize, one after the other, poorly protected cities and regions, which he unified under his own rule. Ivan tripled the size of his domain and set himself above the other princes, declaring himself *czar*, a word meaning "caesar." He then reduced the princes in rank to gentry, or boyars. This began the character of the reign of almost all the Russian czars to come—the concentration of power and expansion of domain.

Ivan the Great sealed the future of Russia, permanently moving the country away from a democratic style of government and making it a dictatorship or autocracy. It was his grandson, though, Ivan IV, "the Terrible," who made the power of the czar absolute.

For fifty-one years, the longest reign of any czar, Ivan the Terrible ruled the Russian Empire. He was only three years old when he first came to the throne all alone, as both his father and mother were dead under suspicious circum-

•

stances. Behind little Ivan, who was trotted out for ceremonial occasions in glorious robes but kept in near starvation the rest of the time, the boyars ruled and systematically looted the treasury. At sixteen, Ivan came into his manhood. He hated the boyars and announced from the throne that he had issued an order for the arrest of a boyar leader. The boyar fled, but was captured and slain by the royal kennel keepers. The boyars, in fear for their lives, capitulated to young Ivan, who was immediately crowned czar, with absolute autocratic powers.

Raising an army that was modern for its time, Ivan began to war against the remaining outposts of the Mongol kingdom and annex land to the south and east. His forays to the north, though, were less successful. Then Ivan's wife, his beloved Anastasia, died, leaving him with two sons, Ivan and Feodor. His paranoia, never deeply hidden beneath the surface, became a driving force. Ivan, for his personal protection, raised an army of six thousand men, dressed in monks' robes, who roamed the land killing, beating, and robbing those the czar saw as a threat. He tried to wipe out the boyars completely. The years that passed brought orgies of blood as Ivan sank deeper into madness. He kept lists of his many victims and prayed for their souls. He considered himself a religious man and ordered built, in 1554, the magnificent church of St. Basil the Blessed in Moscow's Red Square, which is still today symbolic of Russia. He was not so religious in responding to the complaint of the metropolitan (or archbishop) of Moscow about the excesses of Ivan's "monks." He ordered the prelate strangled to death.

Madness and rage were all that was left to him as he slowly deteriorated in the final days of his life. He had married six times after Anastasia's death, but it was the children he had with her that would succeed to the throne.

Two days before his death, in a fit of unexplained rage, he killed his son Ivan with the single blow of a club. On Ivan the Terrible's death, his younger son Feodor, a simpleton, became czar, last of the descendants of Rurik to rule in Russia.

Czar Feodor never lost his idiot's smile. His complete ineptness of rule brought about the Time of Troubles, which lasted for nine years of famine and killing. Feodor died before the troubles really started, and his wife's brother, Boris Godunov, tried to hold the country together. Boris was a handsome and able man with good intentions, but civil unrest and the forces of nature were too much for him. He died in 1605, at the age of fifty-three, in a Kremlin besieged by rebellious Muscovites.

The Time of Troubles and the battle for the throne in the Kremlin continued until 1613, when an assembly made up of all Russian classes, from the boyars and churchmen to the peasantry, met to elect a czar. It chose Mikhail Romanov, a sixteen-year-old relative of Ivan the Terrible's first wife, Anastasia. The Romanov dynasty began.

Isolated, Russia continued to grow. To escape serfdom, military service, and ruinous taxes to finance wars with European neighbors over land and boundaries, Russian peasants kept moving, settling new lands, and expanding Russian culture and influence throughout eastern Europe and western Asia.

While Russian expansion under the rule of Muscovy had ranged to the north as well as east into Siberia, to the south were the fertile lands of the Ukraine. Ukraine (a name that means "borderland") was largely the domain of the Cossacks (from a Tartar word *kazak*, or "free adventurer"), warrior tribesmen who roamed the land and made their services available wherever it was advantageous. By the seventeenth century, the Cossacks were ruled by the king of

•

Poland. But trouble erupted between a Cossack leader and a Polish noble in a jealous row over a woman, and the Cossacks revolted. They were joined by the Ukrainian peasants, whose religion was Orthodox and who resented their Polish landlords, who were Roman Catholic.

Once free of Polish rule, the Cossacks looked to Moscow for protection and in 1654 signed a treaty of union between the Ukraine and the growing Russian Empire. The acquisition of the Ukraine brought to Russia a fertile, productive region that also contributed mightily to the intellectual growth of the fledgling empire.

Russia was now the largest empire in the world, but it was a backward empire bogged down in poverty and slavery and provincialism. Until Peter the Great came to the throne.

The grandson of Mikhail Romanov was born on May 30, 1672. He was a healthy baby who grew into a giant of a man almost seven feet tall, muscular, broad-shouldered and handsome. The first child of Czar Alexis and his young second wife, Natalya Naryshkina, Peter was not first in line to ascend to the Russian throne. After his father's death, Peter's sickly half-brother Feodor wore the crown for six years, and then he also died.

Over his other, older half-brother Ivan, Peter was proclaimed czar by the patriarch of the Russian Orthodox Church and a group of boyars. Peter was then ten years old, although because of his size he looked much older. But Ivan's sister, twenty-five-year-old Sophia, planned a palace revolution to bring a sickly Ivan to the throne, with herself as regent.

On May 15, 1682, Sophia sent riders into the streets of Moscow crying that Peter's mother's family, the Naryshkins, had strangled Ivan. The Streltsy, regiments of riflemen that were first formed by Ivan the Terrible in 1550, immediately marched on the Kremlin shouting for the blood of Peter and his mother. They ranged through the Kremlin for three days, killing all of the Naryshkins, although they spared the life of both Peter and his mother. For the rest of his life, Peter had a facial twitch as a result of the event.

Sophia partly accomplished her plan. Ivan and Peter were to rule as joint czars under her regency. Peter and his mother were sent to live on the outskirts of Moscow, a city Peter now hated, in the village of Preobrazhenskoe. In this little village, Peter set about recruiting and drilling a small army for his personal protection. As Peter grew to manhood, Sophia grew worried about her hold on power. She planned to send a troop of Streltsy to capture Peter, but he was warned and escaped. Now he gathered his troops together and forcibly deposed Sophia, who was sent bitterly protesting to the Novedevichy Monastery, a convent in Moscow, where she remained for the rest of her life. Peter, as 1690 dawned and his ailing half-brother Ivan died, finally became the one czar of all the Russias.

Among the first things that Peter attacked as czar was the institutionalized system of corruption that had existed for many years from top to bottom throughout Russian government and society. This corruption proved an implacable foe for Peter—and every other Russian leader right up to Gorbachev.

Peter was fascinated from an early age with the shipbuilding technology of western Europe. He traveled to the West himself to learn its methods and set about developing for his empire both a navy and a seaport to the West from which to launch it.

Peter modernized much of Russian society and set the pattern of Russian life for the next two hundred years. He encouraged learning and founded school and publishing

houses to educate his people. He moved the capital of his
empire from Moscow to St. Petersburg, the city he founded
and built (on the bones of many Russians) to be Russia's
window on the European world. Today, St. Petersburg
(called Leningrad from 1925 to 1991) is still the most European of Russia's cities.

By the beginning of the eighteenth century, through
Peter's ambition and costly wars, Russia emerged as a
major European power to be reckoned with. But the lot of
most Russians had improved little, and life was still bitterly
hard.

Born a Prussian princess in 1729, Catherine II, "the
Great," became empress in 1762. She had earlier married
Czar Peter III, a weak and brainless grandson of Peter the
Great. Peter was a passionate Prussophile who nevertheless
cared little for his bride—or Russia. With the help of a
regiment of the Russian Guard, Catherine usurped the
throne and then permitted the guard to assassinate Peter.

An enlightened European-style ruler, Catherine instituted a number of reforms, including a system of public
hospitals. She decentralized authority to a certain extent by
introducing local government, but many of her liberal ideas
were not in harmony with Russian life at the time, and the
lives of peasants were no better than before.

Catherine was a cultivated person who loved the arts.
She had a small palace built behind the Winter Palace in St.
Petersburg and furnished it lavishly with paintings and
sculpture. No one aside from her, including servants, was
permitted to enter this palace, which she called her "Hermitage." This palace today is one of the buildings that
make up Russia's most famous museum, and its name was
adopted for the museum. Catherine herself wrote memoirs,
comic operas, and fairy tales; she courted the leading think-
ers of Europe such as Voltaire and Diderot, making French

·

the language that the gentry used, rather than Russian, further separating the upper class from the people it ruled.

During her reign, Russian territory was expanded even further (at the expense of Turkey and Poland), but the institution of serfdom was strengthened and even increased. Although she assumed a "republican" outlook, she was horrified by the American and French revolutions, and much of her liberalism proved to be rhetorical. There was widespread discontent among the people during her reign, although she survived the 1773 people's rebellion, the Peasant War, led by Yemelyan Pugachov, whom Alexander Pushkin immortalized in *The Captain's Daughter*.

In 1801, Catherine's grandson, Alexander I, ascended to the throne. He was a handsome twenty-four-year-old, not at all like his father, Czar Paul I, an ugly and stupid man who paraded his young mistresses before his wife and alienated as many others as he could—until a conspiracy of nobles stabbed and strangled him to death in his bedroom in the Winter Palace. Although Alexander had approved the plan to murder his father, he was not considered one of the cruel and bloodthirsty czars.

He wanted, in fact, to alleviate the plight of the serfs and spoke bitterly of "the state of barbarism in which the country has been left by the traffic in men." As soon as Alexander became czar, he disbanded the secret police and forbade the use of torture in questioning suspects. He released thousands of political prisoners and pardoned exiles, opening the country once more to foreigners and foreign ideas.

While Alexander wished to remove the burden of serfdom from his people, any discussion on his part about freedom for the serfs was strongly opposed by the landowners, upon whom the czar's power depended. But in any case, granting rights to serfs had to be put off with the onset of the Napoleonic Wars. With Napoleon's retreat from Moscow and his eventual defeat in the War of 1812 (called in Russia the War for the Fatherland), Alexander's greatest moment came when he marched into Paris, deposed Napoleon, and convened the Congress of Vienna.

Although Alexander expressed his desire to establish a constitutional government, he was by heredity an autocrat and he held tightly to an autocrat's power. He was visiting the Crimea in 1825 when it was announced that at the age of forty-eight he had come down with a fever and died. Alexander's life was something of a mystery, and his death was an even greater mystery. It was said that he had wanted to retire from public life and chose this way of doing it—that he had not died at all. A hermit appeared sometime later who was treated like a czar by the nobility; it was said by some that he was Alexander, ending his days as a holy man. When Alexander's coffin was opened in the 1920s, it was empty.

After an abortive uprising, called the Decembrist Revolt, by rebellious but ineffectual army officers in 1825, Nicholas I, younger brother of Alexander I, took the throne and ruled Russia with an iron hand for thirty years. The people were ready for reform when Nicholas's son, Alexander II, succeeded to the throne. This Alexander was a more liberal czar than Russia had yet seen and he completely reformed the system of justice, appointing qualified judges and making trials public. In 1861, two years before Abraham Lincoln freed the slaves in America, Alexander emancipated the serfs. Russia began to develop into a modern state.

But the optimism that infected Russia in the early years of Alexander's reign soon turned to disappointment and sullen resentment. Alexander failed to learn what many other future leaders would also fail to learn—that giving a little freedom to people would not satisfy their desires, but only make them want more freedom. Revolutionary movements such as "Land and Freedom," dissatisfied with moderate reform and seeking a constitution and a voice in the governing of the country, flourished throughout Russia, but failed to win the support of the peasants. The terrorist group The People's Will sought even more radical solutions, and in 1881, revolutionaries made many attempts on the life of the Liberator Czar. Finally, Alexander stepped from his carriage after a bomb had been thrown, to see how his injured guards fared. He mildly scolded the bomb thrower and thanked God for his escape. "It is too early to thank God," shouted a second revolutionary, who threw another bomb that wounded Alexander fatally. "Home to the palace to die," he told his driver. But the revolutionaries had made no plans past the assassination to take charge of the government, and the liberal Alexander II was replaced by his reactionary second son, Alexander III.

As has been true throughout Russian history, a period of some expansion or freedom—of looking outward to the rest of the world—was followed by the tightening grip of repression. But during the following repressive years, first under Alexander III and later, Nicholas II, revolutionary groups grew in their influence and activity. One young revolutionary who was involved in a plan to assassinate Alexander III was hanged in the Schlüsselburg Fortress (Petrokrepost) near St. Petersburg. He was Alexander Ilyich Ulyanov, eldest son in a family of revolutionaries. Now, the younger son, Vladimir Ilyich Ulyanov, vowed he would succeed where his brother had failed. Young Vladimir, as was customary for security reasons, took a pseudonym, a "revolutionary" name—Lenin.

In 1903, Lenin, exiled as a revolutionary, and who had written the year before of the need for a centralized organi-

•

zation of professional revolutionaries, called for a congress of Russian Social Democrats. About forty delegates attended the meetings in London. There was much wrangling over largely procedural matters, and the group split into two parts, the Bolsheviks (majority) and the Mensheviks (minority). The Bolsheviks had one more adherent than the minority, a situation that changed when one of their members switched sides; but Lenin, who headed the Bolsheviks, insisted on retaining the title for his group.

Lenin returned to Russia during the "first Russian revolution" in 1905, but could not gather enough adherents to his cause to gain power. During the following years, in Finland, Switzerland, and then Austria, he consolidated his power within the revolutionary movement, while Nicholas II, a weak man who nonetheless insisted on retaining an autocrat's absolute power and was too inflexible to adjust to a changing political situation, grew weaker in his own realm. Russian participation in World War I was disastrous, and the people were finally ready to overthrow the Romanov dynasty.

After one unsuccessful attempt to gain power, Lenin managed to return to Petrograd (as St. Petersburg was renamed in 1914) and, with the help of Leon Trotsky and Joseph Stalin, seized control of the provisional government. On November 9, 1917, Lenin formed the first Soviet (a Russian word meaning "council") government and became its chairman. He concluded a peace treaty with Germany in 1918, taking Russia out of the war. Trotsky objected to the treaty, which he said was not advantageous to Russia. Lenin insisted that it was important for the Communists to consolidate their power in Russia, for from that power base, the revolution could be expanded throughout the world.

Civil war between those loyal to the czar under the

White banner and the revolutionaries under the Red raged in Russia for the next two years.

Nicholas II had abdicated in March of 1917. The Russian royal family first had been confined in the town of Tsarskoye Selo. Later, Nicholas and his family were taken to Yekaterinburg (renamed Sverdlovsk and now Yekaterinburg once again), about 870 miles east of Moscow, where they were imprisoned in an ornate white-washed home requisitioned for the purpose from a retired army engineer named Nikolai Ipatyev. The large residence was surrounded by a stockade and closely watched by the Red Guard. The future of the royal family was uncertain. The Bolsheviks were fearful that Nicholas, even if exiled to another country, would become a rallying point for the White Guard.

Early in the morning of July 17, 1918, the czar and his family were taken to the basement of the house, grouped together against a wall, and shot by local Chekists, members of the Cheka, the Bolshevik secret police. Some bullets failed to reach their mark, ricocheting off jewels hidden in the corsets of the royal daughters. The women were finished off with bayonets.

The firing squad carted the bodies to the countryside, stripped, burned, and threw them into a mine shaft. The next night, to prevent a worshiping cult from growing around the Romanovs, the bodies were exhumed, doused with acid to make them totally unrecognizable, and reburied in a secret grave.

Only in 1990 did the truth come out that Lenin himself—not the secret police—had ordered the executions. The secret was revealed by Lenin's bodyguard, Aleksei Akhimov, and by a telegraph tape confirming the order that was signed by Yakov M. Sverdlov, the state official for

•

whom the city in which the execution took place was re-named.

Although Nicholas was a vacillating, uncharismatic au-tocrat, many Russian Orthodox believers today view him as a martyr, the memory of him driven less by how he ruled than how he died. In 1977, rising cultism prompted the Communist party Politburo to issue a secret order to have the Ipatyev house destroyed. Boris Yeltsin, then party boss in Sverdlovsk, sent bulldozers in the middle of the night to level the house.

Despite the attempt to eradicate the last czar from memory, he and his family have taken on a kind of mythol-ogy among an underground movement that includes small groups of monarchists, descendants of Russian nobility, and other self-styled Russian patriots. Calling themselves *Pamyat*, the Russian word for "memory," some of them rally anti-Semitic passions by noting that both Yurovsky, the leader of the Chekist death squad, and Sverdlov were Jews.

Today, on the site of the execution, someone has boldly placed an iron cross, which has become a focal point for local prayer meetings and political rallies, as well as a favor-ite place for brides and grooms to toast the future after weddings.

The Red Army, under the brilliant leadership of Trotsky, won suzerainty over all of Russia for the Soviet government. Lenin moved the capital from Petrograd to Moscow and in 1919 held there the First Congress of the Communist International.

Lenin's outlook was international, and he saw Russia as the head of an international Communist community. But Lenin's leadership was to be short-lived. In May 1922, he had the first of a series of strokes that finally took his life on January 21, 1924.

Lenin had warned his successors against Stalin, whom he considered brutish and madly ambitious. But Trotsky, Nikolay Bukharin, Grigory Zinoviev, and Lev Kamenev, who might have challenged Stalin for the Soviet leadership, continued to underestimate him. First, Trotsky failed to act when he had the chance to remove Stalin from his Party post. Stalin subsequently convinced Zinoviev and Kamenev to join with him in opposing Trotsky and then joined with Bukharin to oppose Zinoviev and Kamenev. Eventually, he eliminated all of his rivals; all those left in the Party hierarchy owed their positions to Stalin. By the time his opposition realized what had happened, Stalin was firmly in control.

Poised on the brink of internationalism, Stalin turned Russia in on itself once again. Paranoically suspicious of anyone who might dilute his power, Stalin distrusted anything unfamiliar. He had no intellectual or emotional connection with anything outside the Soviet Union, and so he sought to cut it off from the rest of the world. Soviet Jews suffered inordinately under Stalin, not for traditionally Russian anti-Semitic reasons, but because Jews most often had relatives outside the Soviet Union. All personal contacts with the West were to be broken.

Stalin was determined to industrialize Russia, to catch up with and surpass the West. To do this he embarked on one Five-Year Plan, and then another. And he began his program of collectivization—first nationalizing all of the private farmland in the Soviet Union, then putting together a "collective" of farmers to work the land that now belonged to the state and turn over the harvest to the state.

Farmers did not greet collectivization with equanimity. To many of them it seemed like a return to the serfdom they had escaped less than seventy years before. The kulaks in particular, those farmers whose farms were prosperous

•

enough so that they could hire a helper or two to work the land with them, objected to collectivization. Stalin set out to liquidate the kulaks as a class of people.

Repression of the kulaks began in 1929. Their land and crops were confiscated by the state; they were deported, beaten, and murdered. The Stalinist terror against these farmers affected not only the kulaks but also "middle peasants" and other farmers throughout the Soviet Union. Farmers who might have sympathy for the kulaks could be reported and interned or even killed. The government induced famine throughout the land by withholding food particularly from the communities where the food was grown. Famine swept the country and eliminated kulak families and many others as well. By 1933, the kulaks, who had numbered ten million or more, had been wiped out.

The first Five-Year Plan of industrialization set cruelly high goals of attainment. Workers were driven to exhaustion and death, but its goals were accomplished in only four years, at a brutally high cost. The program laid the foundation for an industrial economy, rather than what Russia had always been, an agrarian economy. The new emphasis was on heavy industry—manufacturing machinery, tractors, tanks, and so forth—so that there were few products in the stores. Russians would have to go a little longer, Stalin said, without new shoes or clothing, kitchen utensils, and other consumer goods, while a new economy was being forged. And before, Russians tightened their belts and worked and hoped for a new day.

Into the height of the famine created by the state to destroy the kulaks and many middle peasants, on March 2, 1931, Mikhail Sergeyevich Gorbachev was born into a peasant family. He was born in Privolnoye, a village in the Krasnogvardeisk (a word in Russian meaning "Red Guard") district of the Stavropol Territory, or Krai, the smallest of seven administrative-territorial units in the Russian Republic, known as the Russian Soviet Federated Socialist Republic (RSFSR).

AN OUTLINE OF RUSSIAN-SOVIET HISTORY

862	Rurik founds first Russian state at Novgorod
	Age of Kiev; reception of Christianity
	Tartar invasion
	Alexander Nevsky rules in Novgorod
	Ivan Kalita, Grand Prince of Moscow
	Ivan the Great rules
	Tartar yoke ends
	Ivan the Terrible rules
	Beginning of the conquest of Siberia
	Moscow patriarchate is established
	Boris Godunov rules
	The Time of Troubles
	Mikhail Romanov rules
	Union of the Ukraine and Muscovy
	Peter the Great rules
	The Great Northern War
	Founding of St. Petersburg
	First Partition of Poland
	Catherine the Great rules
	Conquest of the Crimea
	Second Partition of Poland
	Third Partition of Poland
	Alexander I rules
	Conquest of Finland
	The War for the Fatherland
	The Decembrist Revolt
	Nicholas I rules
	First Polish Revolt
	The Crimean War

•

1855–81 Alexander II rules
Emancipation of the serfs
Second Polish Revolt
Conquest of Central Asia
Assassination of Alexander II
Alexander III rules
First major strike
Famine
Nicholas II rules
Wave of strikes
Russo-Japanese War
First Russian revolution
World War I
The October Revolution
Lenin forms first Soviet government
Civil War
Death of Lenin
Trotsky expelled from Communist party
Stalin rules
First Five-Year Plan begins
Collectivization begins
Second Five-Year Plan begins
Moscow trials; the Great Terror
Third Five-Year Plan begins
Soviet-Finnish War
Estonia, Lithuania, Latvia, and Bessarabia are
        incorporated into the USSR
The Great Patriotic War
Death of Stalin
Rise of Khruschev
Fall of Khruschev
Rise of Brezhnev
Era of stagnation
Death of Brezhnev
Andropov named general secretary of the CP
Death of Andropov
Chernenko named general secretary
Death of Chernenko

●

1985 Gorbachev elected general secretary of the CP
      Eastern European Communist bloc countries

      Gorbachev named president of the USSR
      Yeltsin elected president of Russian Federation
      Attempted August putsch
      Dissolution of the USSR

CHAPTER THREE

•

THE MAKING OF A LEADER

•

THE north Caucasus where Mikhail Gorbachev was born was first settled by Russians in the late eighteenth century. They were peasants who moved into the area with the encouragement of Catherine the Great to establish an outpost of Russian presence and religion against the influence of the Ottoman Empire and Islam. The city of Stavropol, which is the capital of the territory, was a fortress in the south for Catherine, and she had one of her favorites, Grigory Alexandrovich Potemkin, lay out the city.

While Potemkin was an excellent architect, he is famous because he was always careful that her majesty's eye should not be offended, and he therefore had pretty facades nailed onto village shacks along her route when she traveled. So was formed the Russian expression *Potemkin Village*, meaning a sham.

The northern Caucasus was then a frontier for Russia, as the West was for America, and warlike Muslim tribes roamed the land. The area figured prominently as a romantic background for the literature of Lermontov, Pushkin, and Tolstoy with its snow-capped mountains, rich black soil and fast-running rivers.

•

After Alexander I freed the serfs in 1861, a new wave of immigrants from less fertile areas of Russia entered the area and founded the village of Privolnoye. These settlers were free peasants—in Russian the name *Privolnoye* means "free," which may signify the difference between these yeomen of the Caucasus and the serfdom they left behind. During this wave of immigration, the forebears of Gorbachev most probably moved into the region.

As was traditional with Soviet leaders, Gorbachev has publicly revealed little about his ancestors, other than that they were (also traditionally) working people. His first official biography said only that he was born "into a peasant family." A subsequent version that the government made available to the international press late in 1985, in which his entire life was outlined in three pages, says: "Gorbachev's parents were genuine peasants who had to earn their daily bread by the sweat of their brows. His grandfather was one of the founders and the chairman of a collective farm. His father, Sergei Andreyevich, proved his mettle first as an agricultural mechanic and later as a frontline soldier in the Great Patriotic War. His competence in his job, his careful husbandry, his Party-inspired sense of justice and his personal modesty earned him universal respect. His mother, Maria Pantelyevna, was and still is equally hard-working, and at the age of 74 refuses to leave her native village."

Remarks that Gorbachev has made in conversation or speeches have led enterprising journalists to discover more about his forebears. Two veteran Moscow correspondents, Dusko Doder and Louise Branson, say that an unnamed source from high inside the government in the Kremlin told them that Gorbachev's grandfather, Andrei Gorbachev, was sent to serve a nine-year sentence (he returned home after a year and a half) to the Gulag in Siberia.

According to Doder and Branson, the elder Gorbachev

•

was charged with storing some forty pounds of grain for his family's use. He was informed on by a jealous neighbor and may not have been guilty of the charge, but merely guilty of inciting a neighbor's envy. That was enough during Stalin's purges to get one sent to the Gulag—or worse.

Andrei Gorbachev, who like his son and grandchildren was born in Privolnoye, had supported the collectivization of the farms in 1930 and was chairman of the village collective, called *kolkhoz* in Russian. It may have been his position as chairman that made it possible for his grandson Misha to survive the famine that would decimate rural families in the 1930s. Death from starvation was common in the Stavropol Krai during the winter of 1931–32, particularly among young children, and in some villages all of the youngest children perished.

Being born at such a time and into such a dire situation must have had a powerful effect in forming Gorbachev's ideas. But even though collectivization brought difficult times to his family and their neighbors and friends, Gorbachev, in his 1987 book *Perestroika*, said: "Collectivization was a great historical act, the most important social change since 1917. . . . Further progress for our country would have been impossible without it." Even though this has been Gorbachev's public stance on collectivization, many of his private remarks belie this position. Collectivization was a heavy blow to the Russian peasantry from which Gorbachev sprung.

Until recently, only scant information had been available about Gorbachev's maternal grandparents, and the new information may not be true. According to American author Gail Sheehy, "Gorbachev has confirmed that his maternal grandparents were Ukrainian—Gopkalo was the family name, according to villagers. . . ." (His maternal grandfather's first name was Panteley, as we know from the

patronymic of Gorbachev's mother, Maria Pantelyevna.)
Like Andrei Gorbachev, he was chairman of a collective in
the Stavropol Territory. According to Sheehy, it was he,
and not grandfather Gorbachev, who was sent to the Gulag.

But it could be any of his grandparents that Gorbachev
described, speaking as general secretary of the Communist
party on the occasion of the seventieth anniversary of the
October Revolution in 1987, as middle peasants who were
victims of "injustice" and "excess" in the 1930s. He called
these middle peasants "a staunch and dependable ally of
the working class, an ally on a new basis." One of these
grandfathers was a staunch supporter at the time of collectivization. This may simply have been a strong instinct for
political survival, rather than agreement with the policy
and philosophy. This instinct is something that Gorbachev
clearly inherited.

We know a little more about Gorbachev's parents. Sergei Andreyevich Gorbachev was twenty-two years old when
his son Misha was born. When the Soviet government provided the first benefits of collectivization in the form of farm
machinery after 1933, Sergei was given special schooling in
mechanization and became a tractor and combine operator
at a machine-tractor station. During World War II, Sergei
Gorbachev fought in the Soviet Army with a combat engineering unit. He was wounded in Poland and returned home
in 1945 heavily decorated with medals and military orders.
Once again, after his return home, Sergei Gorbachev
worked as a combine operator and became chairman of a
combine brigade in the local machine-tractor station. According to exiled Soviet scientist and author Zhores A.
Medvedev, Sergei Gorbachev early became a member of the
Communist party and as such served as a Party official and
an "advisor on economic matters." He received the highly
prestigious Order of Lenin award and was named Honorary

•

Member of the Kolkhoz. He retired in 1971 and on February 22, 1976, "went out in the morning to feed the animals and he just fell down and died," according to family friend Georgi Gorlov in a 1980 interview with David Remnick of the *Washington Post.*

Sergei Gorbachev is generally remembered as a retiring, modest man who was respected by the community for his skill and knowledge. While Medvedev reports that he was a Party member, Doder and Branson say that neither he nor any other of the Gorbachevs, other than Mikhail, were members of the Communist party. It seems that Sergei was one of those men who stay resolutely in the background, although Mikhail has said: "[My father] influenced me intellectually. Even though he was a simple man, I learned much from him." But it is said in the village of Privolnoye that Mikhail Gorbachev "took on his mother's character."

"Emotionally, my mother influenced me more," said Gorbachev to journalist Mainhardt Count Nayhauss. And Maria Pantelyevna is, according to local lore, a "stubborn and willful woman—the first to raise her voice at village meetings." Today, in her eighties, Gorbachev's mother continues to live simply in her small house in Privolnoye on a small widow's pension (recently increased, as all pensions have been).

Gorbachev's mother is a religious woman—a believer in the Russian Orthodox faith—and young Misha was baptized, secretly because of the antireligion stance of the government. When he visited Prime Minister Margaret Thatcher in England before he became general secretary, Gorbachev told people that his grandparents had icons hanging on the walls in their home, but they were covered by portraits of Lenin and Stalin out of fear. His grandparents also took young Misha to church, but he remembers that he had no desire to return. Like the Soviet leaders before him, he is not a follower of any organized religion. But in 1990, for the first time in many years, the Soviet government permitted open celebration of the Russian Orthodox Christmas on January 7.

Later in the year, on September 26, 1990, the Soviet legislature initially approved sweeping legislation on freedom of religion in the Soviet Union. The law prohibited the government from interfering with religious activities, improves the legal status of religious organizations and gave Soviet citizens the right to study religion in homes and private schools. While the constitution of the USSR guaranteed freedom of worship, atheism was the official doctrine of the Communist party, and the Party's opposition to the "opiate of the masses" effectively meant restriction in religious practice. According to Peter Reddaway, an expert on Soviet religious practices at George Washington University, in Washington, D.C., "Official tolerance for religion has increased since President Mikhail Gorbachev came to power in 1985."

Little is known about any Gorbachev siblings. While peasant families had been large, the state-induced famine of 1932–33 and World War II drastically reduced the size of the average farm family. It is rumored that Mikhail had an older brother who was killed in 1943 in the battle of Kursk, and there is another brother, sixteen years younger than Mikhail, named Alexander. The baby of the family, Alexander was doted upon by his mother. Perhaps because of this, or the wide gulf in age between them, the brothers have never been close. Alexander is supposed to be a rather ordinary mid-level government official with little of the spark that sets his brother apart. While there is no evidence of outright hostility, there is also no evidence of affection between them, and according to a Gorbachev family friend, if

Alexander wished to see his brother the president, he was assigned an appointment through official channels.

Like so many of his countrymen, Mikhail Gorbachev was born into national trauma, and it was national trauma that marked the steps of his early life. The famine brought about by collectivization as part of Stalin's Five-Year Plan was followed by further upheaval: Stalin's bloody "political" purges began just five years later and meant death for as many as thirty million people. After another five years the Great Patriotic War began.

The cruel first Five-Year Plan, which cost Russians so dearly in lives and food, paid military dividends when Hitler invaded the Soviet Union. With all of its resources invested in heavy industry, the USSR was one of the world's leading producers of machinery and munitions. Hitler vastly underestimated the USSR's industrial strength, and by the time the Nazis invaded in 1941, the Soviet Union's production of tanks and other war matériel far outstripped the industrial capability of Germany. Even so, Hitler's attack caught Stalin completely off guard, and the Soviet loss of life and property over four years of war was enormous.

The German *Blitzkrieg* hit the north Caucasus in July of 1942, as the Nazis launched a two-pronged attack. One German force moved on Stalingrad (now Volgograd, since the Soviet government erased many of the honors heaped upon Stalin) in the north and another drove toward Baku on the Caspian Sea, where there was Soviet oil in the south. On August 5, 1942, the city of Stavropol was occupied by German troops.

Stavropol in 1935 had been renamed Voroshilovsk by Stalin to honor his defense minister, Kliment Voroshilov. In an attempt to stir up local resentment that had been smoldering for years against Stalin, the Germans immediately reinstated the name Stavropol. (The move was a popular success; when the Soviets reclaimed the city, Stalin permitted the original name to remain.)

The German offensive in the north Caucasus weakened and eventually failed completely, as the Soviet troops began swiftly pushing back the incursion. By January 1943, after an occupation of five months, the German grip on the Stavropol area ended.

The village of Privolnoye was bypassed both by the German offensive and the Soviet counteroffensive and thus never became an active war zone. Although there was no formal German occupation of the village itself, the occupation of the whole area took place during the harvest season when the occupying army was hungry for the grain of the collective.

While it is not part of any public record, Mikhail Gorbachev most probably worked with the other children and the women of the village gathering grain for the conquering army during the late summer and fall of 1942. He was eleven years old at the time. Had he been much older, working for the Germans—even if it was forced labor— would have prevented Gorbachev from ever having a political career in the postwar Soviet Union. As he moved up the Party ladder, Gorbachev needed his mentors to keep any mention of living in an occupied area during the war from becoming public knowledge.

Gorbachev's schooling had been interrupted by the occupation. In September 1943, while the war raged to the north, he returned to school. Misha was a good student, and when he had finished the course at the tiny village school, he was eligible to go on to secondary school, in the educational center for the district at Krasnogvardeisk—a tenmile walk from Privolnoye. Each day, Misha walked to school. Often he was lucky and caught a lift. The roads between the villages were muddy in autumn and spring,

•

snow-covered in winter, and dusty in summer. One needed a sturdy pair of boots, and the villagers passed the hat to help the promising student.

In 1945, with the end of the war, Sergei Gorbachev came home. At the Privolnoye collective, the fourteen-year-old Misha worked with his father as an assistant combine operator. It was grueling work over long hours. In winter, Misha labored after school hours in bitter cold. In summer, the work lasted twelve or more hours a day in unrelenting heat with choking dust thrown up by the harvesting machinery. Still, young Gorbachev enjoyed the physical labor and the comradeship with his father.

But Mikhail knew that he wanted to make a career with the sweat of his intellect and not the sweat of his brow. He had always been an intelligent and intensely curious youngster. He wanted to know things—he wanted to learn. This had been noticed by others in the village. Even though he was very young, his opinion was sought on adult matters. His intense gaze, so often commented upon today, was noted even in his childhood when he first used an ability to influence others that was beyond his years. At fourteen, he joined the Komsomol (the Young Communist League) and began the long journey up through the Party ranks.

This was a path to success that others in Gorbachev's generation trod, but most often with less effect. The Komsomol indoctrinated its younger members in the ways of Communist party thinking and Party life and provided a forum where leadership qualities could be displayed and tested. It was also a sure road to Communist party membership, which in Gorbachev's youth was just about the only path to a good job in the middle echelons of the government. By 1990, because of reforms instituted by Gorbachev, Party membership in the Komsomol was no longer highly prized. According to one survey reported by *Vremya*, the Soviet official nightly news broadcast on television, only 10 percent of young Soviets felt positively about the Komsomol, 40 percent disapproved of the organization, and about 50 percent thought Komsomol membership was irrelevant. Said one young Soviet citizen: "Komsomol is 120,000 aging bureaucrats in search of something to do. They have no constituency."

Every summer during the following years, Gorbachev worked as a temporary employee of the Privolnoye Machine-Tractor Station, which was considered state employment. In 1946, the harvest was bad and food had to be rationed. But some farming areas were able to meet their quotas, and the government instituted a program of incentives, which promised rewards for peasants of the collectives and machine-tractor station workers throughout the country. These awards were still given until the final collapse of the Soviet Union. In the years 1947, 1948, and 1949, the collective at the village of Privolnoye had a good harvest and overfilled its quotas. Chairman of the collective and peasants and combine operators were put forward for the awards. The Presidium (later Politburo) of the Supreme Soviet granted the awards and published a list of those honored. When the list was published at the end of the year, Mikhail Gorbachev was awarded the Order of the Red Banner of Labor, a very great and unusual honor for someone so young.

In his final year at secondary school (the equivalent, in the United States, of high school and the first two years of college), Misha boarded with a teacher in Krasnogvardeisk. It was not as comfortable as home—which, though it was crowded with the addition to the family of baby Sasha, was warm and communal—but it saved the difficult daily trip. There was little fuel to waste on a strong teenager, used to hardship, so the room he shared was cold and bleak. But there was enough lamp oil so that the young student could satisfy his insatiable desire to learn, reading poetry and the great works of Russian literature into the night. He studied hard, but he also played schoolboy sports, at which he was not talented, though he went at them with his typical intensity. His talent shone through in school theatricals, where he displayed the gifts of a natural actor.

The following year, 1950, Mikhail graduated from secondary school, a year late because of the interruption in his schooling due to the occupation. On graduating, he was awarded the silver medal, which placed him at the top of his class, second only to a now-forgotten scholar who won the gold medal. He took and passed the entrance examinations for higher education. Without this, he would have been required to enter the army.

Gorbachev would have had little difficulty in being assigned a place in a provincial institution of higher learning, but he boldly applied to the most prestigious university in the USSR—Moscow State University. Even with his silver medal, competition for entrance to the law faculty at Moscow University was keen. Now, the award he received was invaluable. As a holder of the Order of the Red Banner of Labor, he was highly recommended by the authorities.

Having shown outstanding leadership qualities in the Komsomol, in 1950 Mikhail Gorbachev presented his application to become a candidate member of the Communist party. This first step to full membership in the Party could be taken only after a candidate's eighteenth birthday. After application, there was a probationary period of at least one year, during which the candidate was evaluated for full membership. A university career in Moscow before him and membership in the Communist party all but assured, Gorbachev had emerged as a young man marked for future success.

UNIVERSITY YEARS

And so the poor but ambitious young man from the hinterlands arrives in the big city, determined to make good. It's an old story, and a part of the culture of the rags-to-riches capitalist work ethic. But Mikhail Sergeyevich Gorbachev had his own dreams, and they were more socialist in nature.

Arriving at the Kursk railway station in Moscow that September in 1950, Gorbachev faced the most serious challenge in a young life already filled with challenges. He came to the capital with a sparse wardrobe. A single suitcase was enough for all of his personal belongings. He was stocky, of medium height, and handsome, with striking intense eyes and a self-confident air. Clean-shaven with a full head of dark hair, he wore a gray fur Cossack's hat, cocked at a jaunty angle. Before him were five years that he knew would affect the rest of his life. Here in Moscow he would take the first steps. At the university, he would associate and compete with the elite of the Soviet Union—the new generation that would one day inherit the leadership of one of the world's most powerful nations.

The university, Russia's first, was founded in 1755, while Peter the Great's daughter, Empress Elizabeth, sat on the throne of the vast Russian Empire. Count Ivan Shuvalov and the Russian scientist Mikhail Lomonosov developed a curriculum and opened the school near the Kremlin. The original building was destroyed in the Moscow fire of 1812, but the university was quickly rebuilt. Russia's greatest scientists taught here, and among its graduates are some of the most important people in Russian literature, such as Mikhail Lermontov, Ivan Turgenev, and Anton Chekhov. In 1940, the university was renamed the Moscow Lomonosov State University and was granted the

Order of Lenin. It is today usually referred to as Moscow State University, or more simply, Moscow University.

For more than a hundred years the university operated out of a number of nineteenth-century buildings in the center of Moscow. In 1948, most of its schools were moved to a newly constructed complex on the Lenin Hills in the city's southwestern suburbs. The central building on the campus is one of seven practically identical skyscrapers built at the same time in the "Stalin style" of architecture in various places around the city of Moscow. It has been a landmark on the Moscow skyline for more than forty years.

When Gorbachev arrived in Moscow in 1950, the sciences and mathematics faculties had moved to the Lenin Hills, while the humanities, including the law faculty, were still housed in the old buildings near Gorky Street (now Tverskaya Street), where today Moscow University students of Oriental languages and journalism read and socialize in a nineteenth-century garden setting.

Gorbachev had not initially intended to study law. In an interview with the Italian Communist party newspaper *L'Unita*, he recalled that originally he had wanted to study physics and that he was equally interested in literature, mathematics, and history.

The law as a profession was not respected in the USSR, and is still a profession with little prestige. The role of the lawyer in Stalin's Russia was to discover rationalizations for the torture, imprisonment, and execution of those Stalin and his henchmen considered enemies. There was little or none of the higher purposes of jurisprudence—the rules that a civilized society lives by—in the Soviet Union. There were few lawyers who protected individuals' rights. The career then open to a Soviet lawyer was as a procurator, similar to a prosecutor, for the state. Procurators were particularly despised by country people, of whom Gorbachev was one.

Peasants and others who work on the land and not in the city suffered more at the hands of procurators, who, in the experience of the peasants, offered not justice but coercion, repression, and harsh punishment.

A legal education was not highly valued by most students at the time that Gorbachev entered Moscow University. In the year that he began his university education, 1950–51, out of 1.2 million students in the USSR, only 45,400 were studying law as a profession. By the end of the decade, in the 1958–59 academic year, registration in the various faculties of law in the Soviet Union had dropped to 36,200, while the number of students studying for other professions almost doubled. According to an expert on Soviet law, "Law was not the favorite discipline, because the role of law was not very significant at this time."

Why then did Mikhail Gorbachev go to law school? Among other reasons, it could be that law was the course of study where competition for entrance was the least fierce. Even with his good academic record and glowing recommendations from local Party leaders, Gorbachev was no shoo-in for acceptance at Moscow University. After the war, Stalin, who admired America's development of the atom bomb (he was, like many others, convinced that the only reason the United States bombed Hiroshima and Nagasaki was as a warning example to the USSR), put strong emphasis on the development of scientific education in the Soviet Union. Gorbachev wanted to attend Moscow University, where the very best students with the best recommendations in the Soviet Union would be competing for places, particularly in the sciences. Competition for entrance to Moscow University would have been less difficult through the law faculty. Or there may have been another reason.

Gorbachev clearly did not want to be a lawyer. But he

wanted desperately to be a leader. The most revered leader
in the Soviet Union was Lenin, and Lenin had studied law.
(Of all the Soviet chiefs, only Lenin and Gorbachev were
university educated—both in law.) An education in law
could also be the basis for a political career. In the United
States, where lawyers are usually well paid, although not
always well thought of (opinion polls show Americans rate
lawyers just below used-car salesmen in trustworthiness),
about half of the thousands who attend law school do not
intend to practice law. A legal education is considered good
preparation for many different careers, and often law students intend to go into politics.

The study of law at Moscow University was a rigorous
intellectual exploration of the humanities, discussions
about the laws and culture of other societies, and intense
work on rhetoric and public speaking. Whether he planned
it or not, Mikhail Sergeyevich got just the sort of education
that would be most useful to him in his climb toward the
Soviet leadership.

He lived in the Stromynka student hostel in Moscow's
Sokolniki District in the northeastern part of the city, five
stops on the metro (subway) from the university's downtown campus. They were not luxurious quarters. While students of the sciences were comfortable in the dormitories on
campus in the Lenin Hills, sleeping only two to a room with
relatively private and modern facilities, students at the
"old university" had to make do in the ancient hostels. The
facilities were primitive and crowded, with six or more students sharing a room and an entire corridor using only one
toilet and lavatory.

University students in the Soviet Union were paid a
small amount of money by the state. The amount depended
upon academic year and standing and the school attended.
It was never very much. When Gorbachev was a first-year

•

student in Moscow, he received the equivalent of about twenty rubles a month, hardly enough to buy even the meager meals in the student canteen, certainly too little to replace the threadbare trousers he wore daily during his student days. To live above a bare subsistence level, students needed money from home or an outside job. Since Gorbachev could not count on any money from home, where life was lived frugally from harvest to harvest, he continued to earn money for his extra expenses by working as a combine operator in Privolnoye during the summer recess.

But Gorbachev was not an island of poverty in a sea of affluence. Most of the students at Moscow University lived in pretty much the same way. It was a life dependent for its pleasures on the things that students throughout the world and since time began have used for diversion: reading, friendship, free concerts, and plenty of argument—intellectual and otherwise (although a lot less political argument in Stalin's time than today).

One school friend of Gorbachev's from his initial years at Moscow University was Zdeněk Mlyňar, a Czech student studying in Moscow. In the early 1950s, there were a large number of foreign students from Communist countries enrolled at universities in Moscow. The Chinese kept to themselves and both roomed and did the rounds of classes together. The Eastern Europeans were by far the largest number, and students from Bulgaria, Czechoslovakia, Hungary, Poland, and Romania lived and studied cheek-by-jowl with the Soviet students. In the student jargon of Moscow at the time, these Eastern European students were called *demokraty*, a gibe at the names of their countries, "People's Democracy of . . ."

Since Gorbachev became general secretary, Mlyňar, now living in Austria, has written articles about their friendship. He says that their being assigned to the same room was completely coincidental. While the meeting of any two people can be ascribed to chance, in order to be considered as a roommate of a non-Soviet student in the early 1950s, the authorities would have had to be certain of Gorbachev's total ideological loyalty. Also, Gorbachev was probably asked to report regularly on Mlyňar. But Gorbachev's reports probably were not negative, since Mlyňar's progress through the ranks of the Communist party in Czechoslovakia was far more rapid than Gorbachev's in the USSR.

Zdeňek Mlyňar advanced so rapidly after graduating from Moscow University in 1955 that he was named to the ruling Central Committee of the Communist party of Czechoslovakia in 1967. In 1968, he became one of the leaders of the Prague Spring reformist movement, backing Alexander Dubček. When the reform movement was crushed by the tracks of Soviet tanks in Prague, Mlyňar lost his position and was put out to pasture at a Czechoslovakian research institute. He emigrated to the West in 1977.

According to Mlyňar, Gorbachev early showed liberal feelings and tendencies: "We were studying the official history of Russia. . . . We were led to believe that any ideas that deviated even slightly from the rigid Party line were antiparty, and that any person who held such beliefs should be tried, executed, taken out of the history books. . . . It was then Gorbachev said to me, 'Lenin did not have Martov [the Menshevik leader] arrested, he allowed him to leave the country.' Today, such a remark would not be given much importance. . . . But in 1952 those words signified that the student Gorbachev doubted that there were only two types of Russians, those who adhered strictly to the Party line and the criminals, who did not. What is more, to confide an opinion of this sort to a foreigner, even to a friend, was unusual in those days."

At a showing for students of *Cossacks of the Kuban,* a classic propaganda film from the 1930s, Mlyňar says Gorbachev revealed further doubts that everything Stalin and the Party said was absolutely true. The film is an unabashed tribute to collectivization and shows happy peasant families crowded around tables laden with wholesome food. "It's not like that at all," Gorbachev whispered to his friend Zdeněk.

There was little about peasant life that could be glorified by Stalin's propagandists to the knowledgeable Gorbachev, who lived the life firsthand. According to Mlyňar, "When we were studying collective-farm law, Gorbachev explained to me how insignificant *kolkhoz* legislation was in everyday life and how important, on the other hand, was brute force, which alone secured working discipline on the collective farms."

While working on the collective farm during the summer recess in 1951, Gorbachev was given a graphic example of how officials frowned on contacts with foreigners. Mlyňar had sent him a postcard from Czechoslovakia, and it was delivered to Gorbachev in the fields while he was at work— by the chief of police of Privolnoye. Any contact with the world outside of the Soviet Union was suspicious and would have to be checked out by local authorities.

Gorbachev is not remembered as liberal-minded by all of his fellow law students. In an interview with the *Wall Street Journal* in early 1985, Lev Yudovich remembered Gorbachev as a Komsomol leader in charge of propaganda and ideology who demanded that other Komsomol members studying at the law faculty tow a rigid behavioral line. Yudovich is a former Soviet procurator who has emigrated to the United States. Another fellow law student, former

•

procurator and investigator Fridrich Neznansky, who emigrated to the West in 1977, in a 1985 interview published in *Possev* said he often heard Gorbachev's "steely voice" demanding expulsion from the Komsomol for the least offense.

One story that has been told about Gorbachev during his student days seems to have little basis in fact and is probably apocryphal hindsight. The story goes that Gorbachev, wishing to become a *komsorg*, or leader, of the Komsomol group in the law faculty, took the current leader out on a drinking spree the night before a Komsomol meeting and then denounced him for drunkenness at the meeting.

Whether by fair means or foul, Gorbachev was elected a *komsorg* of the Komsomol in the law faculty at Moscow University in his first year and rose during his university career to be first a member of the committee that ran the Komsomol and then Komsomol organizer for the entire law faculty.

The course of study in the law faculty was a stringent one. Particularly in the first two years, a wide range of subjects was studied in addition to the law. There was, of course, a great deal of reading and work in the study of Marxist-Leninist dialectics. There were studies in literature and the arts as well, and legal history and theory, civil law, labor law, criminal law, Roman law, Soviet law, and international law. After the first two years, there were, in addition to the reading, lectures, and seminars, extensive training in practical legal matters and training in rhetoric and public speaking, which has served Gorbachev well, since he is clearly the best speaker of all the Soviet leaders after Lenin.

Gorbachev was a good, though not brilliant, student. But his real talent lay in his early-recognized leadership ability. It was his Komsomol activity during his university days that would prove a valuable asset later in his career. He also gained another valuable asset at the university.

Raisa Maximovna Titorenko was a smart, pretty, and petite (five feet two inches) student of Marxist-Leninist dialectics at Moscow University. She was the daughter of a railroad engineer from Sterlitamak in the Bashkir Autonomous Soviet Socialist Republic. (The Bashkir ASSR is a division similar to a state within the Russian republic.) A year younger than Gorbachev, she was culturally more sophisticated. She was extremely popular and was often surrounded by eagerly courting fellow students.

The cultural centers (usually a large room on the main floor of a student hostel) were always busy at Moscow University, providing entertainment at little or no cost to overworked students. Mikhail Gorbachev, a serious-minded man, went to the class in ballroom dancing only to jeer at his fellow student Vladimir Lieberman. But the vivacious Raisa Maximovna caught his eye, and they danced together for the first time.

They were both from the hinterlands of Russia. Raisa was intelligent and an avid reader. She had earned a gold medal as the best student in her school, and she had longed in her out-of-the-way home for the culture and excitement of Moscow. Gorbachev, too, thirsted for knowledge and culture. He was a nice-looking young man with an air of confidence about him. Soon they were a couple—Misha and Raya. They went as often as possible to concerts and the theater, which was inexpensive then and still is today. They discussed the plays they saw and the books they read with each other and then with friends. Unlike many Russian men, Gorbachev was no male chauvinist, and Raisa helped shape and direct much of his cultural and intellectual curiosity.

Privacy (there is no word that translates into "privacy"

•

in the Russian language) for the young couple was an exceedingly difficult commodity to come by. Student living space was at a premium, and even student couples who married often had to live separately. Gorbachev's roommate, Zdeněk Mlyňar, had married a fellow Czech student (who was Raisa's roommate), but they each remained in the quarters they were assigned and the marriage did not survive their student days. There was a schedule that provided a little privacy (an hour a week) in Gorbachev's room, but there was little regular time for a relationship to develop.

Early in 1954, Raisa and Misha decided to get married. The wedding was a brief civil ceremony, followed by a modest celebration with their friends in the canteen at the Stromynka student hostel. They spent the night in Misha's room, while all of his roommates found other overnight accommodations. The next day, Raisa went back to her own room and Misha's roommates returned. When the law faculty moved to the Lenin Hills campus, the Gorbachevs were put on the list for married student housing. Some months before they graduated, they finally began living together as husband and wife.

The impressions and recollections people have of Gorbachev in his university days vary widely. According to Mlyňar, Gorbachev did not flaunt his most significant achievement—the emblem of the Red Banner of Labor that he won. This emblem could have impressed his instructors and gotten him some level of favoritism, but according to Mlyňar, it was not in Gorbachev's character to seek favors or display arrogance. Gail Sheehy, on the other hand, says fellow students remarked that Gorbachev wore his labor medal throughout his whole first year at Moscow University.

Lev Yudovich remembers the young Gorbachev as a dogmatic ideologue, harsh in his pursuits of Stalinism. Fri-

drich Neznansky remembers the same. Yudovich, interviewed for *Time*'s biography of Gorbachev, says, "Some of
us regarded him as a two-faced person. He was very good in
his relations with his fellow students. He wanted to help
some of them, but when he took the floor to speak, he didn't
speak out. He just uttered slogans." Neznansky says that
Gorbachev was an unusually strict disciplinarian in his
Komsomol duties, but he also admits that when he, Neznansky, was looking for a good assignment after graduation, Gorbachev used his political influence to help him.

Vladimir Lieberman, who was eight years older than
Gorbachev and a hero of the war, says that Gorbachev did
nothing to dissociate himself from the anti-Semitic fervor
that accompanied the infamous Doctor's Plot early in 1953.
The Doctor's Plot was the public fiction that Stalin in-
vented as the *raison d'être* for his planned last purge. Stalin's main target was chief of secret police Lavrenty Beria,
but he intended to take the entire Presidium along with
Beria. Stalin charged that the doctors, many of whom were
Jewish, who treated the Kremlin hierarchy were poisoning
the leadership. After some persuasion, some of the Jewish
doctors "confessed." An anti-Semitic pogrom was begun
that was halted only after Stalin died later in the year.

Gorbachev may certainly have castigated the "interna-
tionalists" in his Komsomol speeches, but he remained a
friend of Lieberman, who is Jewish. Lieberman has also said
(to Sheehy) that when he was attacked as being guilty by
association in the Doctor's Plot by an anti-Semite in class,
Gorbachev leaped angrily to his defense, shouting "You're
a spineless beast!" at the accuser.

Perhaps it was this event that caused Lieberman, who
believes that Gorbachev is a dedicated Communist, but
with no patience for bureaucratic formality, to say to an
interviewer that in his university years Mikhail Ser-

•

geyevich was "on the verge of nonconformity." Gorbachev's self-confidence did not desert him, even when he
committed a nonconformist act. When one lecturer did little more than read aloud from the textbook in class, Gorbachev wrote him a sarcastic letter saying that everyone in
class was able to read. The teacher, in a rage, condemned
the letter writer as "antisocialist," but Gorbachev coolly
stood his ground and said he thought the instructor's pedantic style was not the best way to approach Stalin's work.
Gorbachev was mildly reproached for showing a lack of
respect, but the lecturer was replaced.

Was Gorbachev a Stalinist? Brought up in a society that
required everyone to worship Stalin like a god, he clearly
was a Stalinist, but he also had some nagging doubts about
some of the policies of the Stalinists. His public face in the
Komsomol and in his classes was that of a hard-line believer
in communism and the cause Joseph Stalin. In late-night
political discussions, he was more pliable, even liberal, although he spoke little.

According to his fellow student and fellow Communist
Zdeněk Mlynař, "He like everyone else at the time was a
Stalinist. In order to be a true reforming Communist, you
have to have been a true Stalinist."

Two major events helped form Gorbachev's generation.
The first was the unexpected death of Stalin, which occurred while Gorbachev was still at the university. Little
changed immediately. Gorbachev and those around him,
whether they doubted or not, felt an enormous loss when
Stalin, who so completely controlled their lives, was gone.
The second event, dependent on the first, did not occur until
1956—after Gorbachev's graduation, when he was an official in the Komsomol in Stavropol. It was Khrushchev's
so-called secret speech in the Presidium, a speech that re-

vealed the nature and extent of Stalin's barbarism. For an entire generation it was as though God had really died.

Both Gorbachev and Mlyñar were awarded "good" degrees (the equivalent in the United States of *cum laude*) from the Moscow State University law faculty, but neither was offered a place in the graduate school or legal jobs in the procuracy. (The procuracy in the USSR was similar to the office of the attorney general in the United States, combined with state and local prosecutors. Its job, however, had little to do with the rights of the people. It was an organization of prosecutors whose job was to legally prosecute those citizens whose loyalty to the regime was questioned. Both opted for Party work in their home districts.

Gorbachev was slated for a job with the Komsomol in Stavropol, a move that could not have been thrilling to Raisa, who so loved the cultural life of Moscow. But they planned to create a cultural life wherever they went. And so they left Moscow, not to return as residents of the capital for twenty-two years.

Mikhail Gorbachev, who arrived in Moscow at nineteen with a desire for education, left Moscow five years later with the best education his country could give him. He also left as a family man. During those five years his intellectual baggage had increased and his character was honed. The picture of the man he became is a complex one, full of contradiction.

WARM SIBERIA

The city of Stavropol is about 1,200 kilometers (750 miles) south of Moscow and light years distant from the capital in sophistication and access to power. It was like being in Siberia, only warmer. It was a warm day in the summer of

1955 when Mikhail Sergeyevich and Raisa Maximovna Gorbachev arrived.

There was a great need in the procuracy throughout the country for young lawyers to process the claims of those who were returning from the Gulag after amnesty had been declared. But Gorbachev did not want to practice law; he saw a career ahead of him in politics—in the Communist party.

In order to avoid assignment to the procuracy, a newly graduated lawyer would have to get a job in the Communist party apparatus, which included the Komsomol. In the reorganization of the security services after Beria's fall, Khrushchev created the KGB and named Alexander Shelepin, first secretary of the Central Committee of the Komsomol, to oversee internal security. Many Komsomol executives moved to the KGB, opening up the ranks of the Young Communists for newcomers.

Gorbachev was offered a job as head of a department in the Stavropol City Komsomol Committee. It was clearly an entry-level position and not the sort of job one would expect to be filled by an honors graduate of Moscow State University who had held top positions in the university Komsomol. For that reason, Gorbachev early stood out, head and shoulders above the others who had similar positions but much lesser credentials. If he planned it that way, it was a good decision.

Raisa got a job teaching in a local school of medicine, but before long got a better job teaching Marxist-Leninist dialectics at the Stavropol Agricultural Institute. Her job had both more status and more pay than her husband's, but he was clearly from the beginning meant for better things.

Stavropol was a provincial capital with a population of about 125,000 in 1955. It is a small city, with a single main street, Karl Marx Prospect, a number of parks, many trees, and the usual monuments. It is not an unattractive place, and the architecture has a pleasant, Russian feeling. Local industry is agricultural in nature, concentrating on such light manufacturing as clothing and leather as well as food processing. Today, there is a theater, a circus (thanks largely to Gorbachev), and a museum.

There was little culture or entertainment available in 1955, so the Gorbachevs indulged themselves in the Russians' favorite pastimes: eating and arguing (preferably at the same time). They became friendly with other young people in the Komsomol and the Party, often hosting long evening dinners with intellectual discussion as the main course. There was obviously great affection between them (in 1987, speaking of the Gorbachevs' strong attachment for each other, Alexander Yakovlev said, "One could only envy them as a family"), and so, when Misha enrolled in Raya's course at the institute, their argumentative classroom dialogues caused no scandal.

Within a year after their arrival in Stavropol, a daughter, Irina, was born. Gorbachev also had a promotion within the same year.

He was named first secretary of the Stavropol City Komsomol Committee in a major promotion after only a year as a minor official in the city Komsomol organization. Gorbachev replaced his boss, Vsevolod Murakhovsky, in the job when he moved into a position in the regular Communist party organization in Stavropol. Murakhovsky had selected Gorbachev for his first job and then recommended him to take his place as he moved on. The two had become friends from the first.

Gorbachev was helped up the ladder by Murakhovsky early in his career, although he quickly surpassed his first mentor. He jumped past Murakhovsky in the Stavropol Communist party organization, and when Gorbachev was finally brought to Moscow, he recommended Murakhovsky to replace him at the head of the local Party. In 1985, Gorbachev repaid the early favor by bringing Murakhovsky to Moscow and appointing him first deputy prime minister.

There are few perks and little prestige in Komsomol work at the territorial level. The mission of the Komsomol was teaching young people and inculcating in them the spirit of Soviet socialism. It was a propaganda organization structured along the same lines as the Communist party.

As head of the Stavropol Komsomol organization, it was Gorbachev's job to visit all of the local Komsomol organizations, which were in every school and factory, every collective and army unit. He spoke at conferences and meetings, monitored lectures, the publishing of educational materials, elections and appointments, and ran the weekly meetings and the programs that provide services for public functions.

Gorbachev's style, which he has retained as much as possible, developed in the Stavropol Komsomol. It is a more relaxed style than the one that marked his Komsomol work during his university years. According to a former editor of the Stavropol Komsomol newspaper, Gorbachev would often drop in casually, share some time with staff members, and discuss politics.

Gorbachev generally adhered to the Party line, but things were easing up in Moscow and the results were being felt even in Stavropol.

On February 25, 1956, an event that profoundly influenced Gorbachev and his entire generation occurred. At the Twentieth Party Congress, Nikita Khrushchev delivered his "secret speech," titled "The Cult of Personality and Its Consequences," and revealed to the people for the first time that Joseph Stalin had been a monster who made an entire empire slaves to his will.

The contents of Khrushchev's speech were not generally known to the people on the street, but within the Communist party, news of the speech spread like wildfire.

To young people brought up to believe completely in Stalin, the very idea was earth-shattering. Since most young people had little personal experience of Stalin's terror, Khrushchev's revelations were mind-boggling. They had grown up during Stalin's regime and believed that the state's intrusion into every area of their private lives was simply the way things were.

But the doubt that was rarely expressed had been exposed, and never again would those of Gorbachev's generation, who often called themselves Children of the Twentieth Party Congress, believe in their government in quite the same way. In the deliberate Russian way, however, de-Stalinization was not accomplished immediately and was still going on thirty years later.

Gorbachev was learning how to deal with influence. As a successful Komsomol secretary, he wielded some influence himself. According to émigré writer Vladimir Maximov, who knew Gorbachev in the early Stavropol days, Gorbachev was asked by a Stavropolitan poet to use his influence and help the poet get a Volga (a Soviet midsize car). Gorbachev helped him out, and so the poet was able to buy his car. But he sold the car on the black market and came back to Gorbachev to ask for another one. Gorbachev exploded in anger, a thing that happened only rarely, and threw the poet out of his office, warning him never to come back.

In 1958, Gorbachev was appointed head of the Department of Propaganda and a second secretary of the Territorial Komsomol organization. This was another step-up within the Komsomol, like being involved in state-level politics as opposed to the city level in the United States.

Meanwhile, upheaval at the national level was having

its effect in the political backwater of Stavropol. Serious failures in the planning and reaping of the 1959 harvest left Khrushchev in need of a scapegoat. He chose Nikolai Belyayev, who was a member of the Central Committee Presidium, and demoted him to first secretary of the territorial Party organization in Stavropol. But Khrushchev wanted Belyayev out altogether, and soon Belyayev was replaced as Stavropol first secretary by Feodor Kulakov.

The appointment to the position of first secretary in Stavropol was a demotion for Kulakov. He was sent from the center of power in Moscow to warm Siberia. In Moscow, Kulakov had been minister of grain products for the RSFSR (the Russian Republic). A tough, authoritarian Party boss, Kulakov had been trained as an agronomist, which included graduate studies in agriculture by correspondence. He was extremely ambitious and took his demotion as an opportunity to turn around the agricultural production record of the Stavropol Territory.

In the shuffling around that went with Khrushchev's reorganizing, Gorbachev was promoted yet again, in 1960, to first secretary of the Territorial Komsomol Committee. He likewise became a member of the ruling Communist party bureau of the territory. This was like a foot in the door from the political organization to the state governing body. It capped an extremely rapid rise for the twenty-nine-year-old Gorbachev. He now met Kulakov, who was to become an important mentor. For the next eighteen years, Gorbachev's career would be linked to Kulakov's rise.

In 1961, Gorbachev, as Territorial Komsomol first secretary, was entitled to attend the Twenty-second Party Congress in Moscow as a delegate. This was an important event in the history of the Soviet Union. While Khrushchev had delivered his "secret speech" denouncing Stalin at the Twentieth Party Congress five years earlier (there was a brief Twenty-first Party Congress, dealing with economic matters only, in 1959), the general Soviet public was still unaware of the extent of Stalin's crimes and Stalin himself had not yet been discredited. His body still lay next to Lenin's in the mausoleum in Red Square, and there were monuments to him across the entire country.

Five thousand delegates attended the congress in the brand-new Palace of Congresses in the Kremlin, with its six thousand seats. At the opening of the congress on October 17, Khrushchev's report had to explain the major changes he had made in the makeup of the Presidium (later called the Politburo) following an abortive attempt to oust him by Kaganovich, Malenkov, and Molotov and supported by Bulganin, Pervukhim, Saburov and Voroshilov.

Khrushchev needed to explain fully their expulsion from the Presidium. He explained it in terms of his de-Stalinization policy and their opposition. He fully detailed Stalin's most horrible crimes for the first time in a public forum. The speakers who came after him in the congress also had to deal with the subject once he opened the can of worms. Now a full public examination of Stalin was launched. This examination made known to all the people of the Soviet Union the full extent of Stalin's despotism.

Right after the congress, Stalin's embalmed remains were removed from the mausoleum (called, strictly, Lenin's Tomb) in Red Square, and monuments to the dictator were toppled throughout the Soviet Union. Later, the name of the city of Stalingrad, famous for its World War II resistance to the Nazis, was changed to Volgograd.

When Gorbachev returned home, there was some difficulty explaining Stalin to new recruits in the blatantly propagandistic Komsomol. The course of Gorbachev's career in the Komsomol had been smooth and his advance rapid, but he chose this time to decide that he wished to move fully into Party work—to concentrate on a career of governing rather than propagandizing.

Gorbachev probably discussed his next move with Kulakov, because at first glance it seems that Gorbachev received a demotion. He applied for and was appointed in March 1962 as Party organizer for a territorial-agricultural unit. The position meant he had to move out of Stavropol into a rural district. It did not bring with it membership in the territorial Party organization, and it was a job for which he had little qualification.

This was a Party organization position to oversee agricultural production in one of sixteen newly created districts in the Stavropol Territory. It was a job that had an element of risk about it, since it was based on Khrushchev's new idea about agricultural production. If the district failed to show an improvement in production, it could be the end of Gorbachev's career. Yet he chose to take the risk, rather than continue in his relatively safe position in the Komsomol.

As throughout his early career, fortune was on Gorbachev's side. He was not up to the task of setting up a new system, and his knowledge of agriculture was too limited for him to adequately perform his job. But the weather was perfect and the harvest was better than it had ever been.

Gorbachev, however, knew that he needed additional training in agriculture. Thus in 1962 he registered for a correspondence course in agricultural economy at the Stavropol Agricultural Institute. But by the end of the highly successful harvest season, Kulakov promoted Gorbachev to head the Department of Party Publications. Gorbachev set up shop at the Stavropol Territory Party headquarters, working directly with Kulakov until Kulakov was called to Moscow. He continued his agricultural studies, and he later received a graduate degree in agriculture, which gave him the credentials he needed to move up even farther.

Khrushchev had denounced Stalin's crimes before the Party congress to separate himself from the others of the Party hierarchy scrambling for power in the wake of Stalin's demise. They all knew that the new leader would not be able to maintain order in the country using Stalin's method of terror. So immediately after Stalin's death there was a general amnesty. Seeking to secure his position at the top of the ladder and gain a reputation as a genius of the new Soviet Union, Khrushchev gambled on making a major national issue of consumerism.

In a 1985 interview between Robert MacNeil of American Public Broadcasting and American industrialist Armand Hammer, who first went to the Soviet Union during the civil war as a doctor to help the new state during a typhus epidemic and stayed on a while to help Lenin industrialize, Hammer said that Khrushchev had told him in the early 1960s that unless the Soviet leadership is able to give the people a standard of living equal to that in the United States, they were doomed to failure.

In the end, Khrushchev's gamble on consumerism and missiles over conventional weapons and industry failed. His behavior was erratic, and he made the bureaucrats nervous. Denouncing Stalin left the Party open to criticism, and that made the *Party* nervous.

On October 13, 1964, before a full meeting of the Presidium and Central Committee, Party ideological watchdog Mikhail Suslov coolly ticked off Khrushchev's "sins." An apoplectic Khrushchev waved his fists and shouted insults. Suslov rose and dispassionately announced, "You can see for yourselves, comrades, there's little point in working with him anymore." It was the end of Khrushchev's eight-year rule.

•

MOVING UP

At a time when the national Communist party leadership was becoming increasingly old and conservative, Gorbachev started his rise to power. At the age of twenty-nine, in 1960, he was Komsomol leader for the entire territory. This was the same year that Feodor Kulakov was appointed first secretary of the Stavropol Territory. Gorbachev attached himself to the senior man, who saw great possibilities in the bright and ambitious young Gorbachev. Two years later, Kulakov brought Gorbachev into the Party leadership in Stavropol, naming him the top official in charge of personnel in industry, farms, and administration.

Five years later, Kulakov was promoted to Moscow to serve as agricultural secretary of the Central Committee. With his mentor's success, Gorbachev's star continued to rise. By 1968 he was the second-ranking official in the province. When the new first secretary, alternate Politburo member Leonid Efremov, was called to Moscow in 1970 to accept a prestigious, but unexciting, position as deputy chairman of a state committee, Gorbachev was his logical replacement.

The position of first secretary of the Stavropol Territory catapulted Gorbachev onto the national scene. There were about a hundred first secretaries in the entire Soviet system. The position was similar to that of a state governor in the United States. First secretaries ran their regions with considerable power and a significant measure of autonomy. They linked Party decisions to the vast territories of the Soviet Union.

Territory secretaries were appointed by the Central Committee, based on recommendations made by one of its members. It is generally accepted that Kulakov, Gorbachev's first important mentor, proposed him for the position; Efremov, who had most recently vacated the post, also undoubtedly lent his approval.

Becoming first secretary also meant that Gorbachev would be nominated as a deputy to the Supreme Soviet, representing his territory. The Supreme Soviet, roughly equivalent to the American Congress, was the permanently sitting legislature. With his new membership in the Supreme Soviet, he was also given a new appointment: chairman of the Standing Commission on Youth Affairs, reflecting his Komsomol experience.

Early in his years as first secretary of Stavropol, Gorbachev began to represent the Soviet Union abroad. In October of 1972 he headed a delegation sent to Brussels to confer with the Communist party in Belgium, important at that time, as Belgium was wavering over its allegiance to NATO.

In May 1975 Gorbachev headed a delegation to West Germany, celebrating at a German Communist party rally the thirtieth anniversary of the fall of Hitler. Gorbachev was sent abroad again in November 1976, heading a delegation to Paris to meet with the French Communist party. These visits were not merely privileges, but served to test Party officials. Gorbachev passed with flying colors.

It was very much a part of Gorbachev's style to maintain contact with his constituents during his years in Stavropol. While first secretary of the territory, Gorbachev and his family lived opposite the KGB headquarters in a one-story nineteenth-century house designated for the first secretary. Gorbachev's office was only a short walk away, and residents would often catch him on his way to work to discuss their business, avoiding having to make an official appointment. Gorbachev was in daily contact with his fellow citizens and was a familiar figure in the town.

Gorbachev was famous for his "walkabouts," strolling

•

on foot through various areas under his jurisdiction, developing a more intimate relationship with the people he met there. On one of these walks he was invited to have dinner with the family of a man who had been decorated Hero of Socialist Labor, one of the nation's most respected medals for dedicated work. Without hesitation, Gorbachev canceled an official dinner to spend the evening with them.

Mikhail and Raisa Gorbachev joined in all the local events, and frequently attended the theater. Gorbachev cheered on the local soccer team and was a devoted parade watcher.

Gorbachev's particular position as first secretary of the Stavropol Territory was an advantage in his rise to power. Working in the countryside meant that Gorbachev could take on larger responsibilities in a smaller arena; in Moscow the hierarchical structure and the intense competition would have worked against him. In Stavropol, Gorbachev could be creative. He could try experimental initiatives, attracting national interest, which might encourage other districts to adopt his ideas.

The geography and economy of the district were also in his favor. Heading up an agricultural region, in a country most interested in increasing agricultural production, Gorbachev had the opportunity to make moves that would be watched with interest by the rest of the nation.

Perhaps the single most important element of Gorbachev's early rise to power was his ability to develop and keep close relationships with those in power. His association with such mentors as Kulakov and Yuri Andropov did more than simply support his ability to govern well; they provided the necessary political connections with which to maneuver through the bureaucratic Soviet hierarchy. Gorbachev's period as first secretary was crucial in developing and consolidating relationships that would ultimately open the doors to the top.

Gorbachev's closeness with Feodor Kulakov, secretary of agriculture in the Central Committee, was already firmly established from their years of working together in Stavropol. Kulakov had supported Gorbachev for the position of first secretary and was a strong ally when it came to negotiating with the bureaucracy in Moscow.

During his time as first secretary, Gorbachev was able to consolidate other important relationships that would serve him well. The exclusive spas and mineral baths of the Stavropol area gave Gorbachev the edge over other territorial first secretaries helping him to develop close relationships with powerful political and military leaders. The Stavropol spas, especially Mineralnye Vody and Kislovodsk, were exclusive retreats often visited by those in positions of power for rest and rejuvenation from the stress of their work. Russians generally believe more in home remedies and mineral baths and such than they do in doctors and the level of medicine practiced in the Soviet Union.

Gorbachev's title as first secretary of the Stavropol Territory put him in a position to host the privileged Kremlin bigwigs who were permitted to frequent these resorts. Mikhail Suslov, chief party ideologist, previously first secretary of Stavropol from 1939 to 1944; Yuri Andropov, chairman of the KGB; and Soviet premier Aleksey Kosygin were regular guests at the Stavropol spas. Suslov regularly visited Kislovodsk as a treatment for a heart condition and a kidney ailment, Andropov for kidney problems, and Kosygin for heart trouble.

Mikhail Suslov had risen to power under Stalin, taking part in the massive purges that occurred in the Stavropol Territory during Gorbachev's boyhood. Suslov was largely responsible for Gorbachev's eventual promotion to Moscow. Suslov, with his nationalistic philosophy and his relatively ascetic life-style, recognized a kindred spirit in Gorbachev more so than in members of the hard-living, decadent Brezhnev clan. Gorbachev's clean record and efforts in agriculture impressed this man whose first priority was the Russian land.

Gorbachev's friendship with Andropov was extremely important to both men, taking on the character of a father-son relationship. The two men were similar in some basic ways. Gorbachev's simple life-style was much more compatible with Andropov's clean living and modest tastes than with the heavy drinking and womanizing of other prominent Party officials at the time. In his interest in the arts Andropov found kindred souls in Mikhail Sergeyevich and Raisa Maximovna, with their extensive interest and knowledge of Russian literature, theater, and art. Andropov was impressed with Gorbachev's character, and attracted by his intelligence and his spotless record. The two men discussed politics searchingly with each other, finding themselves with much in common.

Andropov was an advocate for openness and change, foreseeing economic and social collapse unless the rigidity and stifling bureaucracy of the Soviet system could be opened up to deal with new problems. He was determined to use the KGB and the secret police to break up Brezhnev's tightly connected and corrupt network of power. Both men acknowledged the stark reality of Soviet life in the face of massive and delusionary propaganda.

Gorbachev's relationship with Andropov was crucial to his career. In his moves toward major reform, Andropov was bringing new people onto the main stage of the political arena, and Gorbachev was one of the intelligent and gifted players Andropov chose to maintain as an ally in a position of power.

As KGB chief, Andropov was well aware of the difficulties in Gorbachev's past that would present roadblocks
to advancement in the Party. The imprisonment of his
grandfather and the wartime occupation of his area by the
Nazis would have made advancement after a certain point
impossible, but Andropov would have kept this information
from the public and from the Party hierarchy.

Fewer details are known concerning Gorbachev's relationship with Premier Aleksey Kosygin, although the two
men met often during Kosygin's many trips to Kislovodsk
in the 1960s.

The bond among Gorbachev and these powerful men—
Suslov, Andropov, and Kosygin—was sealed by their status
as outsiders to Brezhnev's inner circle. What fear was to
Stalin, corruption was to Brezhnev. *Blat,* the Russian word
for "grease" or "influence," was the way of doing business
in the Brezhnev era. The Brezhnev gang lived like czars,
skimming money off of every little transaction of the Party
and government. It was a system based on patronage and
favors, a system fueled by heavy drinking, gambling, and
sex. The "perks"—such as dachas, vacations, and access to
the best services and food—that went with good Party jobs
kept the bureaucrats in line.

Politically the Brezhnev circle was conservative, holding relatively primitive concepts of socialism. Gorbachev
saw these men as trying to figure out "how to improve the
economy without changing anything." He later spoke of
Brezhnev's reign as one of exhausting inertia. Gorbachev
had allied himself with men who had adopted much simpler
life-styles, who were working for change politically, not the
least of it being work toward cleaning up the corruption
that was the order of the day. These men recognized the
stagnation in the Soviet Union as a danger, and were in-

•

creasingly pointing out signs of deterioration in the social and economic sectors.

Another important connection made during the years in Stavropol was with Eduard Shevardnadze, first secretary of the Georgian Komsomol. In the early 1970s, Shevardnadze began experimenting with introducing individual initiative among Georgian farmers through organizing work teams that would be given contracts and paid according to production. Gorbachev was impressed by his success and by his strong opposition to corruption. Years later he would choose Shevardnadze as his foreign minister.

Early in his career as first secretary, Gorbachev introduced a similar incentive system linked to productivity. In 1971, groups of farmers signed contracts with their collectives, giving them responsibility for a particular piece of land. They were paid according to what they produced. The press reported a large increase of harvest yields on both irrigated lands and nonirrigated land. Gorbachev later reported that production was increased 20 to 30 percent, with labor and resource costs reduced.

Despite his successful private incentives and his plans for extending the system throughout the Stavropol Territory, he reversed his position when Feodor Kulakov initiated an experiment to centrally coordinate grain production of one district in his region. Gorbachev quickly took on the plan of his mentor, although it meant giving up his own vision. The "Ipatovsky method"—so called for the district where it was first implemented—was a reversal of Gorbachev's experiments in private contracting. Gorbachev was playing his political cards, avoiding alienating his mentor and the conservative Brezhnev clan. This Ipatovsky method, popular with the conservative faction, involved a fleet of mobile "harvesting-transport complexes" made up of combine harvesters and trucks. The fleet would

•

move through an entire area at once, rather than an individual farm, preparing the fields, collecting the harvest, cultivating after the harvest, and so on.

In its very first year, the experiment was an enormous success. The official goal of 120,000 metric tons was far surpassed—the Ipatovsky district delivered 200,000 tons after a record nine-day harvest. On short notice, plans were made to implement the method in other regions as well. The subsequent results, though successful, were not so spectacular as in the district where it originated.

The next year, 1978, the plan was implemented on a wider scale, with results so outstanding that they were never to be repeated. Within seven days, 240,000 metric tons were delivered to the staging area. In the long run the Ipatovsky method would fail, owing to the logistics of moving and maintaining the huge fleets in areas that were better served by one or two simple harvesters. But for now, participation in this successful agricultural experiment helped bring Gorbachev to widespread attention outside his region, and brought awards to many in the Stavropol Territory who participated. Gorbachev himself was awarded the highly prized Order of the October Revolution.

In competition for the higher ranks of the Communist party, Gorbachev faced two formidable rivals in the northern Caucasus. These territorial first secretaries were well-known and well-connected, with impeccable credentials. Sergei Medunov, first secretary in the Krasnodar region, reportedly ran his region as a mafia operation on bribes and patronage. Medunov was friendly with Brezhnev, who often stayed in Krasnodar. His educational credentials were impressive: he was a graduate of the Central Committee Higher Party School and had a Ph.D. in economic sciences, in addition to being a professional agronomist. His wartime service in the Soviet Army was also a political asset. The

•

Krasnodar region had a larger population than Stavropol, and produced twice as much grain, although it was similar in size.

Another candidate for higher office was Ivan Bondarenko, first secretary of the Rostov region. He had been highly successful in leading the development of his region both industrially and agriculturally. The winner of many awards, he was a professional agronomist with broad experience.

With rivals such as these, recognition by his older colleagues and mentors was crucial to Gorbachev's advancement. But according to Zhores Medvedev, "friendly relations with senior colleagues" were not enough to ensure promotion. Economic success in their regions and taking on new programs that could be adopted in other areas and bring national attention were also vitally important to the success of regional secretaries.

Very suddenly, in July 1978, Feodor Kulakov died, creating a gap in the Moscow leadership. The circumstances of his death were mysterious. There was no warning or sign of previous illness; official reports merely stated that his "heart stopped beating." Brezhnev, Chernenko, Kosygin, and Suslov were all absent from the funeral ceremony. Rumors circulated that Kulakov had slashed his wrists. What would have led him to suicide was a matter of conjecture. Medvedev reports that agriculture had been greatly successful in the Stavropol region in 1978 under Kulakov's Ipatovsky method. However, other sources report national agricultural difficulties. Journalist Christian Schmidt-Hauer reports that Kulakov was embroiled in a serious argument within the Party; other sources suggest a major dispute with Brezhnev.

Gorbachev spoke at the funeral, saying farewell to "our friend and comrade." It was his first Red Square speech. He was now in an unclear position. He had lost his first mentor and a strong ally; with luck he might move up to fill his place, or he could find himself with a new superior, at this point an unknown quantity.

Gorbachev was no shoo-in to replace Kulakov. Bondarenko and Medunov, Gorbachev's rivals in the north Caucasus, were likelier candidates, with credentials superior to Gorbachev's. Given the choice himself, Brezhnev would have chosen Ivan Bodyl, his close friend and the first secretary of Moldavia. But Mikhail Gorbachev had strong connections pulling for him in Moscow: Mikhail Suslov, Yuri Andropov, and Aleksey Kosygin. Brezhnev would have difficulty appointing any Central Committee secretary without the approval of these three powerful men.

In September, Andropov set up a meeting with Gorbachev, Brezhnev, and Chernenko. After first stopping in Krasnodar to see Medunov, Brezhnev and Chernenko went on to Mineralnye Vody. Gorbachev and Andropov were waiting for them on the platform of the railway station. For a historic moment the four men who would successively serve as general secretary of the Communist party of the Soviet Union stood together on the train platform. It is known that in their conversation Gorbachev reported a record harvest, far exceeding the official quota for the Stavropol region.

Brezhnev must have been satisfied with the performance of the young official from Stavropol. At the November plenum of the Central Committee in Moscow, on November 27, he announced that Mikhail Sergeyevich Gorbachev would succeed Kulakov as Central Committee secretary for agriculture.

CHAPTER FOUR

·

THE RELUCTANT
REVOLUTIONARY

·

A T the age of forty-seven, Mikhail Sergeyevich Gorba-chev made the move to the center of power in the USSR—Moscow. He had last been a resident of the capital twenty-two years before, when he was a law student at Moscow State University. Now he joined the men who formed the top ranks of leadership in the country.

As a junior secretary of the Central Committee he was, in the autumn of 1978, twentieth in rank among the leaders of the Soviet Union. The Central Committee was the ruling center of the Politburo, the executive branch of government. (The Politburo proposed legislation that was passed on by the Supreme Soviet, the legislative branch.) From the Politburo, the Central Committee was selected; and from the Central Committee was named the general secretary.

By far the youngest member of the leadership, Mikhail Gorbachev was more than twenty years younger than the average member of what had become an aged top circle.

Domestically the move was a smooth one. Raisa joined the philosophy faculty at Moscow State University, taking an appointment there as a lecturer. Irina, their daughter,

•

had already moved to Moscow, where she was studying medicine. She married another physician in 1978 and gave birth to their daughter, Oksana, the next year.

Gorbachev's first few years in Moscow, under Brezhnev's leadership, were not years of domestic bliss for the country, however. After vigorous economic and political expansion through the 1960s and early '70s, the Soviet Union had entered a period of serious economic and political decline. Despite increases in income, the standard of living had not improved, and there was little to buy with the extra rubles. Other than staples, most desired items were available only on the black market. Crime increased, and corruption was a way of life. Service people expected to be paid extra for doing their normal work. Alcoholism had reached epidemic proportions, and life expectancy was actually declining.

Gorbachev was also walking into an increasingly tense, increasingly polarized political scene. After the downfall of Khrushchev in 1964, Brezhnev rose to general secretary. He immediately maneuvered to tighten his hold on power.

The new general secretary moved the powerful Alexander Shelepin—then head of the KGB and a principal figure in Khrushchev's removal—into a trade union job.

Nikolai Podgorny, another power in the Kremlin, made Brezhnev uncomfortable by his close alliance with Aleksey Kosygin. The power struggle was waged in terms of basic political disagreement. Brezhnev differed with Podgorny and Kosygin over economic policy and the ultimate power of the Communist party. Brezhnev felt threatened by these men who wanted to reform the Party-controlled system.

When Mikhail Suslov, ideological head of the Central Committee, threw his support behind Brezhnev, Podgorny was defeated. With both Shelepin and Podgorny out of the way, the aging Brezhnev dug in and solidified his position.

The battles lines remained drawn, however, with tensions building between conservative Brezhnev backers and supporters of reform. Andropov rose quickly through the ranks, becoming head of the KGB and a member of the Politburo. He attracted a following among younger officials such as Gorbachev, who were alarmed by the decay in the country and wanted change. Konstantin Chernenko, an old Brezhnev follower, was also moving up rapidly, first joining the Central Committee and then becoming a full member of the Politburo in 1978. Eventually he was to head the conservative faction backing Brezhnev.

This is the way things were when Mikhail Gorbachev stepped into his new position as secretary of agriculture of the Central Committee. The nation's agricultural picture was no better than any other segment of the Soviet economy and was, at its best, chronically troubled.

The Soviet Union's agricultural problems stemmed from various sources. Despite the huge amount of land area, there is a lack of high-quality arable farmland. Only a small percentage of the land can be used to grow grain. Only about 10 percent is really good-quality farmland; just over 25 percent can be used for food production in any capacity. And the weather is also a problem.

The southern areas of fertile soil are frequently troubled by drought, in spite of extensive irrigation. The cold, damp climate in much of the north is also not conducive to agriculture. The northern latitude of much of the land means there is a short growing season, which makes it difficult to grow such grains as wheat.

Finally, in addition to poor weather and soil, inefficient harvesting of crops, poor transportation, and grossly insufficient storage capability are problems that could leave a bumper crop rotting in the field or on the truck. Gorbachev, as the new secretary of agriculture, was taking on a monster.

The harvest of 1979 was extremely poor. After a wildly successful harvest in 1978, producing 237.4 million tons of grain, too little attention had been paid to preparing for the next season. Production of silage and hay, sowing of winter crops, and application of fertilizer had all been neglected. The grain harvest dropped almost 25 percent in 1979, to 179 million tons. The harvest of other crops was also down significantly. Thirty-one million tons of grain were imported, more than had ever been imported in a single year.

The poor harvest in 1979 became even more significant when President Jimmy Carter imposed a grain embargo on the Soviet Union, following the Soviet invasion of Afghanistan in December 1979. After using their stockpiles, the Soviets bought even more grain in 1980 than in 1979, broadening their dealings to now include imports from Canada, Australia, Argentina, and France.

Despite the difficulties of his first year, Gorbachev became a candidate-member of the Politburo at the plenum of the Central Committee on November 17, 1979. At the same Central Committee session, Gorbachev was appointed head of a committee to examine the legal system in the Soviet Union and suggest changes. This new responsibility expanded his function to include ideological and organizational matters, and strengthened his relationship with Mikhail Suslov, number-two man on the Central Committee and custodian of Party ideology.

The next year, 1980, was plagued by bad weather. Torrential rains, flooding, and a late cold spring meant that the grain harvest would fall far short of target: the yield was just over 189 million tons. Production of other crops also declined significantly. The potato harvest was the lowest it

•

had been in over forty years. Milk and meat production also dropped significantly from the previous year.

The overall picture was bleak. Despite large investments in Soviet agriculture, food imports were increasing exponentially, rising from $700 million in 1970 to $7.2 *billion* in 1980. The cost of these imports was creating havoc in the Soviet economy. One Soviet study showed substantial losses due to lack of storage, negligence, and inadequate transportation, with one-fifth of the grain and one-third of the potatoes grown left to rot, while Moscow was making deals to import food from other countries.

The poor agricultural performance did not hurt Gorbachev politically. In October 1980 he was promoted from candidate-member to full member of the Politburo. Possibly his colleagues felt that Gorbachev's position as the top man in agriculture merited full membership in the Politburo. They may have realized that the difficulties were beyond his control. Despite failure, Gorbachev's career was moving forward.

In fact, that same year Gorbachev became a candidate for the Supreme Soviet. In the elections to this body, candidates choose which constituency they wish to represent, residency not being a requirement. Gorbachev chose to represent Altai Territory, an important agricultural district five times the size of Stavropol geographically, but with the same population. This was the Siberian territory where Raisa was born.

The next year, 1981, was the year of the Twenty-sixth Party Congress, where the new Five-Year Plan was to be adopted. Gorbachev worked extensively with Brezhnev to develop the food program, preparing the reports and speeches that Brezhnev presented.

Brezhnev's program was a mixture of half measures and harebrained publicity ploys. Gorbachev astutely distanced

himself from the program and reportedly set forth proposals of his own. In January 1981, the Central Committee
abolished restrictions on the use of private land for agriculture. Occupants of the land could use it to produce whatever they desired, a move that seemed similar to Lenin's
New Economic Policy. Under the plan, livestock could be
sold at a negotiable price, spelling out the end of the fixed-
price system. Financing was to be provided on easy credit
through the state bank.

Moves had been made in this direction before Gorbachev had come on the scene in Moscow. As early as November 1964, the Central Committee abolished the restrictions
on private plots set by Khrushchev. The permitted size of
the plots was doubled in September 1977, and the Brezhnev
Constitution of 1977 granted the right to use plots of land
for subsidiary small holdings.

The Five-Year Plan beginning in 1981 set targets that
were more unrealistic than ever. The goals of the previous
Five-Year Plan had not been met, yet new targets were
substantially increased.

Despite intensive effort directed toward making the first
year of the plan a success, the 1981 harvest was another
miserable failure. From a failed harvest of 189.1 million
tons the year before, grain production plunged further to
158.2 million tons. Drought and mineral deficiencies from
the previous year's torrential rains resulted in a disastrous
harvest, the worst since 1965, on a per capita basis. Forty-
six million tons of grain were imported that year, and there
were still food shortages in the fall of 1981, partly as a result
of food shipments to Poland.

This time, the poor harvest did have an impact on Gorbachev and the Agricultural Department. The food program was delayed, and as a result of the poor harvest a
number of documents would have to be rewritten, reconsid-

•

ering the target figures. There were serious food shortages throughout the Soviet Union. Shortages were especially severe in Poland, where civil unrest led the Soviet satellite government to impose martial law.

The withdrawal of the U.S. grain embargo in April 1981 provided some relief, allowing the Soviets to increase their imports of grain. But discontent continued to spread as the agricultural system worsened.

As secretary of agriculture, Gorbachev was politically vulnerable. Another disastrous harvest might spell the end of his career. Gorbachev's position grew even more tenuous when his supporter, Mikhail Suslov, died soon after suffering a stroke on January 21, 1982. His death would directly affect the power struggle developing among the leadership of the Communist party of the Soviet Union.

There were two clearly defined factions in the Politburo at this time. The Old Guard of the Brezhnev regime, headed by Chernenko, consisted of men who had matured during the years of Stalin's power and were extremely conservative in their political outlook. Their careers depended on Brezhnev's patronage.

The other faction, headed by Andropov, Dmitri Ustinov, and Andrei Gromyko, supported change, advocating reforms that would give the government more independence from the Party and loosen the Party's grip on economic management. Kosygin, an advocate of reform, had resigned as prime minister in 1980 because of poor health, and was thus out of the power picture. Gorbachev, politically cautious, did not openly display allegiance to Andropov's group.

Suslov had been independent of both factions. When he died, the already tense balance of power was upset, setting off an overt struggle between Andropov and Chernenko for control over the departments previously under Suslov's ju-

•

risdiction. Brezhnev, who supported Chernenko, stayed in Moscow through the late winter, forgoing his usual vacation in Sochi. He left Moscow only to present the Order of Lenin to the Uzbek Republic to mark the sixtieth anniversary of the founding of the USSR. On the trip back to Moscow from Tashkent, Brezhnev had a stroke. He was rushed to a Kremlin hospital close to death, having temporarily lost the ability to speak.

During Brezhnev's absence, Andropov maneuvered to control Suslov's former domain. Although Chernenko had unofficially taken on many of Suslov's functions, Andropov pushed to take over the vacancy left by Suslov in the Central Committee of the Politburo. Andropov had worked closely with Suslov on foreign matters as well as ideology. When the May plenum convened, with a recovering Brezhnev in attendance, Andropov was named as secretary of the Central Committee, with responsibility for what had been Suslov's domain of ideological matters.

The power struggle continued to be played out in indirect ways. Andropov began to discredit Brezhnev's authority by uncovering corruption and scandal close to the general secretary. Andropov used his power at the KGB as part of this tactic. But he did not have to invent a connection between Brezhnev's people and corruption.

General Semyon Tsvigun, Andropov's deputy at the KGB and Brezhnev's wife's brother-in-law, was found in his office, dead of a gunshot wound. An investigation into the death linked Brezhnev's daughter, Galina, with a diamond-smuggling scandal involving Anatoly Kolevatov, director of the State Circus, and Boris Buryatia, a Bolshoi Opera singer. Galina's husband, Lieutenant General Yuri Churbanov, first deputy minister of the MVD (predecessor of the KGB) and her father, the general secretary, were

•

perilously close to the scandal. The episode further under-
mined the strength of Brezhnev's faction.

May 1981 marked the launch of Brezhnev's food program, delayed from its original March date due to the
leader's illness. Many of the program's targets were outra-
geously high, and steps needed to accomplish these goals
were only vaguely laid out. Decision making, according to
the program, would be conducted at the top only, allowing
no part for self-determination for individual collectives and
state farms. The program was simply a hodgepodge of reso-
lutions without any real reform. The farms were permitted
no new freedoms, and the economic mechanism remained
unchanged. It was a plan without substance.

Despite the fanfare and months of effort of thousands of
officials, the 1982 harvest was a failure. With an estimated
175-million-ton harvest (more than 60 million tons short of
the target), Soviet imports again were substantial, amount-
ing to 32 million tons of grain. After the disastrous harvests
of the previous two years, the continued failure—especially
after the launch of the food program—made things look bad
for Gorbachev.

It was an especially humiliating time for Brezhnev to
suffer another agricultural failure. Gorbachev was in a
prime position to be set up as the scapegoat.

Fate, however, would deal a far different hand. The
plenum was scheduled for November 16, when changes in
organization would be addressed. Tension was high, and
Gorbachev was doing everything he could to get Stavropol's grain delivery reports in as soon as possible, working
to ensure his future by whatever means possible.

Chernenko and Andropov were maneuvering for position. Brezhnev was to deliver a speech that was telecast
throughout the nation live from Baku, the capital of Azer-
baijan. Ten minutes into the telecast, an aide quickly

removed the papers from which Brezhnev was reading and replaced them with another speech. Brezhnev was startled and confused. The live telecast ended and the replacement speech was read by an announcer. It appeared afterward as if the incident was set up by Andropov.

Brezhnev stepped up his support for his followers. Andrei Kirilenko, second only to Brezhnev in the Politburo and an obstacle to both Chernenko and Andropov, was quietly reassigned and eased out of the Politburo. Brezhnev conferred the Order of Lenin and the gold medal of the Hero of Socialist Labor award on Nikolai Tikhonov. He was working to prepare the way for Chernenko and for his other close supporters to succeed him.

Throughout the fall, reports of Brezhnev's failing health continued to leak out. In the late autumn, however, he began to appear more frequently in public, first to confer honors on Tikhonov, then to attend the November 7 commemoration of the October Revolution of 1917, the celebration taking place in Red Square. Wearing a heavy overcoat, fur hat, and sunglasses, he remained in the bitter cold for three hours during the parade and demonstration.

Three days later, on November 10, 1982, Brezhnev died suddenly from a heart attack. Gorbachev had escaped any punitive action from the fallen leader. Now, if Andropov could gain the position of general secretary, his continued rise to the top was practically assured.

STIRRINGS OF CHANGE

When all efforts to revive the stricken Leonid Brezhnev failed, the full Politburo, members and candidate-members, and the marshals of the Soviet Union were summoned to a special afternoon emergency session to choose his successor. Marshal Ustinov, a voting Politburo member as well as

•

minister of defense, wasted no time proposing Yuri Andropov for the post of general secretary. By doing so, he
gave everyone to understand that here was a man the military wanted to succeed Brezhnev. The nomination also apparently had the approval of the foreign secretary, Andrei
Gromyko. Then regional party heads—particularly Viktor
Grishin of Moscow and Grigory Romanov of Leningrad—
spoke in favor of Andropov. Certainly Gorbachev was on
the side of his friend and mentor.

There was little doubt that Konstantin Chernenko,
Brezhnev's chief assistant, had long considered himself the
heir apparent to Brezhnev's position and power. But with
two of his allies—Politburo members Andrei Kirilenko and
Arvid Pelshe—too old and too ill to attend the meeting,
Chernenko did not have enough votes to win. Andropov's
nomination was quickly approved.

When his selection as secretary general was announced
on November 12, 1982, Yuri Andropov was sixty-eight
years old—older than anyone before him who had been
chosen for the post. Like his protégé Mikhail Sergeyevich
Gorbachev, Andropov was born in the Stavropol Territory—in the railway-station town of Nagutskaya on June
15, 1914. He had been involved in Party activities since
graduating from technical college in 1936. By 1947 he was
second secretary of the Karelo-Finnish Republic (later
named the Karelian Autonomous Republic, this was land
that had been wrested from Finland in the 1939–40 Winter
War). A few years later he had moved into the Central
Committee secretariat. Within two years he was shifted to
the diplomatic service, and in 1954 became the Soviet ambassador to Hungary. He played a key role in crushing the
1956 Hungarian uprising. His success earned him a higher
post back in Moscow—as head of the Central Committee's
foreign affairs department. Then, in 1967, he was named

head of the KGB, where he remained in power for fifteen years, longer than anyone who had ever held that office. When he at last moved back to the secretariat, it was to be in charge of ideological and personnel matters, an ideal point from which to advance to the pinnacle of leadership. It had taken him more than forty-five years to earn the title of general secretary.

Andropov was an enigmatic man. It is unusual for a KGB chief to move up into the seat of ruling power. In order to move up the ladder, it was imperative that he distance himself from his own reputation. Andropov was a sophisticated intellectual. On his succession he was older and more experienced than any of his predecessors. After fifteen years as KGB chief, he was also better informed than anyone else. Those men he surrounded himself with were also different, in that they did not grasp for wealth or power. Those who did try to take advantage of their power had Andropov himself to contend with. A man of enormous ambition, whose satisfactions came from the artful exercise of power, he was without personal vanity. He could put the interests of the Party and the nation above all else.

Consequently, in a society that seemed to equate ability with advanced age, Andropov was singularly able to appreciate the value of bringing younger men with new ideas, energy, and dedication into the mainstream of the Party. He was also keenly aware of the country's monumental problems.

Under Brezhnev, nepotism and corruption had, in a sense, become legitimized. The Soviet leader had set the example by naming his alcoholic son, Yuri, to the Central Committee and installing him as deputy minister of foreign trade. His daughter had been given a high position in the Intourist organization, which oversaw travel and accommodations of all foreign tourists in the USSR. Other relatives were placed in important posts in the KGB, the Ministry of Internal Affairs, and countless other privileged places. Brezhnev's colleagues had not been slow to follow his lead, similarly placing their relatives in power positions of their own. All of this widened the gap between the entrenched bureaucracy and ordinary citizens.

Russians maintain a delicate balance between idealism and cynicism. This balance was, during Brezhnev's tenure, tipped—perhaps irreversibly—to a cynical view of all Soviet leadership.

The divorce rate climbed to 50 percent. Heavy drinking, if not alcoholism, reached alarming proportions. While scientific advances had lengthened the life expectancy of almost all the peoples of the Western world, life expectancy in the Soviet Union declined for all age groups. Most significant to Andropov was the evidence that economic development had come to a standstill; even food production had declined.

In his first major speech as Kremlin leader, Andropov bluntly announced that the country and the party had to stop relying upon slogans that "won't get us anywhere" and find solutions by assessing "our own and world experience" and the "accumulated knowledge of the best practical workers and scholars." He further astounded his audience by asserting that some party policies were simply wrong, and had "failed the test of time." In short, he said, the Soviet economy was being run "in an irrational manner of trial and error." While he admitted that he had no quick and easy remedies to propose, he was nonetheless determined that discipline and productivity should improve. One thing was certain, "conditions must be provided . . . that will stimulate productive work, initiative, and enterprise."

If Brezhnev had represented the Soviet equivalent of

old-style "boys in the back room" politics, Andropov was the advocate of change. As could be expected, many of the Old Guard considered him dangerous. But with the KGB and the military behind him, no one dared oppose him. It was either follow Andropov or, as the joke went in Moscow at the time, "follow Brezhnev"!

Vague about the precise methods by which to invigorate the Soviet economy, Andropov nevertheless moved swiftly to demonstrate a sense of direction. In his drive for discipline and increased productivity, he called upon the military to crack down on loafers—the habitually late and the chronically drunk—and on workers playing hooky from their jobs by hiding in movie houses or on the long lines of people waiting for hard-to-get foods. At the same time, he directed the stores to stay open later so that diligent workers could have the chance to get the things they needed.

He began a purge of middle-level officials whose reputations were in any way questionable either because their work was inept or their personal behavior was below Andropov's high standards. Among these was Ivan Pavlosky, the minister in charge of the notoriously inefficient railroads. Many of those ousted were past retirement age, old Party members, friends of Brezhnev, whom Andropov simply replaced with younger, more vigorous men. In the case of Minister Nikolai Shchelokov, the investigation of his corruption and transgressions was noisily announced by the press, as if, many said, to demonstrate to the whole nation the seriousness of Andropov's commitment. *The New York Times* estimated that "one-fifth of the regional first secretaries and nine of the twenty-three Central Committee department heads" were ousted.

Many of the purged officials had been in charge of those consumer-oriented industries that were becoming Gorbachev's special area of interest. His close relationship with

•

Andropov (which was not common knowledge at the start of Andropov's term) gave him the opportunity to suggest suitable replacements and place his own allies in positions of power.

Gorbachev also suggested that greater incentives should be offered to the workers to increase production. The Politburo supported his proposal to encourage a limited kind of private ownership: collective farms would be allowed to sell cows or pigs to private farmers. This could be a source of profit for the collectives. In a pilot program, the collective farmers displayed an imaginative approach to their new opportunity. The collective assigned its old pensioners the job of raising the baby animals for sale, thereby expanding both its work force and its profit margin.

With the success of this plan, Gorbachev's responsibilities were almost immediately broadened. His new title was Politburo member and Central Committee secretary responsible for ideology. A position of great power, it was unofficially known as the number-two job in the party—and therefore in the country. It was a signal of Andropov's confidence in Gorbachev, his trusted supporter. Gorbachev's power bases now included agriculture and personnel. Thirty years earlier, Nikita Khrushchev had used the same combination as his springboard to power. Indeed, the appointment is considered to have been the key to Gorbachev's rise to the top, as it gave him visibility within the Politburo, a prominence that could only increase after February 1983, when Andropov's health began to fail. (In fact, Andropov suffered total kidney failure, and was in extremely poor health throughout his reign as general secretary, although this would not be revealed until a year after his death.)

Keeping the deteriorating state of his health secret from the rest of the Party, Andropov began to rely increasingly upon Gorbachev. It was Gorbachev who delivered the keynote speech at the traditional celebration of Lenin's birthday on April 22, where he reported on the reforms and goals of Andropov's new regime. Andropov had delivered the address the year before. Gorbachev called for "a free rein to creativity and initiative" to provide impetus for the people. He pointed to structural changes in the system necessary to bring about a political and economic revival. He argued that control of the ministries and state apparatus was stifling initiative. *Pravda* gave his appearance front-page coverage, setting him up as a man close to the power.

Andropov drew Gorbachev into foreign affairs, including him in meetings with foreign government leaders important to the Soviet Union. As this was an area in which he had no previous experience, Gorbachev extended his own network by establishing contacts with the Soviet foreign affairs specialists. Then, in May 1983, he was put in charge of a Soviet parliamentary delegation on a visit to Canada.

This was Gorbachev's first exposure to the West. As such, it was a test of his ability to deal with Western politicos as well as an opportunity for the Kremlin to introduce its new young star. Canada was the ideal site for his debut: it was a prime source of Soviet grain and it was very similar to its all-important neighbor, the United States.

The success of the visit was almost greater than anyone could have predicted. Gorbachev met with then Prime Minister Pierre Trudeau and the leaders of the opposition political parties.

An unexpected highlight of the visit was Gorbachev's appearance before the Standing Committee of the House of Commons and the Senate on External Affairs and National Defense. Here was a ranking member of the Politburo subjecting himself to questioning by an unknown, potentially hostile group. Many of the Canadian politicians repre-

•

sented Hungarian, Russian, or Polish constituencies. The last time a prominent Soviet had visited Canada had been in 1972, when Premier Aleksey Kosygin had been physically attacked by one Eastern European émigré.

The committee had already subjected the president of Egypt, the prime minister of Greece, and the president of Pakistan to the same sort of no-holds-barred examination.

Gorbachev was ready for them. He spoke to his audience about their mutual concerns—the dangers of nuclear war and the desirability of nuclear disarmament. He spoke in favor of détente and, as he said, "of broadening mutually advantageous collaboration in all areas, and the continuation and deepening of political dialogue. Not confrontation but mutually advantageous collaboration—that is our program."

Nor was he simply spreading sweetness and light. When the Canadians questioned the necessity of Soviet missile forces in Asia, or Soviet policy toward Poland, he staunchly defended his country's position.

He also showed his personal charm, and thanked the Canadians for their cooperation in selling grain to the Soviet Union. Overall, the Westerners found him direct and disarming.

Because he had not yet been spotlighted as a power to be reckoned with in his own country, Gorbachev's visit attracted little attention from the Western press. This afforded him the luxury of informally touring the country, visiting farms and factories, and talking directly to the people. He asked workers how much they were paid, how many cars they owned, whether they took vacations or had summer houses. He asked about their children, their education, their pensions. He asked what made them work so hard. What motivated them?

He was accompanied by Canada's minister of agriculture, Eugene Whalen. They even visited Niagara Falls and, like many other tourists, took the boat ride underneath the falls. In Toronto they dined at the revolving restaurant atop the CN Tower. Gorbachev was the one who mentioned that it was taller than the television tower in Moscow. As their relationship became more informal, Whalen saw that Gorbachev was tremendously impressed by the productivity, efficiency and high quality of the Canadian agricultural system. Whalen began to speak enthusiastically about the benefits of the free-enterprise system and the abundance of cheap food for all.

Gorbachev joked, "Gene, you don't try to convert me to capitalism and I won't try to convert you to communism."

Nevertheless, it was obvious that Whalen's proselytizing plus the obvious success of Canada's economy had stunned Gorbachev. He revealed as much in late-night talks with the Soviet ambassador to Canada, Alexander Yakovlev, with whom he established a warm relationship during this trip. Yakovlev, a friend of Pierre Trudeau's, understood how both systems worked. He had been an exchange student at Columbia University in New York in the late 1950s. The Canadian assignment had further allowed him to acquire a world view. He could talk authoritatively with Gorbachev about the changing power structure of the world.

Yakovlev's judgment and analysis so impressed Gorbachev that he engaged him as his personal advisor. Within a month of Gorbachev's return to Moscow he had Yakovlev recalled home and appointed director of a major institute. (Later, after Gorbachev came to power, he would make Yakovlev a Politburo member and a secretary of the General Committee, which led many to believe that Yakovlev, who in the 1970s had been sent into diplomatic exile for writing an essay critical of the upsurge in Russian national-

•

ism under Brezhnev, had risen to the position of number-two man in the Soviet Union.)

An emergency in Moscow forced Gorbachev to fly home two days earlier than planned. Andropov was facing resistance to his long list of proposed changes for the Party, government leadership, and for Soviet society as a whole. He sensed that his position in the secretariat was not strong, and felt he needed allies. Even though Gorbachev and Andropov agreed on the need to improve the economy, certain factions within the secretariat opposed them. Andropov needed outside support. In June 1983 he brought Grigory Romanov, the Leningrad Party secretary, to Moscow as a ranking Central Committee secretary, and placed him in charge of heavy industry related to defense. Romanov joined Gorbachev and Chernenko as allies of Andropov.

Gorbachev was given the privilege of naming Romanov's successor in Leningrad. He chose Lev Zaikov, chairman of the Leningrad City Soviet. Zaikov was sixty years old, and only sixth in the Party's local chain of command. His superiors were younger and had more Party experience. But Zaikov was popularly known as the only honest man in Party leadership. Gorbachev personally traveled to Leningrad to chair the plenary meeting at which he recommended Zaikov on behalf of the Politburo. To Party *apparatchiki* it was evident that Gorbachev was the Party member in charge of policy and personnel.

Observers saw Romanov as a rival to Gorbachev for the eventual leadership of the country. In public, however, the two men seemed unaware of any potential clash. On his return from a diplomatic mission, Romanov was embraced by Gorbachev at Sheremetyeva Airport. At the meeting of the Supreme Soviet in June 1983 they sat together on the podium, right behind Chernenko and Ustinov. Moscow television viewers could see them in cheerful conversation during the speeches of Foreign Minister Andrei Gromyko and Politburo member Geidar Aliyev.

It was at this June plenary session that Andropov officially became president of the Soviet Union. While the position was largely symbolic—Andropov had all the real power he needed as general secretary—the decision to confer the post on Andropov after only six months showed that he had quickly gained supremacy and wielded full power. (It had taken Brezhnev ten years to achieve the second title of president.)

The nomination was made by Chernenko, the second-ranking member of the Politburo and the secretariat. Gorbachev's recent prominence had given Chernenko the appearance of a political has-been. In nominating Andropov, Chernenko added prestige to Andropov, and simultaneously acquired it for himself. It was said at the time that he had finally stepped into the shoes of Mikhail Suslov, who had been number-two man to Brezhnev. His nominating speech, while praising Andropov, was conservative: he spoke out against permissiveness among artists, writers, and theater people; he criticized Russian youth for adopting Western habits; and he advocated the cultivation of more positive attitudes and heroes.

Frail, stooped, and obviously ill, Andropov was still able to deliver a strong message to his colleagues. He urged them to do more than pay lip service to the notion of progress. He implored them to welcome criticism and allow frank discussions at their meetings. He reminded them, "It is one thing to proclaim socialism as one's goal, and quite another to build it."

In his plans to invigorate the economy, Andropov assailed the principle of *uravnilovka*, the leveling off of wages. He wanted each person to be paid according to the quality

•

and quantity of work performed. Without ever using the word *reform* he spoke of economic levers such as prices and credits, the redefining of the chain of authority, and even a new management structure. He set January 1985 as the target date for the establishment of the changes. He used the term *glasnost,* or "openness," for the first time, which was to become one of Gorbachev's major themes in the years ahead.

Glasnost, he told the assembly, would bring the government and Party closer to the people. To show what he meant, Andropov introduced weekly reports on Politburo sessions, which had always been secret. For the first time since Khrushchev, he permitted publication of plenum speeches.

Important developments had already begun taking place in Soviet industry and agriculture. Two months earlier, in April, a new law dealing with work collectives for industrial projects had been published. Now, workers would be permitted to organize and hold at least two meetings per year at which they could propose changes in the way their particular project was being conducted. Management was required to evaluate their proposals. And management would have the final say on what was done.

Discipline was the prime goal. Workers were encouraged to form work brigades. Under the supervision of a Party-appointed leader, they could decide for themselves how to organize a project and how to divide the payment.

The Hungarians and the Yugoslavs had reorganized their agriculture and industry along similar lines some years earlier. Andropov, who had served in Hungary, was familiar with the Hungarian methods. To many people, it sounded like the introduction of a profit motive.

Gorbachev, who was also familiar with the Hungarian program and with the Hungarian leadership, was host to

•

János Kádár and his staff at talks held in the Kremlin in July of 1983. Andropov's condition improved, and he was able to meet the Hungarian delegation, as well as Chancellor Helmut Kohl of what was then West Germany, and delegations from the Communist parties of France and Portugal.

Aware that time was running short for him, Andropov pushed his protégé to the forefront. For Gorbachev, it was an apprenticeship to power such as few men have ever experienced. Andropov wanted to show a country accustomed to a ruling gerontocracy that younger men would deal more effectively with the new challenges. In August, he took Gorbachev to preside over the meeting of the Old Bolsheviks, the founding fathers of the Soviet Union. It would be the dying premier's last televised speech. He sang the praises of Gorbachev and the new, better-educated generation he represented. Each new generation, he reminded his old friends, is "in some way stronger than the one before. It knows more. It sees further."

At the end of the month, Andropov went to the Caucasus for a vacation. He was never seen in public again.

That same year, the success of Gorbachev's agricultural reforms was amply shown by the significantly larger autumn harvest. However, an unexpected incident robbed him of the chance to take advantage of this good news.

On September 1, a Soviet fighter plane downed a Korean Airlines 747 over Sakhalin. All on board—269 people—were killed, creating a furor in the world press. Andropov was too ill to deal with the situation. As principal deputy to the ailing leader, Gorbachev had to take over as crisis manager. At first, the Soviet authorities appeared to want to tough it out, and refused even to admit that the plane had been shot down. Later, they insisted that the plane had strayed over Soviet territory, including the sensitive military bases at

the Kamchatka Peninsula and the island of Sa\
shal Ogarkov was given the job of trying to
blunder by insisting that the plane had been sp:
CIA. The United States called that assertion a   ......ie.

To foreign observers the fact that the Soviets offered
any explanation at all was seen as an improvement upon
their past practice. Overall, however, the Soviets could not
win, either in world opinion or at home. To the Kremlin
constituency, the incident was seen as a serious failure of
leadership. It was even possible that the military had acted
on its own, without consulting its civilian counterpart.
There was speculation about friction between the two
power centers, stemming from the strong personalities of
Gorbachev and Ogarkov. Ogarkov was subsequently
removed from the center of power.

Andropov's health worsened. Early in October surgeons
removed one kidney. Andropov's apartment became a hospital. Confined to his bed, he ruled the country almost by
remote control. His personal assistants and Gorbachev were
the only people who had access to him. But they lacked
Andropov's power to impose decisions over the Old Guard
Politburo members, who retained a majority of the seats.
And as word of Andropov's operation was whispered
through the Kremlin, his opponents began to band together.

Gorbachev substituted for him at all possible events. He
met with foreign delegations from Communist and non-
Communist countries. He greeted the Canadian parliamentary delegation visiting Moscow, then journeyed to
Hungary for talks with Kádár and his aides. In Portugal, he
supported Alvaro Cunhal, the Communist leader facing re-
election as head of the party. His speech in the leader's
behalf was noteworthy in the tribute he repeatedly paid to

Andropov as the orchestrator of the future of the Soviet people.

When Andropov was unable to stand at the balcony of the Lenin Tomb during the parade commemorating the October 1917 Bolshevik revolution, the nation (and the world press) began to realize the seriousness of his condition. Nevertheless, Andropov continued to devote all of his energy to the task he had embarked upon at the start of his regime—gathering vigorous new leaders around him (and his protégé) and installing them in positions of power.

Andropov brought home Vitaly Vorotnikov from the embassy in Cuba, where he had been exiled by an angry Brezhnev. He assigned him to clean up corruption in Krasnodar, and later named him as premier of the Soviet Union's largest constituent, the Russian Republic, which carried with it promotion to full voting member of the Politburo.

Viktor Chebrikov, Andropov's successor as head of the KGB, was named to the Politburo. Yegor Ligachev was named a Central Committee secretary. Mikhail Solomentsev was appointed a full Politburo member, a blow to the Brezhnev faction, which had organized behind Chernenko.

Unable to attend the important year-end meeting of the Central Committee, Andropov sent this message: "I deeply regret that because of temporary causes I will not be able to attend the sessions." He also sent a speech that was read for him, in which he made it clear that his disability would not deter him from his campaigns for greater efficiency and production, and the elimination of corruption and malingering. He stated that the program had full Party support. While much had been achieved, he told his people, there was still much more to do.

Elections for first secretaries of the country's 150 regions were scheduled to be held in March 1984. As chairman of

•

the election machinery, Gorbachev would personally select the candidates for Party committees. Here was an unparalleled opportunity to strengthen his own position and at the same time weaken the Old Guard.

There had not been such a shake-up in the Party hierarchy since the early years of Leonid Brezhnev. But the Old Guard was still able to marshal its conservative strength for one more try.

On the afternoon of February 10, 1984, Moscow radio announced that Yuri Andropov's heart and kidneys had finally failed during the previous day. Among the Soviet people, who had placed so much faith and hope in Andropov's promises, there was widespread anguish and disappointment. Only fifteen months after the death of Brezhnev, the country was once again without a leader.

Andropov's funeral bier was laid out in the Hall of Columns. Chernenko was in the center of the long line of Politburo members, all of whom had come to pay their last respects. Gromyko and Tikhonov stood at Chernenko's right; Gorbachev and Romanov were at his left—visual representation of the Old Guard–New Guard division within the Party. Yet, in the midst of the Byzantine symbolism and ceremony, there was much deeply felt emotion: as the Politburo members presented themselves to their dead chief's wife and family, Andropov's son, Igor, a member of the diplomatic corps, was unable to hold back his tears. Both Gorbachev and Gromyko rushed to comfort him, as the rest of the Politburo filed slowly out of the hall.

Representatives of all nations attended the funeral services four days later in Red Square. Eulogies were delivered by Chernenko, Ustinov, and Gromyko. As the casket was borne to its Kremlin gravesite, Chernenko was the leading honorary pallbearer, on the left front of the coffin. Mikhail

•

Gorbachev stood directly opposite him on the right side. The arrangement was an indication of things to come.

THE TIDE OF CHANGE IS STEMMED— FOR A TIME

Like much of his personal life, Andropov's rapidly declining health was such a well-kept secret that his death shocked the Central Committee and the Politburo into a state of confusion. In fact, so little was known about the general secretary's personal life that it was only at his funeral that many Party dignitaries learned he had a wife, Tatiana, and a son, Igor. Gorbachev was the only one of the Party to embrace the widow warmly. This showed the leadership how close Gorbachev and Andropov had been.

What was no secret from the Politburo and the Party was that Andropov was grooming Gorbachev to be his successor. Insiders were almost certain that Gorbachev would be announced as the general secretary, to succeed his mentor. And if not Gorbachev, then Grigory Romanov, the Leningrad Party leader and secretary of defense industries, had to be the choice.

But neither Gorbachev nor Romanov controlled enough votes for a clear victory. Observers have often commented upon the Soviet predilection for unanimity, or the appearance of it. As the outcome of the struggle between Gorbachev and Romanov was in doubt, the Politburo and the Central Committee postponed their decision for a few days to let the air clear, and then chose neither contender. They gave the nod, instead, to seventy-two-year-old, ailing Konstantin Chernenko, whose role in leading the eulogies for Andropov had already signified to the Soviet people, viewing the ceremony on television, that he would be their next leader.

•

Born on September 24, 1911, in the Krasnoyarsk region of Siberia, Chernenko had been a Party member since 1931—the year Gorbachev was born. He had no great record of achievement. He owed his progress into the higher Party echelons to his close association with Leonid Brezhnev, whose aide he had been for thirty years. It was said that Chernenko had no program of his own, that all of his ideas on foreign and domestic issues were simply Brezhnev's ideas: he had heard them for thirty years. Chernenko had hoped to be Brezhnev's successor, but had been outmaneuvered by Andropov. So, in a sense, naming him to the post of general secretary at this time was like presenting a reward for loyalty and length of service to the Party.

The choice of Chernenko as general secretary was also a sign that the Old Guard was not yet willing to hand over the reins to the young leaders, which group Gorbachev symbolized. Already fifty-three, Gorbachev was nevertheless perceived by the old-timers as too young and untested for the responsibility. He had gotten so far with the help of his mentors, but now his main mentor was gone and he had not inherited the support of Andropov's followers. In particular, Foreign Minister Andrei Gromyko and Defense Minister Dmitri Ustinov, both men of accomplishment who belonged to no clique, voted against him. Faced with political reality, Gorbachev acquiesced to their decision, and proceeded to use the period of Chernenko's regime as an opportunity to solidify and expand his power base.

Gorbachev was the presiding officer at the Central Committee plenary session at which Chernenko was elected. It was Gorbachev who made the closing speech at the meeting (although Chernenko had the publication of his remarks delayed until a week after the event).

Nevertheless, the choice of Chernenko was hardly greeted with enthusiasm. The old man was obviously in poor health. His emphysema was so bad that he could not effectively shoulder the coffin at Andropov's funeral. There was little doubt that his time in office would be short.

That Gorbachev had risen another degree in the hierarchy was evident from his position in the lineup of official speeches to be delivered at local preelection meetings across the nation. The Soviet practice was to have a simulated political campaign during which the leaders were assigned a day to address the citizens. They spoke in reverse order of importance. As Party leader, Chernenko spoke last. Nikolai Tikhonov, the government leader, spoke the day before him. Scheduled to speak the day before Tikhonov (and after Gromyko and Ustinov), Gorbachev had apparently earned the sobriquet Second General Secretary.

Speaking in the village of Ipatovo, Gorbachev took the opportunity to declare that he stood for the same things as their deceased leader, Andropov, and that his priorities were the same. In addition to continuing the campaign against corruption and for tighter discipline, he wanted to modernize technology, improve management and increase agricultural production.

At the April 1984 plenary session of the Supreme Soviet, it was Gorbachev who made the speech formally proposing Chernenko as the Soviet leader. He also made a powerful argument for combining the posts of general secretary and president (actually, chairman of the Supreme Soviet). While this may have been construed as a way for the Old Guard to flaunt its victory, it has also been interpreted as an indication that the Chernenko forces had agreed not to reverse the programs that Andropov had initiated.

Gorbachev's election as chairman of the Foreign Affairs Commission of the Council of the Soviet Union at the same session was, for him, a big step in a new direction. Previously, his sphere had been agriculture and domestic issues.

•

Chernenko, who nominated him, had held the same post under Brezhnev. The assignment was seen as Gorbachev's chance to take an active part in the implementation of foreign policy.

As he had done for Andropov, Gorbachev substituted for Chernenko whenever illness prevented the general secretary from fulfilling his obligations. But with a difference. He was no longer the loyal assistant to an admired mentor. He was now an independent political professional seeking power. The statements he made, the policies he advanced, the opinions he offered, were his own. He dared to call attention to the need for incentives, for greater productivity, for creative solutions. He was running for office.

He had begun to educate himself about all aspects of Soviet life, holding seminars to which he invited economists, sociologists, and other experts to speak freely about the problems of the economy. How, he wanted to know, could they hasten economic development? What would it take to mobilize the people in their own behalf?

Gorbachev has been described as a good listener. He has great vitality, yet is able to listen and focus completely on whoever is speaking to him. Able to say exactly what they thought without fear of reprisal, the experts were enthusiastic in offering ideas.

It was at such sessions that Gorbachev first learned of the work of Soviet sociologist Tatiana Zaslavskaya. Soviet doctrine had stated that there was no such thing as human nature; there was only class nature. The nonexploitive, classless Soviet society would create a selfless human being, of courage and diligence. Zaslavskaya's research disagreed with this notion. Her years of study indicated that "we must accept man as he is." Gorbachev's desires to motivate the people through incentives and a degree of privatization stemmed from the same conviction.

Despite his illness, Chernenko, on the other hand, was attempting to maintain the status quo. While he could not cancel Andropov's programs or dismiss his appointees, he let it be known that he was in no hurry to carry out his predecessor's wishes. The Brezhnev bureaucrats began to reappear in their old familiar haunts.

There is a Russian word, *pokazukha,* which means "for show." A ceremony takes place simply to give the illusion that something has happened—an achievement of some sort has taken place and is being rightly celebrated. On September 27, 1984, the completion of the Baikal–Amur Railroad was celebrated. Television viewers saw the laying of the final link in the two-thousand-mile railway that was supposed to complement the Trans-Siberian Railway and move traffic away from the Chinese border. However, the press was not permitted to take a ride on the history-making first train between Irkutsk in the heart of the country to the shores of the Pacific Ocean.

Gorbachev knew what was going on, but was powerless to interfere. It was not until he came to power in 1985 did the press finally learn that the railway had not been finished. Its miles of uncompleted track were turning to rust. Chernenko had staged the 1984 event because the railway was supposed to have been completed by that date. The Politburo wanted to give the people the feeling that they were doing everything according to plan. It was *pokazukha.* The term, according to Kremlin watchers, symbolized Chernenko's leadership.

Chernenko had two other impressive projects in mind: he wanted to irrigate southern Russia and Soviet central Asia by diverting Russia's rivers, and he wanted to reclaim more land for farming (rather than increase the efficiency of the vast acreage already under cultivation). A more realistic Gorbachev, at pains to distance himself from the Cher-

•

nenko leadership, opposed the first measure and, as the expert in agricultural affairs, simply ignored the second.

Chernenko made a positive contribution in the area of foreign affairs. He forced a change in the Soviet policy toward the United States, resuming the Soviet-American arms talks, which Andropov had broken off the previous year.

In June of 1984, as chairman of the Foreign Affairs Commission, Gorbachev represented the Soviet Union in Rome at the funeral of Enrico Berlinguer, the Italian Communist leader. The Italian Communist party had long been a problem to Moscow because of its pragmatism and progressive outlook. Gorbachev met representatives from the Spanish and French Communist parties, whose attitudes were similar to those of the Italians. He was quoted in the Italian papers as saying that there was too much centralization within the Soviet Union, and that the fifteen republics should have more autonomy. He was also tremendously impressed by the Italians, hundreds of thousands of them crowding the streets, paying tribute to the leader—without being commanded by the authorities to do so.

Meanwhile, relations between the two Germanys were noticeably improving. Erich Honecker, the East German leader, had arranged for a line of credit from Chancellor Helmut Kohl of West Germany. Honecker was also planning visits to Romania and Bulgaria. The Bulgarian leader, Todor Zhivkov, was planning to visit West Germany, as was the Romanian chief, Nicolae Ceauşescu. To make matters more peculiar, this independent East-West diplomatic maneuvering supposedly had the approval of the general secretary of the Party in Moscow.

Chernenko was not seen in public during the summer. The Soviet press strongly attacked the East German–West German accommodation in a lengthy campaign. Then Ho-

necker changed his plans, postponing his meeting with
Kohl. A few days later, Gorbachev flew to Sofia, the Bulgarian capital. That evening the West German government
was informed that the visit of Party chief Zhivkov had been
canceled.

Ceauşescu alone persisted in asserting his independence
from Moscow. During the summer, Romania had been the
sole Communist nation to send a team of athletes to the Los
Angeles Olympic Games. In October, Ceauşescu visited
West Germany. He modified the apparent blow to Warsaw
Pact unity by speaking out against the nuclear policy of the
United States. (János Kádár of Hungary chose the same
season to visit France. However, as France's NATO con-
nections were not as important as those of West Germany,
Moscow paid scant attention.)

Western observers interpreted these goings-on as indica-
tive of serious policy differences within the Kremlin. The
decision to keep the satellite countries tightly in line was
presumably made by Foreign Minister Gromyko, with the
support of Marshal Ustinov, and not by Chernenko at all.
Gorbachev, in the role of "bad cop," had been effective in
persuading Honecker and Zhivkov to change their plans. In
this he had earned the further admiration of Gromyko, who
was known to have been impressed by Gorbachev's show of
strength presiding over the weekly Politburo meetings in
Chernenko's absence.

By the end of 1984, Chernenko was rarely seen in public.
When he did make the effort to go to the ballet, he was
literally carried to and from his chair. The entire audience
could see that the man was almost too frail to sit through
the performance.

Chernenko was too ill to attend a conference on ideology
in Moscow on December 10. Substituting for him, Gorbachev gave the main speech, in which he used publicly for the

•

first time the term *glasnost*. Andropov had used the word in his speech to the Politburo and Secretariat when he became president in June of 1983. Translated as "openness" by the Western press, the actual meaning, as Soviet experts were quick to note, is more like "publicity" than "frankness." Gorbachev's words were that "openness is a compulsory condition of socialist democracy and a norm of public life." But the experts saw that statement as yet another sign of Gorbachev's increasing confidence in his own power.

A few days later, on December 15, Gorbachev once again headed a thirty-member parliamentary delegation visiting a foreign country. The Soviets had decided to accept Prime Minister Margaret Thatcher's invitation to send a high-ranking official to Great Britain. While there had been almost no press coverage of Gorbachev's visit to Canada the previous year, because few in the West knew who he was or guessed his importance, the British press treated this trip almost as a royal visit. Accompanied this time by Raisa, smiling and modishly outfitted, the two of them projected an image of worldly sophistication that surprised and charmed their British hosts, who were used to sterner and dowdier Soviet visitors. Television crews gleefully followed them everywhere. Raisa used an American Express card on a shopping trip through Harrod's, and the world saw her leaning on the same counters that so frequently beckoned Princess Di. For the first time, the Soviet people saw one of their own high Party officials on television, every day, interacting with the leaders of another powerful nation. Television became Gorbachev's ally, enhancing his popularity at home as he was forging alliances abroad.

Ever mindful of details (and thanks to the excellent briefings of Alexander Yakovlev), Gorbachev managed to include witty remarks about the British satirist

C. Northcote Parkinson in his banter with interviewers. In the reading room of the British Museum, where Karl Marx is known to have done his research for *Das Kapital*, he quipped that people who don't like Marx should blame the museum.

As he had done in Canada, he appeared before the British Parliament, speaking to the Select Committee on Foreign Relations. As nuclear arms talks between Foreign Minister Gromyko and U.S. secretary of state George Shultz were shortly to be resumed, the British—and presumably, the other nations of the world—were eager to hear what he had to say. Gorbachev was reassuring. He agreed that the USSR was interested in seeing a limit to, and an eventual ban on, nuclear arms.

"We still believe that there is and can be no rational alternative to the policy of peaceful coexistence," he said, "and I would like to emphasize this point with all certainty. ... We are ready to go as far as our Western partners in the talks. Naturally enough, equality and equal security shall underlie any agreements in this field. And, of course, any course that seeks military superiority over the USSR and its allies is unacceptable and has no prospects."

Gorbachev refused to be put on the defensive when questioned about human rights in the Soviet Union. Rather, he reminded the offending member of Parliament that Britain persecuted "entire communities, entire nationalities." At this reference to the continuing struggle in Northern Ireland, his audience visibly chafed. Later, he shrugged the matter off, saying, "Truth comes out of heated discussion."

Gorbachev's successful meeting with Prime Minister Margaret Thatcher was surely the high point of the trip to Britain. She entertained the couple at the prime minister's country home, Chequers, and after their lengthy discussion

•

period, Mrs. Thatcher announced to Britain and the world,
"I like Mr. Gorbachev. We can do business together."

The sudden death of Defense Minister Dmitri Ustinov
brought the Gorbachevs' London visit to an abrupt halt.
Gorbachev flew to Moscow to attend the funeral. Grigory
Romanov, his chief rival, was chairman of the funeral commission, and was the main speaker at the funeral meeting in
Red Square on December 24. It was a bitterly cold day.
Chernenko had been present for the Guard of Honor ceremony, which had been held indoors the previous day. He
could not tolerate the cold and was absent from the final
outdoor ceremony.

The balance of power was shifting once again. Seventy-
three-year-old Marshal Sergei Sokolov was appointed defense minister. Commander of the Leningrad district in the
1970s, he was assumed to be a Romanov supporter.

In his year-end speech to the Central Committee, Gorbachev stated, "We cannot remain a major power in world
affairs unless we put our domestic house in order." He said
that a new industrial revolution was necessary, which
would require sacrifices. "Without the hard work and complete dedication of each and every one," he said, "it is not
even possible to retain what has been achieved." The Soviet
Union was in a period of decline that could become irreversible, he warned, admitting that in his search for a solution
he was tending toward a type of market socialism, under
which he could apply such economic levers as price, cost,
profit, and any others which would increase the efficiency of
the economy. He expressed the view that the Communist
party program needed revision to bring it in step with pre-
sent-day reality.

The speech, if publicly published, would probably have
created a sensation. It was printed, instead, as a Party

pamphlet, and one hundred thousand copies were distributed to the Party organizations a week later.

Chernenko disagreed with every idea Gorbachev expressed, and issued a statement that he intended to retain every past accomplishment. "This is how it was in the past; this will always remain so in the future."

In February of 1985, when the preelection rallies were to be held, Chernenko's speech was read for him. (Elections were staged to give a democratic appearance to a predetermined outcome.) Viktor Grishin, Moscow Party chief, told the nation that its leader was home because of doctor's orders. Two days later, escorted by Grishin, a weak Chernenko was shown casting his vote. (Journalists, who were not allowed to watch Chernenko cast his ballot, believed that this was a staged shot, and that Chernenko never left the Kremlin hospital.)

Chernenko was shown on television again on March 2, again accompanied by Grishin, greeting a group of Party officials. It was his last public appearance.

Business was conducted in his name by Chernenko's aides. Gorbachev and Romanov were nowhere to be seen. As if he realized that the struggle for power would soon come to a head, and that he had better be on hand to protect his own position, Gorbachev canceled a scheduled trip to the United States, sending Vladimir Shcherbitsky, Party leader of the Ukraine, in his stead.

Suddenly, Chernenko's wife, Anna, gave a lavish reception for the women of Moscow's diplomatic community, to which even Brezhnev's widow was invited. Raisa Gorbacheva's outfit was remarked upon by other guests: instead of the chic sandals, pearl earrings and satin party gown that she wore in London, she appeared in a plain dark suit, with no jewelry. She remained in the background, deferring always to the senior Kremlin women.

•

The following week, on March 10, 1985, Chernenko's death was announced over Soviet radio and television.

Within four hours Moscow Radio and Tass announced the election of Mikhail Sergeyevich Gorbachev as general secretary of the Communist party.

There had been little doubt among Soviet watchers around the world that Gorbachev was the logical successor. As it turned out, his victory was a close call.

CHAPTER FIVE

•

THE POLITICS
OF *GLASNOST*

•

AFTER Andropov's death, Gorbachev had lacked sufficient support among the voting members of the Politburo to prevail over Chernenko. And during the ensuing year, while Chernenko was general secretary, he had not noticeably strengthened his list of supporters. To the Old Guard, he was still too young, too new, too untried, and too dangerous. Outspoken in his antagonism to the entrenched bureaucracy, he had apparently made no new friends among them.

As expected, Gorbachev's rival, Leningrad Party chief Grigory Romanov, nominated Viktor Grishin, the powerful head of the Moscow Party organization, to become general secretary. As luck would have it, two of his supporters were unable to attend the hurriedly called Politburo meeting— Vladimir Shcherbitsky was in San Francisco, and Kazakhstan Party chief Dinmukhamed Kunaev was still en route from his home in Alma-Ata to Moscow.

Another lucky break for Gorbachev was unexpected, at least by the majority attending the meeting. During the year that he had substituted for Chernenko at meetings, political functions, debates and ceremonies, Gorbachev had steadily earned the admiration and support of the one Politburo member who was truly respected by all the others— Andrei Gromyko, the living symbol of more than forty years of Soviet history. It was Gromyko who nominated Gorbachev for the post of general secretary. Then the usually dispassionate foreign minister delivered an emotionally charged, extemporaneous speech to the Central Committee in which he depicted Gorbachev as a gifted politician, a man of superb analytical skill, whose sharp mind was always working in the interests of the Party, the man to whom the Soviet Union could look for brilliant leadership in all areas. Gromyko's description of Gorbachev has become famous, "Comrades, this man has a nice smile, but he has teeth of iron."

Also articulate on Gorbachev's behalf were such nonvoting (younger) members as the Georgian leader Eduard Shevardnadze and Viktor Chebrikov, head of the KGB. Gradually, the Old Guard was persuaded that Gorbachev was tough enough and shrewd enough and conservative enough, his cries for reform notwithstanding, to deserve their vote. He won by the slimmest of margins.

News of Gorbachev's election was received with enthusiasm by the people. He was young (at fifty-four, Gorbachev was the youngest member of the leadership), and in good health, and he seemed to offer the promise of something new, something lasting, possibly something better.

On the day of Chernenko's funeral, March 14, 1985, Gorbachev appeared before the Soviet people for the first time as their leader. His message was short and conventional. There was a slight change in the traditional funeral service—soldiers, rather than the aging Politburo members, carried the dead leader's coffin. And the lineup at the mausoleum included only three military leaders. Then the

•

1,500-man military band segued from Chopin's "Funeral March" to livelier tunes and the troops led a spirited parade back to the Kremlin.

Representatives of more than 120 nations attended Chernenko's funeral. Gorbachev presented himself to all of them. He then scheduled private conversations with as many of them as he could. On his list was Prime Minister Margaret Thatcher, who had already told the world that she believed Gorbachev was someone she (and the West) could do business with. He chatted for eighty-five minutes with Vice-president George Bush, who described him as "an impressive idea salesman." Canadian prime minister Brian Mulroney, French president François Mitterrand, West Germany's chancellor Helmut Kohl, the Chinese deputy premier Li Peng, and President Zia ul-Haq of Pakistan all came away impressed by this man who, they agreed, was clearly in command.

Gorbachev then proceeded to make himself accessible to his own people. He toured factories, schools, hospitals, always breaking away from the official tour routes to chat with onlookers, questioning them about their concerns, their hopes, their ideas. He wanted to take people by surprise, explaining that that was his way of finding out what was genuine and what was, possibly, *pokazukha*. He imparted a message to the workers as well, one that was carried to the entire nation on TV newscasts: "I know that you *can* work better, but *can* is not enough. You *must* work better."

The serious political and economic problems that Andropov had only begun to deal with, and Chernenko had attempted to ignore, were now Gorbachev's to solve. The country's continuing inability to feed its people was not altogether due to bad weather or poor soil, but to frustrating conditions that Gorbachev, having seen the effectiveness of the Canadian farmers (as well as the impact of his own local agricultural reforms), was convinced properly motivated workers could overcome. Soviet industry lacked basic quality control, produced goods that the people did not need, and failed to provide the everyday household commodities they wanted. As he saw them, the difficulties were almost entirely man-made—caused by corruption, ignorance, laziness, and inefficiency, resulting in mass inertia and a sense of hopelessness. Significant changes in attitudes and in the way the system worked were required.

In his efforts to reorganize the Party machinery and reenergize the nation, Gorbachev made particularly effective use of television. Unlike his predecessors, he was aware of the medium's potential; its ability to reach all parts of the country (there are eleven time zones in the Soviet Union, compared with four in the United States); command the attention of a vast audience at all educational levels; and, by providing role models for the people to emulate, create at least a climate for change in that audience's attitudes and expectations. The government increased the number of live news and direct-response call-in shows to give viewers the sense of being in touch with reality. Live coverage of Gorbachev's meetings with leaders of other countries gave the people a sense of their nation as a participant in world events. This was in distinct contrast to the policies of previous leaders, where little was broadcast about the outside world other than that it was a hostile environment.

Among the first of Gorbachev's official acts was his May 16, 1985, decree ordering substantial cuts in the production and sale of vodka. Alcohol abuse, and its cost in worker productivity, had long been one of the nation's most serious problems. The number of liquor outlets was reduced and their hours shortened. The legal drinking age was raised from eighteen to twenty-one. Fines for drunkenness were

•

increased. Vodka was no longer freely served at Party functions. Social occasions were no longer competitive drinking fests. Gorbachev's nickname became *"Gen Sok,"* translated as "General Juice," instead of *"gen sec,"* or "general secretary."

In the spring of 1985, Gorbachev delivered what appeared to be an impromptu speech to Leningrad Party members at the historic Smolny Institute. The Smolny Institute in Leningrad had been, at the turn of the century, a finishing school for young women of the Russian aristocracy. One of the buildings that was a part of the elaborate blue and white Smolny Monastery, it was commandeered as Bolshevik headquarters by Lenin in 1917. It was here that Lenin planned the overthrow of the Duma (Parliament) and the Bolshevik takeover of the government. During World War II, the entire space occupied by buildings and gardens was covered with camouflage netting to protect the site from German bombardiers. It was in this impeccably maintained building, today one of St. Petersburg's premier tourist attractions, that Gorbachev chose to introduce what he called a necessary revolution from above.

He called it *perestroika*—a "restructuring." Gorbachev warned that everyone, from the worker to the minister, "must change attitudes. Anyone who is not prepared to do so must simply get out of the way!" He followed his words with action of his own, launching what many have called a bloodless purge—a wholesale Party and government housecleaning, during which some 60 percent of the government ministers were replaced. He swept through the armed forces, regional power centers, and local Party organizations, transforming the Party leadership. Through dismissal or retirement he replaced corrupt or aging Brezhnev-era bureaucrats with dynamic, younger men who shared his attitudes.

To no one's surprise, Grigory Romanov of Leningrad was among the first to be ousted. Gorbachev's rival since the death of Andropov, it was Romanov who had put forth Grishin for the post of general secretary. Rumor had it that Romanov was an alcoholic who consistently abused his authority as head of the Leningrad Party. For his daughter's wedding banquet he reportedly ordered the Hermitage Museum to supply the priceless set of Sèvres porcelain that had belonged to the royal family. The party got out of hand, and numerous pieces of porcelain were shattered by drunken guests. Soon after, Romanov was officially retired for reasons of health. Gossips whispered that he was hospitalized for alcoholism.

Possibly the most stunning change Gorbachev made was to name Foreign Minister Andrei Gromyko to the largely ceremonial post of president of the Soviet Union. Gromyko had been instrumental in helping Gorbachev gain acceptance by the Old Guard of the Politburo and Central Committee, yet the so-called promotion essentially removed him from power. As president, Gromyko kept his place in the Politburo, and also the many perquisites to which he had become accustomed over his decades in power. Selected to replace him as foreign minister was Eduard Shevardnadze, an amiable Georgian with virtually no diplomatic experience. With this move, the Foreign Ministry ceased to be an independent conservative power center. Shevardnadze would prove to be a talented negotiator capable of revamping foreign policy to suit Gorbachev's design.

Gorbachev understood that decades of keeping pace with the United States in the escalating arms race had become more than the country's economy could bear. The military was consuming the nation's resources and, ultimately, producing nothing of value for the people. To match the dizzying technology of the latest nuclear weap-

•

onry described by President Ronald Reagan, the Soviet Union would have to build, at enormous cost, factories capable of producing those weapons systems. This strain on the Soviet economy, once accomplished, would not improve the dismal quality of life or create one item of desperately needed consumer goods.

In a historic interview with representatives of *Time* in the summer of 1985, Gorbachev stated his concern about arms control and Soviet relations with the United States, saying that the world situation was complex to the point of being explosive. "Time is passing and it might be too late. The train might already have left the station." He suggested that it was time to consider eliminating weaponry and improving the relations between the two superpowers.

Outlining his plans for reviving his nation's failing economy, he spoke of profit, pricing, and credit as tools that he would employ. Then he asked the interviewers, "What are the external conditions we need to fulfill those domestic plans? I leave the answer to that question to you." The answer had to be relief from the economic burden of nuclear armament.

Gorbachev kept up his disarmament campaign throughout the year. That summer, he chose the fortieth anniversary of the bombing of Hiroshima to declare a Soviet moratorium on underground testing of nuclear weapons, and challenged the United States to do the same. The Reagan administration called it a propaganda ploy.

During his visit with President Mitterrand in Paris in October, Gorbachev offered the British and French a separate nuclear-arms agreement. The offer was rejected, but his message remained clear.

Finally, President Reagan agreed to meet with Gorbachev for two days in Geneva in November of 1985. It was called the Fireside Summit, because the two world leaders

•

strolled to a secluded cottage and, with only two interpreters present, chatted in front of a cozy fire for more than an hour. Their first meeting had originally been scheduled to last only fifteen minutes.

They saw each other six times during the two-day period, discussing nuclear arms (Reagan offered a disarmament proposal that Gorbachev scanned and dismissed), human rights, Afghanistan and so forth, and found that, despite their disagreements, they had a great deal to talk about. Both agreed that the meetings were productive. Reagan then invited Gorbachev to visit the United States. Gorbachev accepted and returned the invitation, which Reagan also accepted. Reagan agreed with Prime Minister Margaret Thatcher: Gorbachev was a man they could do business with.

Gorbachev's busy first year created an atmosphere of excitement and altered the tone of U.S.-Soviet relations for the first time in forty years. The sheer number of changes was impressive. In twelve short months he replaced thirty heads of the eighty government ministries, consolidated five ministries into one state-farm industry committee, and ousted the leaders of ten of the twenty-four departments of the Central Committee.

Outside Moscow he replaced numerous republic secretaries and more than 50 of the 159 regional secretaries. He also recast a significant number of deputy ministers and ambassadors. It was not easy to find replacements. "Officials should develop out of *perestroika*," he said. "We should replace them. But where will we get new ones? If only we could bake them, like pancakes!"

His close advisor, Alexander Yakovlev, said later that he knew there would be changes, but "in 1985 if you had said that all these things would happen, I'd have given my arm that it was not possible."

•

And yet, in his five-and-a-half-hour speech to the Twenty-seventh Party Congress in February 1986, Gorbachev promised, or warned, that there was a great deal more to be done. *Perestroika* was no whim. To the agricultural leaders, he said that produce quotas should go to central locations for storage, adding that the farmers could keep any surplus for local use or sale. He wanted each area to work on an individual system of cost accounting. Job-by-job payment systems were to become widespread. He spoke of personal initiative and individual responsibility for meeting production goals. He also declared that those in charge must think of ways to prevent mismanagement and sponging. When he said that prices would have to reflect economic and social realities, he sent a shiver through many in the audience—for decades Soviet prices had been stabilized by artificial price controls.

Was Gorbachev actually proposing fundamental changes? Or was he merely tinkering with externals? Western observers differed in their reactions. How, they wondered, could he make the plan work? How, in a socialist system, could a plant be closed for inefficiency? What happened to the concept of full employment if unnecessary operations were canceled?

Gorbachev believed that slavish attention to the centralized command economy had stifled economic development. He urged his people to accept his proposals because, despite their seeming contradictions of the system, he believed they would work. It was more important to produce necessary goods, he said, than argue about philosophy. Times had changed since Lenin. To remain relevant to the modern world, Soviet socialism would have to change, too.

Possibly Gorbachev overestimated their capacity for change and failed to foresee the resistance he would face within the system. Years of enforced obedience had, according to his close advisor, Yakovlev, turned the people "into a nation of political idiots." In addition, the Gorbachev team were mostly young men from the provinces who had not had the opportunity to cultivate the intricate network of alliances needed to be politically effective. Many observers felt that in this respect, Gorbachev resembled Jimmy Carter during the latter's presidency—intelligent, educated, dedicated, and with a deep sense of mission, but with no ties to the entrenched political establishment. Gorbachev's rolling pronunciation also recalled Carter. Carter's southern accent to northerners in America seems as foreign as Gorbachev's "country" Russian did to Muscovites.

To broaden his sphere of influence Gorbachev embarked upon the policy of *glasnost*. Gorbachev referred to it as a substitute for multiparty politics. The policy brought about the release of previously banned films and novels, and a subsequent blossoming in the film and publishing industries. Writers now able to criticize the leadership established a number of "opposition" newsletters and an ongoing official reexamination of the country's Stalinist past. The press and TV news staffs began to behave like investigative reporters, exposing corruption and crusading with unexpected zeal against mismanagement, particularly on the local level.

Glasnost had its severest test on April 26, 1986. Without warning, reactor number 4 of the Chernobyl nuclear-power station exploded, ejecting a giant geyser of radioactive matter into the atmosphere and immediately killing two people. The largest nuclear generator in the USSR and the pride of Russian technology, Chernobyl had promised to be the key to increased production of nuclear power, the main source of energy for the Ukraine, the fulfillment of the Soviet dream of a superefficient nuclear-industrial complex,

•

wherein even the hot water from reactor cooling systems would be used—for central heating, for greenhouses, and to provide ponds for fish breeding. The explosion at Chernobyl blew the dream apart.

The actual sequence of events remains confused. Thirty minutes after the blast, the first firemen arrived on the scene from the nearby town of Pripyat. As they fought to control the leaping two-hundred-foot flames, they were unaware that underneath, the graphite core of the reactor was fiercely burning. The highest-ranking officer at the site was the leader of the local fire department, Major Telyatnikov. With fifteen men, Telyatnikov fought to stop the fire in reactor number 4 from spreading to the three other reactors. (The fire was extremely difficult to contain because flammable plastic had been used to isolate the electric cables.) The roof of reactor number 4 had already collapsed, and the other three were in danger of falling.

A call for help went out to the Kiev fire department eighty miles away. The extra men did not arrive in time to save Telyatnikov's heroes, who received an estimated twenty times the lethal dose of radiation. They did succeed in shutting down the other reactors, and then had to work around the clock to keep them from heating up again. Engineers from other power stations were flown in to help.

As far as is known, Gorbachev heard about the accident about five hours after it occurred. Chaos ruled through the night. Early in the morning, medical teams evaluated the firemen and members of the crew manning the plant.

The next day, rescue teams were dispatched to the burning power station. More than two thousand people were immediately known to have been exposed to radiation; 299 of the most seriously ill were evacuated to Moscow, the rest to neighboring Kiev.

The accident occurred on a Saturday. The nearby Pri-

•

pyat-Kiev artificial reservoir, a popular fishing and recrea-
tion site, was crowded with tourists. Residents of nearby
towns were not evacuated, nor were they instructed to remain indoors. The local radio and TV stations broadcast no
announcement of the explosion, nor any warnings or instructions to the people. For almost thirty-six hours, no one
in the nearby town of Pripyat was informed of the danger.
Not until Sunday morning were the town's forty thousand
residents evacuated.

Sweden reported indications of a major nuclear accident; two days later, the Swedes detected a radioactive
cloud and requested information. On April 28, Soviet television news briefly mentioned the incident, but made no further comment. Over the wishes of Gorbachev and
Vorotnikov, the Politburo voted to maintain a news black-
out. Plans for the traditional May Day celebrations in Kiev
went forward as usual.

For several days hundreds of helicopters dropped tons of
neutron-absorbing sand, lead, clay, and boron on the fire.
Because the reactor core was in danger of melting down—
the China Syndrome nightmare—thousands of workers
were brought in to dig a tunnel beneath the thin concrete
foundation, pump out the water beneath the reactors and
then pump concrete into the tunnel to support the sinking
reactor.

When the wind changed direction a week later, another
fifty thousand people were evacuated.

A special secret department within the State Committee
for Meteorology was assigned the task of monitoring the
amount of radioactivity in the air. The monitoring system
consisted of a network of towers and a counter for measur-
ing radioactivity, but it turned out that no one really knew
how the system worked.

There were no civilian emergency evacuation plans, nor

In the Soviet Parliament, the leaders of the country express happy cooperation and unguarded distrust, all in the blink of an eye. (NOVASTI PRESS)

Late 1950s photo of Soviet leadership, including Gorbachev's important mentors Kulakov (seventh from left), Andropov (behind Brezhnev), and Suslov (fourth from right). (ARCHIVES OF THE USSR)

Gorbachev's first mentor, Feodor Kulakov, a member of the Presidium in the 1960s. He was rumored to have committed suicide shortly after this picture was taken.

(ARCHIVES OF THE USSR)

Above: Mikhail Gorbachev as party official in Stavropol in the 1950s.
(ARCHIVES OF THE USSR)

Right: Mikhail and Raisa Gorbachev at the time of their marriage in 1954.
(NOVOSTI PRESS)

Mikhail Suslov, a ruling member of the Politburo, attacking the United States incursion in Vietnam in 1968 before the Supreme Soviet. (TASS)

Suslov arriving for a visit in Stavropol; Party boss Gorbachev beaming, early 1970s. (TASS)

General Secretary Andropov with soon-to-be General Secretary Chernenko and Gorbachev laying wreath at Lenin's tomb, 1981. (TASS)

Yuri Andropov addressing the Supreme Soviet in the late 1970s. All four general secretaries of the Soviet Union from 1964 through 1991 are in this picture. In the front row, Gorbachev (fourth from left), Chernenko (sixth from left), Brezhnev (seventh from left). (TASS)

Mikhail Gorbachev as general secretary addressing Supreme Soviet, flanked by Yegor Ligachev (left), and Andrei Gromyko (right). Boris Yeltsin, in a rare moment of applause, in the first row behind Ligachev. (TASS)

Raisa Gorbachev was an interested, but uninvolved, spectator at Soviet parliamentary sessions. (TASS)

Boris Yeltsin and Moscow mayor Gavriil Popov. (NOVOSTI PRESS*)*

Yeltsin working the crowd. (NOVOSTI PRESS)

Yeltsin supporters demonstrate outside Kremlin, March 21, 1991.

Boris Yeltsin mounts a friendly Soviet tank in front of the Russian "White House" on the coup's first day and courageously calls for a general strike and the arrest of the coup plotters. (TASS)

Above: Believed to be one of the Gorbachevs' two residences in Moscow. It is not known by the general public where Gorbachev lives.

Opposite: Trucks lined up in preparation for anti-rally maneuvers, March 28, 1992.

Mikhail Gorbachev returns to Moscow from the Crimea after the abortive coup. (TASS)

even one agency in charge of the situation. The power station was under the aegis of the Ministry of Power and Electrification; the Ministry of Medium Machine Building governed the fuel cycle and reactor core; the medical system of the power station was the responsibility of a secret department within the Ministry of Health, but the medical services in the surrounding towns were handled by the Ukrainian health network. No one was really in charge.

While the Chernobyl accident is attributable to no single agency, clearly it was the way such projects were put together in the Soviet Union that laid the groundwork for the disaster's severity. In order to finish the job within an unrealistically forecast time, welders did a slapdash job on pipes that carried radioactive fluids. This was only one area in which an accident was waiting to happen.

It was not until two weeks after the explosion that Gorbachev addressed the nation. He said little about the cause of the accident, but promised to take corrective action. He called for a nuclear-test ban in the face of the international dimensions of the disaster. Critics considered his avoidance of the issue of what caused the accident unworthy of a leader of his stature. Nevertheless, from that time on, all disasters and calamities have been promptly reported in the Soviet media.

Only a few months earlier, the Twenty-seventh Party Congress had endorsed a Five-Year Plan that called for the doubling of Soviet nuclear capacity. While most nations were reconsidering the wisdom of relying upon nuclear power (no plants had been built in the United States since the Three Mile Island accident in 1979), the Soviet Union had opted to build nuclear-power stations that would generate thermal energy as the way to command the future. There had been no public discussion prior to the acceptance of the plan.

•

The effect of the Chernobyl disaster upon the Soviet economic plans must surely have been numbing. A million hectares of agricultural land were contaminated. All told, more than a million people were evacuated. Villages were abandoned, cattle slain, and thousands of tons of contaminated topsoil scraped away for burial. About eight hundred scattered shallow burial pits bulldozed around Chernobyl were filled with contaminated material from houses, forests, and farms.

An estimated fifty million curies of radioactive iodine and six million curies of radioactive cesium (the two most volatile radioactive products) were released into the atmosphere during the first week after the explosion. About six million curies of less volatile radioactive strontium were released. Radioactive strontium binds with soil; cesium with water. The isotopes have a half-life of more than thirty years. It is conceivable that the environment will be contaminated for centuries.

In August, a full report about the disaster was presented at a meeting of the International Atomic Energy Agency in Vienna. The Soviet delegation identified the cause as a singular sequence of human errors, set in motion by an unauthorized test of the reactor that violated stringent safety regulations. Western experts, who criticized the design of the Soviet reactor, recognizing it as obsolete, were mollified by the frankness of the report. The two-volume document was never made public in the Soviet Union. This was not an impressive example of *glasnost*.

During the cleanup, Soviet film director Vladimir Shevchenko entered the contaminated zone to document the aftermath of the disaster. *Chernobyl—Chronicle of Difficult Weeks* is a heart-wrenching record of the event and the brave response of Soviet firemen, scientists, and workers to the danger. To record the facts cost Shevchenko his life: six months after the film was completed, in 1988, he was dead from radiation poisoning.

Local and republic governments criticized the national government about the cleanup, accusing officials of being slow to evacuate people to safety, exposing cleanup workers to high doses of radiation, using slipshod methods to bury contaminated wastes, and then building resettlement homes in contaminated regions. Almost five years after the accident, Soviet prosecutor general Nikolai Trubin conceded that there had been gross failures in the government's cleanup plan, and some officials are now facing criminal charges for failing to protect the public from fallout, for ignoring radiation levels, and for violating health norms in burying radiation debris.

As the charges continue to be made, the cleanup still causes problems. Local officials in Chernobyl are debating the solutions to such problems as a string of thirty railroad cars in which tons of contaminated beef have supposedly been kept refrigerated since the accident—this for lack of a safe disposal site.

One result of the Chernobyl explosion was that farm products from within a twenty- or thirty-mile radius of the area had to be tested for radioactivity. Contaminated produce was confiscated on the spot, with the farmers receiving no compensation. Only "clean" produce was accepted for marketing, and a great portion of that was trucked in from the outer areas to supply Moscow and Leningrad.

To avoid ruin, many farmers tried to transport their fruits and vegetables to markets far to the north and east, where, they had heard, there was no testing. The government then prohibited them to move their crops outside the area without a special permit. As a result, there were serious fruit and vegetable shortages in Siberia and the Arctic regions. Where food was available, prices rose to new heights.

As shelves emptied of food in the state stores during the spring through the end of 1990, the housewives of Kiev and Moscow and Leningrad and the rest of the Soviet Union sought their vegetables, meat and dairy products in the "free" markets. Products there were not only expensive, but no one could tell them whether or not the food they bought for their families was contaminated. Mothers worried, and they blamed Gorbachev for their worry.

According to Dr. Tamara Belookaya, head of diagnostics at the Institute of Radiation Medicine near Minsk, in Byelorussia, "The medical and biological consequences of Chernobyl appear much more serious and diverse than had been expected during the first years."

In an October 1991 article in *Chernobyl Digest* Dr. Belookaya wrote: "Radiation, heavy metals, chemical pollution, inadequate nutrition and psychological stress have caused essential changes in the health status of the Byelorussian population."

While fallout from the Chernobyl disaster continues to be felt in the Ukraine, where the nuclear power plant is situated, 70 percent of the contamination from the Chernobyl explosion that rained on the Soviet Union hit Byelorussia, to the north. Dr. Belookaya says that the number of illnesses in infected areas of Byelorussia have tripled since the accident.

Through the end of 1991, Soviet authorities acknowledged only thirty-one deaths due to the accident. But since the end of the Union and the rise of the independent countries of Russia, Byelorussia, and Ukraine, officials have no vested interest in minimizing and covering up the damage done by the nuclear accident at Chernobyl. Therefore, we may learn of many more Chernobyl-related deaths soon.

Meanwhile, the Chernobyl power station has still been functioning with its two remaining nuclear reactors. But in

•

October and November 1991, two separate incidents of fire prompted the Ukraine Parliament to vote to close down the facility sometime in 1993. It may be many years before the full cost in lives and money is known.

The success of Gorbachev's antialcohol campaign also had an unexpected result: a marked increase in drug abuse, a problem the health service could not handle. There are no Soviet hospitals specializing in the treatment of drug addiction. The existence of the problem has been officially denied for many years, although according to Soviet law, addicts who commit crimes while under the influence of drugs must be treated.

During Gorbachev's first year in office, the housing shortage had been identified as a major source of discontent. Under the complicated Russian system, different ministries controlled cities and their suburbs. Local authorities determined housing priorities. When an important construction—a power plant or a new hospital—was behind schedule, less important works were abandoned to allow the number-one project to be completed on time. Consequently, very few living quarters have been completed over the past twenty years. Hundreds of thousands of houses had been built during Khrushchev's emergency housing push from 1955 to 1962, but they had been thrown together with little attention, care, or skill. After thirty years, they were ready to fall apart. The Twenty-seventh Party Congress voted to remedy the situation by building new, high-quality housing, but after the Chernobyl explosion all available building materials were commandeered to rebuild housing for the 150,000 people who had lost their homes.

The emergency housing program was nearly completed when the province of Moldavia suffered an earthquake on August 31, 1986. This part of the Ukraine was known to be a seismic zone, and buildings there were supposedly con-

•

structed according to special safety plans. The post-1978 buildings, which had been put up during the Brezhnev era—by corrupt contractors who violated safety standards and pocketed huge profits—collapsed. The scale of destruction was gargantuan: 49,000 houses, 1,100 schools, 350 hospitals, 230 office buildings, and thousands of shops and farmhouses crumbled into dust.

Soon after, the cruise ship *Admiral Nakhimov* mysteriously sank in the Black Sea. Four hundred lives were lost. The sixty-year-old vessel had been resurrected after being sunk during World War II. Too fragile to sail, it had been condemned and was to have been scrapped. No one could explain why the ship was still carrying passengers.

To raise morale, probably his own as well as the public's, Gorbachev took to the road on a highly publicized fact-finding expedition. He headed first for the Soviet Far East, to Primorski and Khabarovsk, sparsely populated regions as large as Japan and Korea combined. Despite special government incentives, the plentiful land has attracted few settlers. Consequently, the area suffers chronic food and fuel shortages and depends heavily upon neighboring China for trade.

Gorbachev, realizing the importance of cooperation between the nations, made a strong peace overture to the Chinese government. He announced that the Soviet Union would remove its troops from the Chinese border at Mongolia. Of greater importance was his resolution of the border dispute that dated from 1969. The Amur and Ussuri rivers mark the long Sino-Soviet boundary. The Soviet Union had always insisted that it owned the land up to the Chinese bank of the rivers—thus claiming control of the waterways and the numerous fish swimming in both rivers. The Chinese maintained that the boundary line was in the middle of the waterways, implying that both nations shared the

•

travel lane as well as the fish. Gorbachev's acceptance of the Chinese position opened a new chapter in Sino-Soviet relations. For reasons no one understood, he mentioned the concession offhandedly, almost as an aside in the context of a long speech. It was as if it were impossible for him, or the Soviet Union, to apologize to the Chinese government and accept responsibility for the tortuous border conflict that had lasted nearly two decades.

In an effort to rally the people to work harder and meet the goals of the first year of the Five-Year Plan, Gorbachev continued making public speeches highly critical of the bureaucrats. His thesis was always that local bureaucracies stubbornly preferred to continue doing business the same old inefficient way, and because of inertia and conservatism the excellent decisions of his administration were not being translated into action. Soviet technology would be stalled for decades, he said, because new factories were being built according to old plans!

Some observers considered Gorbachev naive to believe that pep talks and rallying cries would automatically result in economic development. Change, they said, would come only when there are changes in the way the system operates. In the Soviet Union the government controlled every aspect of people's lives: no entity existed without government knowledge and regulation. For all his talk of new energy and ideas, Gorbachev in 1986 had not yet actually changed a single domestic policy.

Internationally, Gorbachev was able to end the year on a promising note. President Reagan apparently agreed with Gorbachev that it would be to the advantage of both to lessen the antagonism between the United States and the Soviet Union. However, the two men seemed unwilling to test their seemingly compatible relationship with a formal

•

state visit by Gorbachev to Washington. Instead, they opted for another mini-summit. They agreed to meet in Iceland.

Gorbachev managed to turn what could have been another disaster into a bargaining chip. On August 30, 1986, the American journalist Nicholas Daniloff of *U.S. News and World Report* was arrested as a spy. Since Stalin's regime, there had been an unwritten rule against using members of the press in these sorts of cloak-and-dagger games. Apparently, Daniloff had been seized by the KGB in clumsy retaliation for the FBI's arrest of a Soviet United Nations employee. The world press was figuratively booing loudly at the Soviets for their unacceptable behavior. But Gorbachev, who had already shown that he never apologized, traded Daniloff's release for the meeting at Reykjavik.

Gorbachev had already made several unilateral peace concessions. He had extended the moratorium on Soviet nuclear testing, and had accepted the principle of on-site inspection. He had even backed down on his demand that the United States cease Star Wars (Strategic Defense Initiative) research. The Western interpretation of those actions was that he was using the peace initiatives to relieve the pressure of his own domestic economic problems, and that Reagan's tough stance was showing results.

At their 1985 meeting in Geneva, Gorbachev had hinted that if the United States continued with its SDI program, Soviet scientists would be forced to develop a better, cheaper, quicker program. In reality, the Soviets were in no position to compete on a technological level and Gorbachev was unwilling to underwrite the huge cost of development. In the United States, the estimated price tag on the initial research had reached thirty billion dollars. Faced with shortages of food, housing, and consumer goods, Gorbachev considered additional weaponry a waste of human and material resources. He hoped that the meeting in Reykjavik would result in agreement on nuclear disarmament. Gorbachev wanted an end to SDI, and the sooner the better.

Knowing that it would take ten to fifteen years for the Americans to put SDI in working order, Gorbachev suggested an agreement that, over fifteen years, would eventually eliminate intercontinental missiles; SDI would therefore be unnecessary. Why waste money and matériel developing and testing a system whose targets were systematically disappearing?

The press considered his offer bold and imaginative, a real breakthrough. There was a worldwide shiver of excitement, as it was suddenly possible that the two leaders might arrive at what was arguably the most far-reaching decision since President Harry S Truman agreed to use the atomic bomb.

But President Reagan would not cancel Star Wars. He was quite willing to eliminate ballistic missiles, he said, but he wanted SDI for protection against possible cheating. It appeared that the Soviet Union was being asked to jettison its ballistic missiles, while permitting the United States and Europe to continue the buildup of their high-tech antimissile system.

Nevertheless, Gorbachev apparently made major concessions. The Soviet Union agreed to the removal of Soviet and American missiles from Europe. This was the "zero-zero option" that had previously been rejected by Brezhnev, Andropov, and Chernenko. Gorbachev accepted the American position on testing—a verification of yields rather than a test ban—and the American proposal to cut nuclear arms in half over the next five years. The Soviets saw Reagan's offer to share the Star Wars technology as a ploy: the Soviet economy could not afford it and their territory was so large that it would be relatively useless.

Reykjavik was a disappointment for Gorbachev. To a
world obsessed by the fear of nuclear holocaust (the accident at Chernobyl had offered a terrifying hint of the cost
of such an adventure), Gorbachev had signaled that he was
willing to walk more than halfway toward an arms agreement. He had shown the Western world that, given the
freedom or the opportunity to operate on his own, he was
able to offer innovative solutions. He had also shown that
he could be both flexible and decisive. He had increased his
standing with the watchful world. In an end-of-the-meeting
press conference, he blamed the American "military-indus-
trial complex" for Reagan's refusal to come to terms.

Back home, Gorbachev next turned his attention to
human rights. On his foreign visits, Gorbachev was invari-
ably questioned about, and criticized for, the Soviets' dismal record in that area. He scored brilliantly with his
end-of-the-year gift of freedom to Andrei Sakharov, the
physicist and Nobel Prize winner who had been banished to
the closed city of Gorky seven years earlier because of his
dissident views. As the story goes, Sakharov was surprised
by workers who came, without warning, to install a telephone in his apartment. The next afternoon he received a
telephone call from the general secretary. Gorbachev personally told Sakharov that he was free to return to Moscow.
There were no conditions attached to his pardon. A few
days later, his countrymen cheered his return, and Sakharov immediately repeated the statement that had sent
him to Gorky to begin with—that Soviet troops should get
out of Afghanistan. This time, the KGB left him alone.

Gorbachev happened to agree with Sakharov that the
Afghanistan invasion was a mistake. Sakharov was also
against the United States's Strategic Defense Initiative.
Freeing Sakharov was not only smart public relations, but
it provided Gorbachev with another voice in his corner,

that of a highly respected world figure whose ideas on many important issues were surprisingly like his own.

Sakharov's release was part of a series of human rights initiatives. Hundreds of exiles and people serving prison terms were permitted to return to their homes during what has been called a broad amnesty for political crimes. The offenses ranged from teaching Hebrew to speaking out against the government. Many of the newly freed returned to the activities that had originally placed them at risk—this time without government intrusion.

Among the least heralded of Gorbachev's reforms was the easing of foreign travel restrictions. Young Soviet men and women now expected to be able to vacation in Canada or the United States, or in St. Petersburg or Moscow, or all of Europe. Sports and cultural stars were able to arrange personal tours abroad, a change that served to make them Soviet ambassadors rather than probable defectors. There was even a steady increase in the number of people permitted to emigrate from the Soviet Union.

More than any leader in history, Gorbachev brought the Russian nation out of isolation and to the threshold of real partnership with the other industrialized nations of the world. He did more in his six years than Peter the Great did in thirty. But his personal commitment to socialism was strong.

On February 27, 1991, in a television address from the Republic of Byelorussia, Gorbachev said, "I am not ashamed to say that I am a Communist and adhere to the Communist ideal, and with this, I will leave for the other world." But he is also a reformer, and as such he wanted to adapt the Soviet version of socialism to make it more successful in the marketplace of nations and in the USSR itself. In a 1990 interview with *Time* magazine staffers, Gorbachev stated: "The Stalinist model of socialism should not be confused with true socialist theory. As we dismantle the Stalinist system, we are not retreating from socialism, but are moving toward it."

Gorbachev was also unique in that he let his wife become a public figure. Raisa Maximovna is chic and attractive as well as intelligent. She visibly accompanied her husband on all his official trips abroad and charmed people around the world. She has been less visible within the Soviet Union, however. The Gorbachevs' daughter Irina is married to a physician named Anatoly. (His surname is not known to the public.) Irina's favorite author is Isaac Asimov, according to her father's good-natured sally to Asimov at a Washington reception.

In a society where equal rights for women were guaranteed by law but ignored in practice, Gorbachev was a proponent of women's rights in rhetoric, but did little to advance the voice of women in the country's seats of power. At the Twenty-eighth Party Congress in 1990 Gorbachev said, "We have to admit that the women's question is among the most burning issues facing us. Despite all the slogans, of which there have been more than enough, the working and living conditions of our women require considerable attention and radical improvement."

In the first two years of his tenure as general secretary of the Communist party of the USSR, Gorbachev was welcomed with open arms by the intelligentsia. The freedom he fostered to exchange ideas was a warm wind off the Black Sea.

Even though sophisticated Muscovites smiled condescendingly at his rolling country accent, they warmed to his appreciation of the great Russian culture and they hurried to profit from the opening of the boundaries to communication and exchange with the West.

At a 1989 dinner party in Moscow, Soviet scientist

•

Maxim, forty-five, was excited about his coming trip to the United States. "Six months ago I couldn't travel outside Moscow," he grinned. "Now I can go anywhere. I love Gorbachev."

A year later, back in Moscow after his journey, he was complaining. "In all of Moscow I cannot get a fur hat for rubles. How can I think with a cold head? Gorbachev is slipping."

The freedom to travel was a double-edged sword. Nora, a twenty-eight-year-old television editor in Leningrad, was invited to visit Los Angeles by an American documentary filmmaker. On her visit she walked into a California supermarket. Stunned by the sight of so much food, she sank to the floor and sobbed. "Only now do I realize how deprived I have been all my life," she cried.

Gorbachev was the first Soviet leader to use television, a medium that dominates American politics. Gorbachev spoke often on television and made sure that parliamentary sessions were televised. (These sessions were at first shown live, during the daytime, but so many people watched that no work got done. After a short time, the sessions were taped and broadcast during the evening hours. Then people often dozed off during the day at their desks after staying awake viewing until after midnight.)

Here, too, increasing openness between the Soviet Union and the West meant television programming from the West is seen in Soviet homes. Political observers think that television significantly sped the demand for autonomy by the Eastern European Soviet satellites. In the Soviet Union, too, television has become pervasive. Stalin told a deprived people they were doing better than everyone else—that there was starvation and rioting in the streets of Washington and London—and the people believed him, since they were forbidden to see for themselves. Today, such barriers do not exist. State-controlled television still eagerly shows racial strife and homelessness in America, but the picture of plenty outside the country, while store shelves are empty within, is one with which most citizens are familiar.

As some of the windows opened by *glasnost* began to close during Gorbachev's move to the right, the irreverent Friday-night discussion program *Vzglyad (View)* that often featured progressive young journalist Artyom Borovik, who had earlier gained attention when he revealed dissent over the Afghanistan invasion, was taken off the air. The probing stories which had begun to be seen on the national news program *Vremya (Time)* disappeared.

Through television, Russians have become more familiar with America. And they generally like Americans. If they live in a major city such as Moscow or Leningrad, they may actually have met one. Mikhail Gorbachev's good relationship with Americans was a plus for him, although Soviets thought Americans politically naive in their devotion to the Soviet leader. A joke going around Moscow at the time Gorbachev was named president of the USSR went

"Q: What is the difference between the Soviet Union and the United States?

"A: In the United States, Gorbachev could be elected President."

By the time of Gorbachev's elevation to the new, more powerful presidency, criticism of his economic policies had reached new heights. While many had complained vigorously before that the economy was only getting worse, people were afraid that removal of Gorbachev would mean a right-wing coup and a return to the old ways before *glasnost*.

While Gorbachev had been the first to look toward a market-type economy as a solution to the Soviet Union's economic troubles, he had been dragging his feet and looking for a market system that was compatible with socialism.

Perestroika seemed to be a bust. Boris Yeltsin, who had criticized Gorbachev's policies in 1987 and succumbed to humiliating defeat, was now receiving widespread support for his plan to rapidly turn the economy into a market system.

Gorbachev asked the people's deputies of the largest Soviet republic, the Russian Republic, to deny Yeltsin the republic's presidency. But Yeltsin was elected with just a four-vote majority of the hundreds of ballots cast, and seizing the time to show in which direction he was headed, Yeltsin resigned his Communist party membership.

By the summer of 1990, Muscovites were calling the Soviet Union "the world's largest anti-Communist country."

On October 15, 1990, banner headlines from Maui to Moscow proclaimed that Mikhail Sergeyevich Gorbachev had won the Nobel Peace Prize. Walking in the footsteps of Albert Schweitzer and Mother Teresa, Martin Luther King, Jr., and Gorbachev's own countryman Andrei Sakharov, the heir to the mantle of Stalin had been given the West's highest international accolade for peacemaking. Gorbachev had been uncomfortable in Stalin's mantle, and he had tried to push the memory of the despotic Georgian further into the past, to make the Soviet Union a powerful but peaceful member of the fellowship of nations.

In the West, Gorbachev had been called the "greatest statesman of the second half of the twentieth century." The Soviet people cheered the award, but since they had long been told that such Western honors were "political pornography," there was little dancing in the streets. The people recognized Gorbachev's achievements in foreign affairs, but shortages at home in food and consumer goods, housing, and the amenities of life had eroded his popularity. Political pundits throughout the world predicted his imminent demise.

According to the official announcement of the Nobel Prize Committee,

> During the last few years dramatic changes have taken place in the relationship between East and West. Confrontation has been replaced by negotiations. Old European nation-states have regained their freedom.
>
> The arms race is slowing down, and we see a definite and active process in the direction of arms control and disarmament. Several regional conflicts have been solved or have at least come closer to a solution. The U.N. is beginning to play the role which was originally planned for it in an international community governed by law.
>
> These historic changes spring from several factors, but in 1990 the Nobel Committee wants to honor Mikhail Gorbachev for his many and decisive contributions. The greater openness he has brought about in Soviet society has also helped promote international trust.

Gorbachev had been previously nominated, but now won out over about a hundred candidates following a year that saw the Soviet-dominated Eastern European nations politically set free by the Soviet president to rule themselves. The Nobel Peace Prize has often been given to those who have achieved success in international power politics, such as Theodore Roosevelt and Woodrow Wilson, rather than those who represent humanitarian ideals. But previous winners within the Soviet bloc had been anti-Communists such as Sakharov and the Polish labor activist (later president) Lech Walesa.

•

In the USSR, Gorbachev was "thrilled" at receiving the prize and said that he felt energized "intellectually, emotionally and physically." Initially, he said that he would travel to Oslo to accept the award, but as he continued to be politically beset at home, he asked the committee for a delay of the scheduled ceremony. The committee responded that a delay was impossible.

On December 10, 1990, Gorbachev remained in Moscow to defend his policies at a Communist party plenum, while an aide, First Deputy Foreign Minister Anatoly Kovalev, received the gold medal, diploma, and check for $715,000 that represent the award, at the ceremony in Oslo's Town Hall. Gorbachev sent a message that was read by Kovalev. In it, he said there was a "unique opportunity for reason and the logic of peace to prevail over that of war and annihilation." But, he continued, "there are some very grave threats that have not been eliminated: the potential for conflict, aggressive intentions, and totalitarian traditions."

On December 14, Gorbachev officially accepted the Nobel Prize from Kovalev in televised proceedings in Moscow. He then announced that he was donating more than $1 million, which included the $715,000 Nobel Prize money, to help children's health care in the Soviet Union. Gorbachev said, "When thinking how to dispose of this money, I decided that it should first of all serve children, especially those in ecological disaster zones and in need of special care and treatment."

According to Tass, the Soviet press agency, Gorbachev donated a total of $1,167,000 to children's hospitals, including two that treat children who had been injured by the nuclear accident in 1986 at Chernobyl. Gorbachev had previously donated royalties from his book *Perestroika*, amounting to $1.1 million, to the Communist party.

The Nobel Prize made no appreciable difference in Gor-

•

bachev's popularity at home. Critics were everywhere, and even in the field of international diplomacy it was charged that Gorbachev had weakened the Soviet Union by liberating Eastern Europe and cutting military funding. A maverick people's deputy in the Soviet Parliament, Colonel Nikolai Petrushenko, said, "Even I could defend the interests of the Soviet Union in this way, by making concessions, unjustified concessions."

Most Soviet citizens were willing, though, to acknowledge Gorbachev's successes in the international arena. People's deputy and historian Roy Medvedev, a victim of Stalinist repression, said he thought that Gorbachev's success in making peace would eventually help the beleaguered Soviet economy by slashing military costs and paving the way for Western aid.

Where most of Gorbachev's fellow citizens were unwilling to give praise was in the area closest to them—the economy. The widow of former Soviet Nobel laureate Andrei Sakharov, Elena Bonner, said, "It's shocking, the West's blindness to the tragedies our country has lived through during the five years of *perestroika* headed by Gorbachev."

People's deputy Georgi Arbatov said, "I am sure that he deserves the Peace Prize. I wouldn't think he has deserved the Nobel Prize for Economics."

From the very beginning, the Soviet economy did not work. At various times in more than seventy years of Soviet socialism it appeared to be working, but the appearance had little to do with productivity. What held the Soviet economy together was fear.

Stalin's reign of terror ended with his death. While repression still controlled the people of the Soviet Union, the fear began to wane. Corruption took its place.

Corruption was not new to the Russian people. *Blat* has

•

been the way the government operated from the time of the
early czars. In the two decades between 1960 and 1980,
Leonid Brezhnev and his followers turned ordinary corruption into high art. Nothing moved or was built or processed
without payoffs. The way in which the system ran—the
way that goals were set and production accomplished—was
expensive in terms of labor and materials. Waste was endemic. Corruption, always an expensive vice, cost far more
than the Soviet people could afford.

More and more, the black market became the economy
where goods were available and sold. By the time Gorbachev was embarking on his third year as general secretary,
the black market had become healthier than the regular
economy.

On Soviet television one evening in 1989, a Soviet economist explained how in one week one could turn an investment of $200 into $9,000. "You buy for $200 a VCR in the
United States, which you bring to Moscow and sell on the
black market for 6,000 rubles [the official exchange of currency was then about $1.50 for 1 ruble, while on the black
market 20 rubles were offered for $1]. Then you take your
6,000 rubles and buy 1 ton of aluminum. You sell the ton of
aluminum to a company in the U.S. for $9,000, and you
have a profit of $8,800."

The opportunity to make money in the Soviet Union has
existed in the last few years. Gorbachev sanctioned some
private enterprise in the form of cooperative ventures,
which may be owned by the people who operate them.
These cooperatives may also have some foreign investment
and participation. So far, most successful cooperatives have
been restaurants that cater to tourists and foreign businessmen. Russians, however, have little tradition or experience
of doing business and few have taken advantage of the new
opportunity.

•

Some people, however, are making a lot of money. One thirty-eight-year-old entrepreneur says he heads eighty different cooperatives in Moscow, some to sell metals abroad. He boasts of millions of dollars (not rubles) in foreign banks. Yet he says he is a "good communist." The revolution was right to try to eradicate poverty and express the sentiment in the cry "no poor." Where the revolution went wrong, he thought, was in the cry "no rich."

"They resent me because I am rich," he said, "they call me 'mafia,' but I am not mafia, just a hardworking businessman."

He dresses like Moscow mafia, however, in five-hundred-ruble American jeans and Reebok hightops that cost more than two thousand rubles on the black market.

Unlike money in America, money in Soviet society has not automatically conveyed status. Nor do such professions as medicine and the law guarantee either income or status.

Traditionally at the bottom of the social scale have been waiters and taxi drivers. The Muscovite white-collar worker would say with a sneer, "They have to beg for their money [tips]." Today, with money and goods most available to those with access to foreign currency, society has been turned on its ear. Waiters and taxi drivers frequently earned upwards of three thousand rubles per week. This at a time when the average salary was about four hundred rubles per month, and the average physician made about five hundred rubles, lawyers considerably less. The situation created the feeling of a society out of control.

CHAPTER SIX

•

THE FALL AND RISE
OF BORIS YELTSIN

•

BORIS Yeltsin was born a month before Mikhail Gorbachev and less than 1,400 kilometers (a little more than 1,000 miles) to the northeast. The circumstances into which they were born were similar. The Gorbachevs and the Yeltsins were both working-class families. At the time the two sons were born, the Soviet Union was mired in a Stalin-engineered famine, and both families were desperately poor.

Yeltsin and Gorbachev are both ethnic Russians born in Russia. Their political careers were not developed in the center of power, but in their home agricultural-industrial districts, each about a thousand miles from Moscow. They both rose through the ranks of the Communist party to become Party leaders in their home districts and were then brought to Moscow to participate in the central government.

While their careers were not exactly parallel, they both came out of the *apparat,* or bureaucracy, without which the strongmen who have ruled the Russian and Soviet empires could not have operated. Coming to the center of power almost at the same time (conservative Yegor Ligachev brought Yeltsin to Moscow soon after Gorbachev came to power), they were both reformers. Both wanted change, and about most issues they agreed more than they disagreed. Yet they became opponents and enemies. While Yeltsin eventually defeated Gorbachev, without Gorbachev, Yeltsin, as we know him, would not exist.

Boris Yeltsin was born on February 1, 1931, in the village of Butko near Sverdlovsk (now called Yekaterinburg, its prerevolutionary name) one of the Soviet Union's most important industrial centers.

In the Middle Ural Mountains about a thousand miles east of Moscow, Sverdlovsk was known as the Soviet Pittsburgh. First (and now) named for Catherine the Great, the city was renamed in the 1920s after Yakov Sverdlov, a Bolshevik leader who was active in the revolutionary movement in the Urals. From 1917 to 1918 Sverdlov ran the Soviet Union along with Lenin and Trotsky. He died suddenly in 1919 at the age of thirty-four.

Yeltsin remembers, in his autobiography *Against the Grain*, that times were very hard—the harvests were bad and there was little food. Like Gorbachev's family, the Yeltsins were members of a collective farm. There was a horse, but when he died and there was no way to pull the plow, Boris's father Nikolai Ignatievich moved the family to nearby Perm, where he got work as a laborer on a construction site.

The entire family—Boris, his younger brother and sister, father, grandfather, and mother, Klavdia Vasilievna—all lived in a small communal hut which they shared with a goat they had bought for milking. The goat, according to Yeltsin, was their salvation. She gave milk and they huddled against her for warmth in the cold winter.

Yeltsin was tough right from the start. His parents took the baby boy to the small village church for christening

•

(Yeltsin, like Gorbachev, is not a believer), and the priest, who was somewhat the worse for many traditional toasts of vodka, left the infant in the bottom of the baptismal font while he argued a fine point with a parishioner. Yeltsin's mother hauled him, sputtering, from the water. The priest, unruffled, said, "If he can survive such an ordeal, it means he's a good, tough lad—and I name him Boris."

From early in life, Yeltsin says, he was tough, energetic, ambitious and, most of all, rebellious. He was a ringleader in classroom high jinks and throughout early school days received reprimands about his behavior, although he says he always knew his lessons and studied hard. The reprimands from school were met with harsh punishment from his father at home.

At his graduation from primary school, young Boris, who had gotten excellent grades on his examinations and was receiving a diploma which led to secondary education, asked to be allowed to address the assembled students, teachers and parents. Assuming that he would thank his teachers for his education, the school authorities granted permission. Yeltsin tore into his homeroom teacher, saying she was incompetent and cruel and had no right to teach children. The ceremony was brought to a quick end in an uproar.

Young Yeltsin was immediately expelled from the school and his diploma withdrawn. He was given a piece of paper (colloquially called a "wolf's ticket") that merely testified he had completed seven years of primary schooling with no recommendation for additional education.

Later, at home, when his father readied the strap to teach him a lesson, Boris, who had become a big, muscular young man, stopped him. "That's enough," he said. "From now on, I'm going to educate myself." Nobody ever tried to punish him again, according to Yeltsin.

Boris Yeltsin continued his education at the Pushkin School in Sverdlovsk, where he began to participate actively in sports. Volleyball became his passion; Boris even slept with a ball. Sports were an activity that consumed Yeltsin through much of his school days and after. Today, Yeltsin still finds time to actively play the sports that he enjoys. He is an avid, if inexpert, tennis player.

At the Pushkin School, Yeltsin successfully completed his secondary education. He then applied for admission to the department of civil engineering at the Urals Polytechnic Institute. There, he was again active in sports, particularly volleyball, not only playing for the institute's men's team and the Sverdlovsk city team, but also training the institute's men's and women's second teams.

At the end of his first year at the institute, Yeltsin decided to spend the summer vacation seeing the USSR. He left Sverdlovsk with no money—just the clothes on his back and one extra shirt. In two months he visited Kazan, Moscow, Leningrad, Minsk, Kiev, Zaporozhye, Simferopol, Eupatoria, Yalta, Novorossisk, Sochi, Sukhumi, Batumi, Rostov-on-Don, Volgograd, Saratov, Kuibyshev, Zlatoust, and Chelyabinsk. He returned home in tatters and practically barefoot.

Back at school, Yeltsin's commitment to volleyball continued. He estimated that he spent six hours a day at the sport. In order to keep up with his studies, Yeltsin trained himself to get along on three and a half hours sleep a night—a regimen he adheres to still.

Yeltsin graduated from Urals Polytechnic Institute in 1955. His was a graduating class that has remained closely knit, spending their vacations together every five years since graduation.

After graduation, Yeltsin was made the same job offer all graduates receive—foreman on an industrial building

•

site. But Yeltsin decided to spend a year learning the twelve basic trades, one each month. That same year, at the age of twenty-five, he married Anastasia Girina, called Naya, who has remained in the background like most wives of the Soviet Union's public men and decidedly unlike Raisa Gorbacheva.

During a period of record growth throughout the Soviet Union, Yeltsin became a hard-working foreman and then supervisor on construction projects in Sverdlovsk, the industrial center of the country. With a management style Yeltsin himself characterizes as "tough," he rose through the ranks to become chief engineer of a new house-building organization with a modern factory and thousands of workers. At age thirty-two, when the general manager retired, Yeltsin became head of this large building-manufacturing complex.

Yeltsin had joined the Communist party early in his career. Although much of his Party work was part time after working hours, he had made a reputation as a good manager who got things done. In 1969 he received an invitation from the leadership to head the Sverdlovsk Province's construction committee of the Communist party. It was a big step forward on the leadership track of the Soviet Union.

In 1976, Yeltsin was called to Moscow, ostensibly to take a Party leadership course. He was called out of the course for meetings at the Central Committee of the Communist party. He had what seemed to him senseless talks with party organizational chiefs Kapitonov and Kirilenko, after which he was closely questioned by the powerful Party ideological chief Mikhail Suslov. Suslov asked Yeltsin if he thought he was up to a bigger job, so Yeltsin knew there was something in the wind, but he still did not know what it was.

Two of the Central Committee secretaries hustled Yeltsin into a car and told him he had an important meeting in the Kremlin. The group went into a suite of offices and entered an anteroom where they were told they were "expected." Yeltsin led the way into a large office where General Secretary Leonid Brezhnev sat at the end of a long conference table. Brezhnev rose and greeted Yeltsin. Then he turned to one of the Central Committee secretaries and said, "So, he's decided to assume power in Sverdlovsk province, has he?"

Both Yeltsin and his escort were taken aback. The escort said, "We haven't asked him yet." Brezhnev then told Yeltsin that the Politburo had recommended him to be first secretary of the Communist party in Sverdlovsk. It was an important position, comparable then to being governor of a large industrial state in the United States. Yeltsin accepted.

Just days later, on November 2, 1976, a Party plenum of the Sverdlovsk Provincial Committee met and nominated Yeltsin as its first secretary. Yeltsin had the populist touch that many liked, and he became a popular first secretary in Sverdlovsk, although he was known as a man who liked to get his own way.

As first secretary he began to make the acquaintance of other important and becoming-important leaders throughout the Soviet Union. He began to get to know Mikhail Gorbachev.

Gorbachev, first secretary of Stavropol Province, was on an equal footing with Yeltsin. They first spoke together over the telephone, doing the business of running their different provinces. When they later met, a warm personal regard grew between the two men. Yeltsin became a supporter of Gorbachev as he moved forward on the path to becoming general secretary.

On April 12, 1985, with a great deal of misgiving, Boris

Yeltsin came to Moscow to take a position on the Central Committee as head of construction for the Soviet Union.

Yeltsin had been used to getting his own way. He had not been in a subordinate position for a long time, and he chafed at the strict Party hierarchy, what he called the "structure of subordination" on the Central Committee. According to Yeltsin, "Working within such a frigidly bureaucratic framework was an ordeal for someone of my freewheeling and self-confident temperament."

The chance to get out of the structure of subordination came on December 22, 1985, when Yeltsin was sent for by the Politburo. He was told that the Politburo had decided that Yeltsin should leave his post on the Central Committee and take over as head of the Moscow City Committee of the Communist party—equivalent then to the job of mayor.

Gorbachev told Yeltsin that the current head of the Party in Moscow, Viktor Grishin, had allowed the situation in Moscow to decline precipitously and that he had to be replaced. Gorbachev wanted Yeltsin for the job.

Grishin was truly one of the Old Guard of the Brezhnev era, living off corruption—the bribes that he both accepted and doled out. Even though he had supported the reformer Andropov (who was head of the KGB at the time), Grishin expected that in his fiefdom it would be business as usual. But Gorbachev had brought with him to the top levels of government the people who were not tainted by corruption, such as Ligachev and Yeltsin. He was now getting rid of the most egregious examples of the old ways. On December 24, 1985, at a plenum of the Moscow City Committee, Gorbachev announced that Grishin was being "retired at his own request." He then surprised nobody by introducing Yeltsin as the new committee head.

Yeltsin immediately fired all of Grishin's aides. He then

fired all of those people he felt he couldn't trust and set about building his own organization.

During 1986, Yeltsin felt that the Central Committee at Gorbachev's urging supported him in his attempts to revive the Moscow organization. He began by developing permanent "fairs" on empty lots in Moscow to bring fruits and vegetables from other regions to the capital and provide spaces for amusements.

He stood on lines to see if service was adequate and if the products that were supposed to be in the shops were actually available. When he found management corruptly selling their goods out the back door to the black market, while nothing remained on the shelves to buy at state-supported prices, he fired management. But Yeltsin could not be everywhere, and corruption was endemic. There seemed to be no way to stem the tide.

While many of the politicians Gorbachev brought to Moscow were reformers who saw in the kind of wholesale corruption practiced under Brezhnev a disaster for their country, they also saw the simple perquisites of office as only right. Yeltsin began attacking these perquisites. He was offered a dacha that had been assigned to Gorbachev before he became general secretary and had a new one built. Yeltsin said the marble-walled dacha was too grand for him. Sometimes he did not ride in his limousine, but took the trolley or bus (with a camera crew along), although he always looked uncomfortable in those situations. More and more he began to publicly criticize officials who took "perks." His instincts as a populist made him appear to be just "one of the boys." Many Muscovites liked his style.

Since there was basically no private property in the Soviet Union, government officials and Party members depended on their perks for living well. When Yeltsin attacked them there, he hit them where they lived. Yeltsin went to war with the people he depended upon for his influence and power.

Within months, the battle lines were drawn. By the time the Politburo gathered at Lenin's Tomb for the 1987 May Day celebration, they were deeply divided. The first to break ranks was Boris Yeltsin.

He picked up the banner of populism, saying, "I believe in real ties with the people. I believe that's imperative and vital for any politician."

But more conservative people in the Party said the Party must remain on top. They were led by Yegor Ligachev, Gorbachev's right-hand man, then at the height of his powers.

This conflict between the Party Man and the Populist would come to dominate Kremlin politics. It grew into a battle of such size that at a Party conference fourteen months later, Gorbachev was forced to break all tradition and show the world how the Party had been unable to deal with one maverick.

The story Gorbachev told began when Boris Yeltsin was still a provincial Party boss. Ironically, it was Yegor Ligachev who first spotted Yeltsin's talents. During a trip to Sverdlovsk, Ligachev visited people in the factories, shops, and markets. People would stop him and say, "Our first secretary Boris Yeltsin is a good leader. Don't even think of taking him away from us to Moscow." That impressed Ligachev.

Ligachev said, "That's why Yeltsin was proposed as Moscow Party leader. At first, Boris Yeltsin threw himself into his work. He identified problems, and he dealt with them. He did a lot of things to turn around Moscow, and we supported him. We knew that the Moscow party faced a very difficult task."

From the start, Yeltsin didn't like Ligachev's style and

way of working on the Central Committee. Even at the 1986 Party Congress Yeltsin was critical, of the Secretariat and specifically of Ligachev.

From his office in the labyrinth of the Kremlin, Ligachev ran the Party bureaucracy, and this bureaucracy ran the Soviet Union. It was the source of his enormous power.

Ligachev didn't see himself that way. He said, "They say that I am omnipotent. It's not true. I'm just one member of the Politburo. I accept the discipline and abide by the rules of the Politburo."

Yeltsin complained on many occasions about Ligachev. He said that Ligachev was petty, concentrating on minor issues, that he was unprincipled and inconsistent. "We faced each other in the Politburo and we just locked horns. It was an open war," Yeltsin said.

"Yeltsin is all talk," Ligachev replied. "And when push comes to shove, he's never actually achieved anything. So let's judge by the record and then decide."

According to Yeltsin, they had violent arguments over the question of privileges. "He believed there was no such thing as privilege. He'd say, 'That's just what my people deserve. So what?' "

Ligachev's bureaucrats were a caste apart, separated from the rest of Soviet society by power and privilege. In Moscow, Yeltsin took on the bureaucrats. He campaigned against Party perks and privileges. He was the first Kremlin politician to make sure he was seen as the man on the street.

With these simple steps, Yeltsin turned *perestroika* into populism. Never before had a Soviet leader dared take the people's side against the Party establishment. And the Party establishment didn't like it.

"They didn't understand," Yeltsin said. "They said, 'Why are you doing this?' They seemed surprised. I said, 'If I'm going to a factory, I want to travel like the workers.

What's so special about that? If I want to give my driver a day off and have no car, I take the bus."

Yeltsin's campaign was more than just photo opportunities. Behind the scenes he was taking the Moscow Party apart. Yeltsin fired all six of the city secretaries, fifteen of nineteen section heads, and twenty-two of thirty-three district first secretaries.

Gorbachev said, "At first we accepted that these people had to go. Then, he started a second, then a third round of firings. It began to worry us. I personally criticized Yeltsin at the Politburo. I said, 'Boris, we are for *perestroika*. But *perestroika* means restructuring, not mindless upheaval.'"

"I can't say I never made mistakes," Yeltsin replied. "Of course, I made some mistakes, but not many."

As usual, when Gorbachev took his summer vacation, the deputy leader, Ligachev, was left in charge. Throughout the summer of 1987 the Politburo continued to criticize Yeltsin and the way he was running Moscow. The capital city had always been a showcase for the Party, with public displays limited to the proud and patriotic. But under Yeltsin things began to change.

All kinds of characters began to use Moscow's new pedestrian precinct, the Arbat, as a hangout. To Yeltsin's more conservative colleagues, it all smacked of bourgeois decadence.

Ligachev toured the area and reported to the Politburo on his findings. There was a flood of complaints, he said, about the noise and disorder. So the Politburo ordered Yeltsin to fix the problem. Yeltsin was in favor of allowing demonstrations and suggested something along the lines of a speakers' corner, like the one in London's Hyde Park.

Yeltsin allowed nationalists to demonstrate on the streets of Moscow. These first protests were tame enough, but more followed.

Yeltsin's popularity grew, everywhere but on the Politburo. He said, "I decided that whatever my ideas were at that time, it was useless to try to get anyone there to pay attention to my view, my plans. Nobody took them into account. So, I thought, why make it hard for myself? And for them."

Yeltsin wrote a letter to Gorbachev. Gorbachev said, "In August 1987, when I was on vacation, I received a personal letter from Boris Yeltsin. He asked to be released from his duties as Moscow Party leader. I didn't rush into anything. I kept the letter to myself. I didn't even tell the Politburo."

Yeltsin's offer to resign was not the bombshell he had expected. Gorbachev was preoccupied with his next step for *perestroika*, a speech telling the truth about Stalin's crimes. The conservatives in the Central Committee who had blocked Gorbachev's free election proposals in January were again expected to put up a fight. So, the last thing Gorbachev needed was controversy from Yeltsin.

On October 21, 1987, the Central Committee met in secret. Until the very end of the meeting, everything went as Gorbachev had planned it. The Central Committee listened to Gorbachev speak. The deputy leader, Yegor Ligachev, presided over the meeting.

At the end of the meeting, Ligachev asked if there were any questions. The question was only a formality since everybody was getting up to leave. Suddenly, there was a commotion.

Gorbachev stopped Ligachev. He said, "Wait a minute, Boris Yeltsin wants to speak."

Ligachev said, "The session's over, I'm winding it up."

Gorbachev said, "No." "Boris Nikolayevich, did you ask to speak?"

Yeltsin said, "Yes, I did."

Gorbachev said, "Then, please, let him speak."

Yeltsin got up and tore apart the official line. Until then, no senior Party member had dared question Gorbachev's policy of *perestroika*. Yeltsin did. He said that *perestroika* was not delivering the goods to the Soviet people. Life was not getting better, but worse. In effect, Yeltsin accused the emperor of *perestroika* of having no clothes.

"God knows why I did it," Yeltsin said. "Maybe it's just the way I am. I didn't prepare a text. I simply had an outline, seven items on a piece of paper, just to be on the safe side. But I decided I had to seize the moment. I had to declare my position. My fight was really with Ligachev. Gorbachev tried to act as referee, he played the role of peacekeeper."

For Gorbachev, what had been a successful meeting turned into a disaster. Only what Yeltsin said mattered; Gorbachev's speech was forgotten.

After the meeting, Yeltsin admitted, "I let down the Central Committee, the Politburo, and my own Moscow Party. All the Central Committee and the Politburo are against me. So, I repeat, I ask to be released, both from the Politburo, and as leader of the Moscow Party. Perhaps I made some mistakes. I did say some things that weren't right at the meeting. But the problem wasn't what I said, but when I said it."

Yeltsin's resignation as Moscow Party boss could be accepted only by the Moscow Party. And the last act of the Yeltsin resignation drama would be something of a show trial. The strain of waiting took its toll. When the day came, Boris Yeltsin was in the hospital.

There were rumors about a heart attack. Some said he had tried to stab himself with a paper knife. Yeltsin was used to being honored and respected. Now he was to be condemned. Yeltsin's doctor insisted he was fit enough to attend the meeting.

The meeting was attended by Gorbachev himself. What followed was a ritual public humiliation. The members of the Moscow Party, especially those Yeltsin had treated harshly, seized their chance to settle old scores. One said, "It was as if each speaker had taken a garbage can full of trash and just dumped it on Yeltsin."

Yuri Prokofiev, who had clashed often with Yeltsin, said, "There are some people who rise on their own merits. Others do it by stepping on other people around them." Yeltsin, he said, fell into the second category.

It went on for over four hours. Gorbachev's face got redder and redder and redder. His eyes darted around the hall.

Suddenly, the ordeal was over. The last speeches had been made and the crowd was leaving. Yeltsin sat slumped over the table, his head in his hands. Gorbachev looked back from the doorway and saw Yeltsin. Then, he went back, took his arm, and helped him out of the hall.

Even though Gorbachev himself spoke quite harshly, when he had to act he just shifted Yeltsin into an administrative post. That way, he protected him from even harsher consequences or from being sent to some remote and irrelevant part of the world. But now, after twenty years of service to the Party, Boris Yeltsin was out in the cold, no longer Moscow Party boss. No longer on the Politburo, no longer on the way up.

After, Yeltsin said, "I never felt so bad before. I've had my ups and downs in life. But nothing like this. This time I was really knocked down."

But the lower Yeltsin fell in the eyes of the Party, the higher his reputation rose among the people as the rumors spread. Nobody knew exactly what he had done, but they believed he had stood up to the Communist party and he was suffering for it. But Yeltsin was not through with the Communist party.

Wanting to push through his ideas about reforming the elective process to make it more responsive to the people, Gorbachev called a full party conference, the first of its kind in half a century. On June 28, 1988, five thousand delegates gathered in the Kremlin. Gorbachev opened the conference with an all-day speech. He abandoned his plans to make Communist party officials face elections. Instead, he proposed to bypass them. If he could not make the Party democratic, he would try to bring democracy to the Soviet Parliament. Gorbachev said, "This will be a new body of supreme political power with elected deputies. It will be called the USSR Congress of People's Deputies."

Gorbachev gave the delegates free reign to discuss the issues. But on the fourth and final day, one subject had still not been mentioned. Yeltsin was sitting in the balcony. Then suddenly, during the session, he appeared in the back of the hall. He walked down the aisle and sat in the front row. Every eye was on him now and no one was listening to the speaker anymore. Suddenly he made a dash for the platform.

After twenty minutes of hard-hitting diatribe, Yeltsin came to the question on everyone's mind: "Comrade delegates, a delicate matter. It's a question of my own political rehabilitation. I deeply resent what was done to me. I ask the conference to withdraw the resolution against me. I ask you to rehabilitate me before the Party. Yes, the road to reform is a difficult one. But we have begun our journey and destiny tells us we must continue on this road and no other."

Yeltsin had thrown down the gauntlet to the conference

and to Ligachev personally. Revenge was in the air. A smile crossed Ligachev's face as he walked to the platform, confident of his own power. Everyone waited for him to tear Yeltsin apart.

Ligachev said, "Hard to believe, but it's a fact. Yeltsin sat silent in the Politburo. Hours of crucial discussions went by, and he took no part at all. He just bided his time and let others tackle the problems. Sounds outrageous, but it's a fact. Is that Party comradeship, my friend Boris? I was expecting his speech. I knew he would speak. Not everything he said was incorrect. But on the whole it shows that you, Boris, are wrong."

In using Yeltsin's name, Ligachev referred to him simply as "Boris," rather than as was polite, "Boris Nikolayevich." It was the way you would address a naughty child, totally without respect.

A long round of applause followed Ligachev. Ligachev won that day. There would be no Party rehabilitation for Boris Yeltsin.

The conference ended with a vote. A massive majority followed Gorbachev and voted for an elected parliament. It seemed these apparatchiks were voting to put their own jobs on the line, but many of them thought democratic reform would take ten years. So they would be sitting pretty for at least another decade.

But Gorbachev, in the closing seconds of the conference, pulled a rabbit out of his hat. Standing before the conference, he took a small piece of paper from his file. It was a timetable for putting all the decisions of the conference into effect. The deadlines were minimal: immediate adoption of the new laws on election, with elections to follow just as soon, everything within a year. It took everyone by surprise.

Nine months later, the Soviet Union was in the throes of

its first-ever democratic election campaign. Boris Yeltsin, the party's pariah, was the people's choice. Never before had going to the polls meant anything in the Soviet Union. The very idea of more than one candidate was a novelty. An epidemic of election fever gripped the people.

Anyone who could garner five hundred signatures could be nominated. But before their names appeared on the ballot, they had to be approved at meetings controlled by the Party.

The Party planned that Gorbachev's new Congress of People's Deputies would be dominated by the Party. But many people, especially in the big cities, thought otherwise.

Boris Yeltsin felt he knew the people. He was still in the Party, although he had been disgraced and stripped of his top Party post. He was once again challenging the Party's leadership.

Yeltsin said, "Of course I didn't expect it to be all smiling faces. But to go about it, like that, to use pressure in that way, organized by the whole propaganda machine, the entire propaganda machine used to back my opponent, and I was left with only my volunteer army."

The more he was reviled and persecuted by the Party power, the more popular he became with the people. He was accorded rock-star adulation by the middle-aged women who form the base of his support.

According to Yeltsin, "My political enemies tried to get all kinds of information on me. There were all sorts of innuendos and slander. They even published this booklet on how to criticize me during election meetings. The city Party committee handed out these booklets to everyone."

Boris Yeltsin won with 89 percent of votes cast in Moscow. Though radicals won fewer than 20 percent of the seats all over the Soviet Union, they humiliated the Party. In Leningrad, all the official candidates were defeated.

When the large, unwieldy Congress of People's Deputies met, Yeltsin had little chance of being chosen from it to vote in its select, permanently sitting legislature, the Supreme Soviet. He said, "We need to elect a progressive Supreme Soviet. I don't want to offend anyone, but if they elect a bunch of yes men, well, then . . ."

Predictably, the conservative majority followed form. They voted for the "yes" men and rejected Yeltsin. But a little-known deputy from Siberia came to his rescue.

Alexei Kazannik said, "Fifteen minutes before the session started, I said to Yeltsin, 'I want you to take my seat in the Supreme Soviet.' He was very surprised. He said, 'Don't do it. A seat there is really worth having.' "

According to Yeltsin, "I started half-heartedly to dissuade him. But he said, no, the voters wouldn't forgive him unless he did this. So, then, Gorbachev and Lukyanov, two lawyers, debated whether this was legal. There was a vote, and it was passed." But the conservative Supreme Soviet of the USSR was not to be the forum for Boris Yeltsin.

The legislative body of the RSFSR—the Russian Soviet Federated Socialist Republic—had little power in a country dominated both by the Communist party and the central government. But that was to change radically.

While the RSFSR was the jewel of the Soviet empire, with about 80 percent of its people and about the same amount of its resources, it got back much less from the center than it gave. The nationalistic feelings being experienced in other republics of the Soviet Union were also being felt in Russia.

The center was not Russian, it was Communist. While it had almost always been Russian Communists (only Stalin was not, he was a Georgian) who ran the empire, they had gone out of their way to assure the other republics that they would have an equal voice in running the country

•

along with Russia. Sometimes this worked to the detriment of Russia, since the other republics were wary of the Russians' empire-building past.

As the Communist party weakened, so did the center. In every republic, there was a call for more autonomy. As a delegate to the Parliament of the Russian Federation, Yeltsin had a voice that would be listened to.

In the Federation Parliament, Yeltsin's name, in the spring of 1990, was placed in nomination for the post of chairman of the RSFSR Supreme Soviet.

Gorbachev, about to leave the country on a diplomatic mission to Canada and the United States, tried to use what influence he had to keep Yeltsin from the chairman's seat. But his machinations backfired. Beginning to feel their oats as independent legislators, the deputies to the Russian congress resented the interference from the center. Yeltsin was elected to the top post by four votes.

A year later, in general elections, Yeltsin became the first popularly elected president of Russia—what was soon to become an independent nation.

CHAPTER SEVEN

•

RAISA MAXIMOVNA, FOOTNOTE TO HISTORY

•

THE woman with whom Gorbachev shares his personal life is unlike any other in Russian history. She is sometimes compared to Lenin's wife, the famed revolutionary Nadezhda Krupskaya, who fought shoulder to shoulder with her husband through years of planning, exile, and eventual success of the Revolution. Krupskaya was a political firebrand, an educator, and a member of the Central Committee. Like her political forebear, Raisa Maximovna Gorbacheva is complex and individualistic, with strong opinions and a modern sensibility.

When Gorbachev prepared to make his move for general secretary in the winter of 1984, he made certain that he introduced Raisa to the world at the same time. He was the first Soviet leader in history to present himself with his wife at his side, rather than three steps behind. Soviet leaders had always fostered an image of isolated, dominant despots in service to the state. The existence of their wives and families was practically a state secret. Konstantin Chernenko displayed his aging wife at the 1984 elections, but she was never again seen in public. It is said that Brezhnev, a notorious womanizer, preferred almost any woman to his wife. Joseph Stalin had two wives—the first, a Georgian peasant, died of tuberculosis before the Revolution. He married his second wife, Nadezhda Allilueva, in 1919, when she was seventeen and he was forty. Allilueva, a Party activist, died suddenly in 1932. The circumstances surrounding her death were mysterious: some say she committed suicide, others say Stalin shot her to death.

The murky heritage of Soviet first ladies did not give Raisa Gorbacheva much to go on when it came time for her to help her husband storm the citadels of the Western world. She took up the challenge with characteristic bravado.

Three months before he came to power as general secretary, Gorbachev presented his wife to the world. The occasion was a trip to London to meet with Prime Minister Margaret Thatcher. Jaded British reporters, with faded visions of the grandmotherly Nina Khrushcheva lurking in their heads, immediately fell for the youthful Raisa, who made her first evening appearance wearing a white satin gown and gold high-heeled sandals. This did not jibe with any Soviet woman they had ever seen. Here was a lovely, sparkling woman, with silken skin and a dazzling smile. The next morning, the *Sunday Times* called her "the Bo Derek of the steppes."

As if in response, Raisa wasted no time showing off her intellect. At an official dinner she discussed English literature knowledgeably with a Foreign Ministry official and then caught him flat-footed by asking his view of modern Soviet writers.

The press knew a story when they saw one. Reporters and photographers followed her everywhere. Catching her shopping at Cartier, they were delirious when Raisa trotted out her American Express card and purchased a pair of

•

diamond earrings for $2,100. Reporters looking for a new epithet daily, happily dubbed her the "Gucci comrade."

It is difficult for most Westerners today to remember just how mysterious the Soviets seemed in 1984. Raisa's glamour and outgoing manner floored the British, who for several decades viewed the Soviets as secretive, dour, and badly dressed adversaries.

The photographers who followed Raisa everywhere were so enchanted with her vivacity and spontaneity that on her last day they chipped in to buy her a farewell bouquet of flowers.

Ever since her London debut, Raisa's clothes, style, and shopping habits have received as much attention as her comments, which early in her public career struck many people as being preachy. Few people have been able to get close enough to the first lady to actually hear her speak. Even in the few interviews she grants, she almost never comments on her personal life. For example, the public was surprised to learn that she is a grandmother, and there is still speculation that, in addition to their daughter, Irina, the Gorbachevs have a second, unidentified child. Thus, what is most observed is the way Raisa looks. By anyone's standards she is an attractive woman, with the fresh, porcelain complexion characteristic of many Slavic women and a ready smile.

By Western standards Raisa displays conservative good taste in fashion. When she first set foot in Paris, in October of 1985, wearing her furs and high-heeled boots, the French fashion press was waiting to ambush her. The flinty-eyed Parisians were more critical than the English had been. Fashion reporters found fault with her unseasonable dark wool suits and her fondness for stripes. Said *Le Monde*'s fashion editor, "She has to support the one Moscow couture house and apparently they are having a season on stripes."

•

When Raisa appeared at an official dinner at the Élysée Palace wearing a pleated brown chiffon evening dress striped with gold, one snide observer called it a "Muscovite gown." When she had the temerity to wear the same outfit twice, the snipers opened fire: "Princess Diana of England wears the same dress twice in public, but at least she waits two years," complained the society reporter for Monte Carlo radio. On top of everything else, the French did not like Raisa's very high heels. (Raisa stands five feet two inches and likes to add some leverage to her height by wearing heels.)

If Raisa's feelings were hurt, she did not show it. On the contrary, she turned up smiling at private showings at the salons of Pierre Cardin and Yves Saint Laurent. She was relaxed and friendly with the great French designers, plying Saint Laurent with questions about fashion. "How do you find me?" she is said to have asked Cardin. "Beautiful," he replied. After Raisa had viewed forty outfits from his couture collection, Cardin was even more voluble: "She is a woman of great charm, of style and most of all, of intelligence and culture," the famed designer said. "She is a formidable woman."

Raisa prevailed. By the time the visit was over, the French, like the British, were enthralled. *Match* put it most succinctly, and most accurately: "The image of the Soviet Union has changed by virtue of a woman's face." *Le Figaro* called her Gorbachev's "secret weapon."

Raisa's background remains typically obscure, her official Kremlin biography only a scant few lines. Even her date of birth is unclear, with dates ranging from January 5, 1932, according to the diplomats who processed her visa papers, to as late as 1934. She was born Raisa Maximovna Titorenko in the town of Rubtsovsk in Siberia. There has been some question regarding her ethnic background, a subject that carries some weight in Soviet society. Her name is Ukrainian and her broad cheekbones suggest Mongol ancestry. (During Gorbachev's 1985 interview with the Italian Communist newspaper *L'Unita*, he expressed his admiration for his wife and said that she was one-quarter Jewish.) At Revolution Day celebrations in Red Square, Raisa publicly insisted that she is "absolutely Russian."

Her father's occupation and social status is also a subject of debate. Her official biography says that her father was a railway engineer, but the editors of *Time* report rumors that he may have been an economist exiled to Siberia by Stalin. Gail Sheehy states emphatically that Raisa's father worked for the railway, but his job may have been of high or low level. Throwing a spanner into the works, other reporters describe Raisa's parents as "physicians."

Not much is said about her mother or her siblings, although some sources say she has a sister, others a brother. This veil of secrecy concerning family background was typical of Soviet style and attitude. Gorbachev's own official biography carried almost no personal information.

Regardless of her parents' occupations, Raisa was well-read and knowledgeable in the arts even as a young girl, so it is presumed that she came from an educated family. She grew up and went to school in Sterlitamak, a drab industrial center of 248,000 people set in the rolling farmlands and oilfields about eight hundred miles east of Moscow at the southern foot of the Urals. (Today the air and water of Sterlitamak are contaminated by the foul effluent of five chemical plants on the outskirts of town.) Raisa attended Middle School No. 3, where she won a secondary-school gold medal, signifying the highest academic achievement in her scholastic district. She went on to receive a first-class education at Moscow State University, the showpiece of the Soviet educational system.

•

At the university, Raisa studied philosophy and earned praise for her academic performance. She was also fun-loving and adventurous and had many admirers until young Mikhail Gorbachev took her out of circulation. It would seem that even as a young woman Raisa had the same ability to charm that continues to captivate reporters today.

Both Raisa and Mikhail lived in the Stromynka student hostel, and their romance quickly blossomed. If she was beautiful and naturally elegant, he was a handsome, virile-looking young man. They both had sharp, inquiring minds. However, according to Raisa herself, it was neither Mikhail's brains nor good looks that attracted her: it was his "reliability," a word with many layers of importance in Soviet society.

Gorbachev as a young man was hardworking, dedicated, and undeniably intelligent. Raisa proceeded to add another important dimension to his developing character. She took him to art museums, plays, and concerts. They read together and haunted bookstores and libraries. From the beginning, they were more than in love—they were also friends and partners.

Early in 1954, while both were still students, they married. The following year, both graduated and moved to Mikhail's home region of Stavropol, where he had taken a position in the city Komsomol. Raisa took a position teaching in a medical institute, but soon left to accept a more lucrative job teaching in the philosophy department at Stavropol Agricultural Institute, the local community college. In these early years of their marriage, her position was more prestigious than her husband's (there has been no more prestigious job in the Soviet Union than that of a university professor), and she earned a larger salary. Mikhail actually enrolled in her class in philosophy, and the two

•

were famous in the classroom for their heated ideological arguments.

Nor did Raisa hesitate to argue with party officials who supervised the courses she taught. When still a young teacher, Raisa objected to the secretive way that she and her colleagues were observed and evaluated. When one of her lectures was secretively taped, she asked to meet with the offending authorities and the directors of the institute and openly admonished them for spying on her.

Despite her outburst, Raisa kept her job. She soon was in hot water again when she refused to teach atheism, a standard part of the official agenda. Gail Sheehy reports her protest: "I don't like to teach atheism, and I'm not going to do it anymore." She got away with it.

If today Raisa seems too outspoken, too well dressed and too clever for much of Soviet society, it is easy to imagine the impact she must have had on Stavropol, so far removed from the nation's cultural life in the 1950s. The cultivated Raisa did not have much in common with the other women, most of whom performed unskilled work and thought her arrogant. Domestic life, which has never been easy for Russian women, also posed problems. While homes in Stavropol were charming and old-fashioned, they often were without indoor plumbing or electricity. Like millions of Russian women before and since, Raisa coped.

Soon after moving to Stavropol, a daughter, Irina Mikhailovna, was born to the Gorbachevs. Raisa continued to teach. When she was thirty-four, she submitted her doctoral thesis in sociology to the V. I. Lenin Pedagogical Institute in Moscow. She called it, *Emergence of New Characteristics in the Daily Lives of the Collective Farm Peasantry (Based on Sociological Investigations in the Stavropol Region)*.

Even though some have said that the thesis was "pretty

banal," in a way Raisa is considered a Soviet pioneer in sociology, until recently a barely recognized science in the Soviet Union. The study of sociology was considered antirevolutionary and associated with bourgeois decadence. Even the word *sociologist* is unknown, and in her country Raisa is called a "philosopher."

At the time of her thesis, there was little agreement on the nature of this new area of study or on its limits of inquiry. Most early investigations were conducted in small towns and rural regions far from Moscow. Quantitative techniques had not yet been widely developed, and were ignored completely if the results did not match the officially desired outcome.

Raisa's thesis concerned the living conditions of farm workers in the Stavropol region. Her central theme was "Difficulties and Contradictions." As the wife of the regional Party organizer for agriculture, she had first-hand information about her subject.

In her analysis, she brought up the troubling issues of class differences in the supposedly "classless" society. She observed the differences in wages and education between groups of farm workers. She also exposed sexual discrimination in rural regions, documenting the burden of labor put on women.

Raisa accurately reported her findings, even though her observations did not conform to Party philosophy. She stood by her story and, as before, there is no evidence that she suffered any repercussions from it.

On the contrary, the report most probably helped advance her academic career. The continued rise of her husband in Party politics did not hurt. When Mikhail Sergeyevich was called to Moscow in 1978, Raisa was invited to join the faculty of her alma mater. She was appointed lecturer in Marxist-Leninist philosophy at Moscow

State University, a prestigious and much-desired position. In order to graduate, all university students must take this course. In fact, almost one-third of each student's total course of study was then devoted to Marxist-Leninist philosophy. Mass lectures and seminars are used to provide endless drill on the material, which must be mastered. Good marks count for future careers.

Sophisticated Muscovites, however, quip that Marxist-Leninist dialectics is to philosophy as "Potemkin Architecture" is to architecture; that is to say, there is little intellectual or philosophical content in dialectics.

As her husband began to move higher and higher into the upper circles of Party leadership, Raisa's own sphere of influence at the university also increased. "I am a working woman," she liked to say. She continued at her university post until her husband was named general secretary, and then she became a world figure.

Was Raisa privy to the inside workings of Soviet politics? Did she have her husband's ear when it came to policymaking? Possibly. Although she keeps her comments about her husband to a minimum, she has been quoted as saying, "I'm very lucky with Mikhail. We are really friends—or, if you prefer, we have a great complicity."

Those who have known the couple over the years say that while they argue together, they are very similar in character. Both ask searching questions, and neither hesitates to speak out.

Other public clues of their closeness comes from this much publicized episode: when Gorbachev gave his first major speech in the West before French legislators in Paris, he scanned the audience until he found Raisa, then, according to *Match*, "gave her a look full of tenderness and smiled at her."

Raisa's role in Gorbachev's political life was down-

•

played in the Soviet Union during his tenure. She often was not even identified in photographs, or was simply mentioned as "spouse." But it is obvious that a woman with a doctoral degree in philosophy, a woman who has taught the nation's future careerists the national political philosophy, had something to say about the political intricacies of that nation's government. And it is also clear that a woman with Raisa's inquiring mind and outspoken views will make her presence felt wherever she can.

As general secretary, Gorbachev himself hinted that his wife had political influence. Late in 1987, journalist Tom Brokaw had a historic interview with Gorbachev for NBC television news. Brokaw asked him, "Do you go home in the evenings and discuss with her national politics, political difficulties and so on in this country?"

Gorbachev replied, "We discuss everything."

Brokaw pushed further: "Including Soviet affairs at the highest level?"

Gorbachev repeated his previous response, "We discuss everything."

The Soviet version of the interview dropped the second question and edited the first to Brokaw querying Gorbachev on whether he discussed with Raisa "questions of public life."

The actual extent of Raisa's influence remains a matter of speculation. She may have been instrumental in Gorbachev's campaign for openness, particularly in the realm of the arts. While visiting Washington, D.C., during the 1990 summit meeting between her husband and President Bush, Raisa opened an exhibit of Russian religious texts at the Library of Congress. The exhibit celebrated the faith of those practicing the oldest form of Russian Christianity. According to people involved in the long negotiations that resulted in the exhibit, Communist party officials had at-

•

tempted to hinder her participation. "It's a sign of the times," said the Russian émigré novelist Vassily Aksyonov, a guest at the reception at the Library of Congress. "She's putting herself closer to the center of the country, closer to the mood of the Russian nation."

Raisa did not as easily captivate America as she had Europe. The best and most avidly watched sideshow was between Raisa and Nancy Reagan, the so-called "teacup summits."

Raisa and Nancy first jockeyed for position in Geneva in 1985 at the first Reagan-Gorbachev summit. On this occasion they exchanged tea parties and made small talk. Nancy's aides reported that Mrs. Reagan found Raisa a bit pedantic and inflexible. There was no comment from Raisa's side. The two women smiled, linked hands, and faced the cameras. For the record, Nancy said, "I think she's a very nice lady."

One year later, Raisa unexpectedly decided to attend the working summit at Reykjavik, Iceland. Some Americans objected, saying that Mrs. Gorbachev had upstaged Mrs. Reagan, who had not planned to attend. Even some Soviet officials were unhappy with Raisa's participation. No one knows whose idea it was for Raisa to accompany her husband to the Reykjavik summit, but it is certain that, despite her willfulness, she would not have gone if Mikhail Sergeyevich had thought otherwise.

Once on the scene, Raisa made good use of her time and scored points with Westerners. Visiting a simple farm chapel, she said, "I am an atheist, but I know the church, and I respect all faiths. It is, after all, a personal matter. . . . I believe in the natural goodness of people, and I firmly believe that no one wants war, especially nuclear war."

In November of 1987, the Gorbachevs came to the United States for the first time to participate in the third summit. Americans were eager to get a look at the Soviet first lady. Raisa, vivacious and talkative, gave them an eyeful—and an earful. She had something to say on virtually every subject, from literature to social and family obligations. One diplomat told *Time* magazine that Mrs. Gorbacheva seemed well informed but nervous, "like a student who had studied hard for an exam and wanted to show off everything she knew." At one State Department luncheon, Raisa, anxious to make a good impression, tried to speak to all 180 people in the receiving line. Lunch was not over until four o'clock in the afternoon.

While Raisa captivated Americans at large, trouble was brewing between the two first ladies. Nancy Reagan had invited Raisa Gorbacheva to tea and a tour of the White House personal quarters before the summit began. When she received no response after two weeks, a White House aide sent a reminder, demanding a reply within twenty-four hours. Two days later, the answer came: the Soviet first lady would prefer morning coffee to afternoon tea. (Other American sources would later say that Nancy was late in issuing the invitation.)

Their face-off began with Raisa asserting, "We missed you in Reykjavik." Nancy, caught off guard, replied, "I was told women weren't invited." It was downhill from there.

The two women could not seem to get a fix on each other. Nancy, still recovering from cancer surgery, was clearly not feeling well. Raisa plunged ahead, lecturing Nancy on everything that popped into her head, including the American Civil War. ("Who does that dame think she is?" Nancy said under her breath.) Raisa's enthusiastic questioning about the nineteenth-century furnishings of the White House seemed to fluster Nancy, who had to turn Raisa's questions over to an assistant curator.

Another tiff occurred over the question of dress for a state dinner at the White House. Normal dress code for such occasions is black tie, but the Soviets did not wear black tie. The Reagans insisted. The Soviets refused. The men all wore dark suits.

By week's end, it was clear that Mrs. Gorbacheva and Mrs. Reagan would never be best friends. Both women gamely tried to put a good face on it, shook hands, and agreed to keep their feelings to themselves.

Unaccustomed to her every word and move being scrutinized by millions of people, Raisa had come across as pedantic and lecturing. She would change.

Two years later, at the Bush-Gorbachev summit, Raisa set a new tone. The prickly and self-assertive manner had disappeared. Raisa now emerged as a graceful and gracious guest. On her second visit to the capital, she seemed more natural, more conversational. She seemed to enjoy herself more. *The New York Times* quoted Rebecca Matlock, wife of the then United States ambassador to Moscow, as saying, "This is very different than last time."

Raisa now toured the White House family quarters with Barbara Bush, a woman known for her formidable informality. Whether it was the influence of Mrs. Bush, or simply a newfound ease amidst the frenetic political socializing, Raisa charmed the socks off the Washington press corps. Her obvious enjoyment of children completely won over the Americans. On a tour of the Capital Children's Museum, Raisa took the hand of John Benton, Ambassador Matlock's grandson, and said, smiling, "You lead me and show me everything you know." The shy little boy obligingly helped her turn the Archimedean water screw, then played a quick game of electronic ticktacktoe with her. Even Millie, the Bushes' English springer spaniel, succumbed to

Raisa's warmth and openness, cuddling as close to Mrs. Gorbacheva as she could get.

From the beginning, Raisa's relationship with Barbara Bush was easier and more comfortable, testimony to both Raisa's greater confidence and also to Mrs. Bush's own winning ways.

Appearing with Barbara Bush at commencement exercises at Wellesley College in Massachusetts, on the platform, Raisa spoke first. She stuck to a friendly talk that echoed her husband's themes, and expressed safe sentiments about peace and *perestroika*. Her speech may have lacked wallop (many said they were "disappointed"), but both Mikhail and Raisa have always been intuitive about where and when to defer to other powerful people. (While her husband was generally acknowledged to be the best speaker in the Soviet hierarchy since Lenin, Raisa hardly ever speaks publicly in the Soviet Union, particularly not in Moscow. It may be her low-profile stance at home or perhaps that she also has the "country" accent that makes the city people smile when Mikhail Sergeyevich speaks.)

Undoubtedly, Raisa had previewed her speech for her husband. In any case, she knew that her task that day was to set the stage for Barbara Bush. She very astutely and courteously took a step back and let Mrs. Bush take center stage.

The American first lady was in top form. To an audience of graduating seniors, their families and professors, Barbara talked about the importance of family values. With characteristic good humor she concluded by saying, "Who knows, somewhere out in this audience may even be someone who will one day follow in my footsteps and preside over the White House as the president's spouse."

Then, after a pause, she added, "And I wish him well."

•

The audience of 5,400 people roared with laughter and gave Mrs. Bush a ringing ovation.

As the two first ladies were leaving the commencement tent, a woman asked Raisa in Russian, "Are you a feminist?" The usually loquacious Raisa, who earlier that day had been voluble on the subject of civil rights, the right to travel, and independence for Lithuanians, demurred.

It is hard to know what Raisa thinks about the role of women in Soviet society. In the Soviet Union women are overworked and underpaid. At best, the Soviet male attitude toward women is contradictory. The Soviet government was the first in history to write female emancipation into its Constitution. In this new world, women would be equal to men and participate fully in the work force.

Nearly half the female work-force is employed in unskilled, often backbreaking manual labor. Men operate machines, while women do the dirty manual jobs, such as hauling bushels of potatoes, shoveling refuse, and collecting garbage. It is true that more than 70 percent of Soviet doctors and teachers are women, but in the Soviet Union these jobs pay poorly, and few women ever reach the top of their professions. Only about a quarter of the Party were women, which meant few women had the opportunity to reach any position of power in public affairs. Only about 5 percent of senior Party positions such as regional first secretary were held by women. This percentage is not much different from that in the United States, where there are only two women in the Senate and women constitute less than 5 percent of the House of Representatives. And just like her counterpart in the United States, Russian women receive only about two-thirds the salary that men do.

But if American women are pressing up against a glass ceiling, Russian women are being pressed down upon by what seems like a cast iron block through which they cannot even see.

Russian women are completely responsible for domestic life. In Russia, this is not a task that can be shared with housekeepers and baby-sitters. There are no microwave pizzas or Chinese take-out. A woman who has worked at her job all day is likely to find herself standing in line for hours to shop for food, which she then has to prepare, serve, and clean up after. She is now being blamed for social ills, including soaring divorce rates, juvenile delinquency, and drugs. She is supposed to do the dirty work that men refuse, and also take care of the babies, young children, and men. Russian women find little humor in the old Russian proverb that translates into "women do everything; men do the rest."

Author Francine du Plessix Gray has observed that while Russian men blatantly discriminate against women, they do not dominate them. Russian women are formidable in their ability to cope. They are strong and selfless. On first meeting, Russian women—whether bureaucrats, teachers, doctors or the babushkas sweeping the sidewalks—can be fearsome. Russian women know what it takes to overcome sometimes insurmountable odds, and sometimes the strain shows on their faces and in their outward behavior.

Gorbachev also walked a double line regarding feminism, sounding very much like any conservative American politician. In the Tom Brokaw interview, Gorbachev said, "I think that a woman should take part in all spheres in life, in all of the processes taking place in society." But almost in the same breath he spoke of women's "predestination, that is, as keeper of the home fires." In his book *Perestroika*, Gorbachev writes of a "weakening of family ties and slack attitude to family responsibilities" as a "paradoxical result

·

of our sincere and politically justified desire to make women equal with men in everything."

Some say that Raisa is the one who pushed Gorbachev toward reform to help working women. There is speculation that she was behind Gorbachev's pledge to institute paid leaves for new mothers, shorter workdays or workweeks for mothers, as well as nursery school or kindergarten for every Soviet child.

It is unlikely that Americans will ever know as much about Raisa Gorbacheva as they would like—either about what she thinks or how she feels.

Gorbachev wanted to show off his bright and stylish wife at home and abroad without breaking too sharply from Soviet custom. Raisa Gorbacheva is a naturally outgoing woman and, like her husband, has grown into a polished public performer. Although not fluent in languages, she speaks English and some French, which she says she learned on her own. Early in her public career, she was often accused of speaking or lecturing in a pedantic manner. This was largely due to inexperience and language difficulties. She learned fast. Today, even when speaking through an interpreter, she manages to give the impression that she is having a conversation, one of the more difficult feats of human communication.

Famous on the world stage, Raisa has not been so highly regarded at home. Russian men resent her altogether. In the Soviet Union, leaders were best advised to serve the state and keep their private lives, if they had any, to themselves. From Khrushchev through Gorbachev, personality cults have been considered evil in the Soviet Union. (By contrast, virtually anyone who wants to run for office in America has to appear with a family, and even the president's dog makes "news.")

In the face of hardship at home, conservative Soviet

●

women tended to resent her taste and indulgence in clothes. Her apparent life of privilege was not always well received. Her dress far surpassed the clothing of most Soviet women, and expensive clothing was not admired in the Soviet Union.

Raisa had two roles to play—one abroad and one at home—and both of them were new. She had virtually no role models upon which to base her performance. She had to practice, experiment, and modulate her performance every day. The public kept a fascinated eye on her, watching her develop the role. Little by little, by virtue of television appearances, the Soviet public began to know her and appreciate her. She appeared at Soviet public functions, shaking hands in receiving lines, taking the wives of visiting heads of state on tours of art galleries.

While she herself had no role model, it is possible that Raisa Gorbacheva may herself become a role model for future generations of Russian women. Raisa created a part for herself as the wife of the Soviet general secretary. Unwilling to silently follow him, unwilling to remain invisible, she came out as an intelligent and outspoken partner to one of the most important and controversial players on the world stage today.

CHAPTER EIGHT

•

ECONOMICS—UP TO *PERESTROIKA* AND BEYOND

•

I N the earliest days of what became the Russian and then
Soviet empire, the land was farmed by the freemen who
owned the land they worked, and passed down the land
from father to son, generation to generation.

From the eleventh century on, the family farms were
gobbled up by large estates owned by the Russian princes,
the boyars, and the Orthodox Church. These upper classes
often took over the farmland by force, with roving hand-
picked armies of mercenaries, or sometimes, after a poor
harvest, bought the land at bargain prices from individual
farmers. Eventually, the small farms disappeared. Instead,
there were now huge estates manned by free tenant farmers
who worked the land and became increasingly dependent on
their landowners. The landowners' rents were ruinous, and
the taxes of the state took whatever was left. Farming became a life of bare survival. There was no longer any way
to prosper. One bad crop could drive a family in debt
enough to change the family's status from free to serf.

The Mongol invasion led to the Tartar Yoke, which
lasted from the middle of the thirteenth century to the end

of the fifteenth. It brought to a halt any economic progress that might have been made. While the Tartars did not interfere with the developing political structure of Russia, heavy tribute to the absent lords stripped the land of wealth without enriching its inhabitants.

The expansion of Russian territory at the end of the Tartar occupation increased the economic power of the burgeoning Russian empire. But the growth of the economy did not filter down to the people. By the close of the sixteenth century, the rights of tenant farmers to move from farm to farm and to work new lands had ended. Peasants now were permanently attached to the land they worked.

There were two kinds of peasants: those who worked for the state on land owned by the state, and the serfs who were the personal property of their landowner masters. State peasants were bound to the land and were part of it; serfs were themselves property, to be disposed of as their lord wished. Being a serf was like being a slave, only with certain disadvantages—a serf was not exempt from either military service or taxes.

Russia was predominantly agrarian throughout the sixteenth and seventeenth centuries, and economic progress in its cities was sluggish or nonexistent. While the reign of Peter the Great is generally regarded as a major turning point in the political history of Russia, the structure of the economy was barely disturbed by his rule. However, the changes wrought by Peter in the political and social life of the Russian empire eventually began to have a subtle effect on the economy.

With the "Europeanization" of Russian society came a demand for consumer goods and products that could not be met with existing capabilities. The state began to invest in this area of the economy by offering tax exemptions, tariff protection, and subsidies to manufacturers. These state-

•

subsidized entrepreneurs now began to make silks, bro-
cades, hosiery, and other consumer products, as well as
armaments. The manufacturers employed thousands of
workers; employees of smaller manufacturers worked in
their own homes.

The workers were largely state peasants and serfs who
were permitted to take some outside employment. The industries that grew most rapidly were the pig iron industry,
which by 1725 was as big in Russia as it was in England, and
the industries of sugar production and textiles.

In the early eighteenth century, a new class of serfs was
created: *possessionary* serfs, who belonged to an industrial
enterprise, rather than a landowner or the state. By the
time Czar Alexander II freed the serfs in 1861, the total
number of industrial workers in Russian amounted to about
1.5 million people.

Without the emancipation of the serfs, Russia would
have remained mired in a medieval economy. But Alexander made the first tentative steps toward bringing Russia
into the modern age by releasing the serfs from their absolute bondage, so they could become contributing citizens
and help in improving the welfare and growth of the Russian state.

After emancipation, industrial growth boomed, even
though the major force of the country's economy remained
agriculture. The total value of industrial production
reached 1.5 billion rubles in 1890 and grew to 5.7 billion
rubles in 1913. Industrial employment also grew, and by
1913 more than three million workers were employed—
about 2 percent of the total population.

Although the peasants living in this period before the
revolution had some legal and economic hope, they did not
grow rich. The yield of crops per acre remained low and was
far less than that in the western European countries. Never-

theless, the Stolypin land reform of 1906–11 reduced further the holdings of the nobility so that fully half of the land that the nobility had held before emancipation was by 1911 owned by free peasants.

At the turn of the century, Russia began exploiting some of its vast mineral wealth in the Donets Basin, north of the Black Sea in the south of European Russia. The state economy, bolstered by the rich deposits of coal and iron ore, began to improve.

Even so, four-fifths of the state's income came from indirect taxation of goods, rather than direct taxation on income. The poor paid as much tax on whatever they bought as the rich, assuming they had any money with which to purchase goods. (Fully a quarter of the state's income came from its monopoly on vodka production.) The people, from peasants and workers to merchants and professionals, had a standard of living well below that of the rest of Europe.

When World War I broke out, things got worse. This was not a war to defend the homeland or strengthen the cause of Russian civilization. It was a war that the people neither understood nor desired. The entire system, governing and economic, was strained to the breaking point. In 1917, with dissatisfaction from every quarter—deserting soldiers sick of the privation of the front joined with suffering workers at home and exiled revolutionaries pouring back into Russia—the system snapped. The scramble for power began. The ensuing civil war raged as the Bolsheviks sought to destroy those still loyal to Czar Nicholas II and impose their own Marxist system of government and economics on the giant Russian empire.

From that moment in 1917 the Soviet economy has gone through eight stages until today, when the books have been closed on Soviet socialist-style economics—for the immedi-

•

ate future, at any rate. The economic stages in Soviet history have been Civil War Communism (1917–21); NEP, or the New Economic Policy (1921–28); the Five-Year Plans before the war (1928–41); the War Economy (1941–45); War Recovery Economy (1945–53); Economic Expansion (1953–74); Stagnation (1974–85); and *Perestroika* (1985–91).

Civil War Communism meant the imposition of communism by fiat on the population of Russia. There was no organized economic force, only chaos and hardship. Little manufacturing was done, since raw materials were difficult, if not impossible, to come by and workers were occupied with the civil war. Food and any available goods were seized for the Red Army and the Bolshevik government. What industry existed, as well as banks, public utilities, land, and other natural resources, were all nationalized.

The New Economic Policy was introduced by Lenin into the fledgling Soviet state in 1921. In March of that year, Lenin had been graphically convinced of the need for a new approach to economic policy when sailors at the Kronstadt fortress and naval base near Petrograd, the pride of the revolution, supported the strikes and demonstrations of that city's workers against labor regimentation and food shortages. Rallying under the cry, "Soviets without Bolsheviks," the sailors demanded greater economic and political freedom for the both workers and peasants. The sailors demanded freedom for peasants to work the land as they pleased, freedom of speech and of the press. All attempts at conciliation with the renegade sailors failed. The government resorted to military force. Trotsky and Mikhail Tukhachevsky, an ex-czarist officer who had joined the Bolsheviks after fighting valiantly in World War I, led a military attack across the ice and put down the revolt. Survivors of the attack were shot or imprisoned. Even though the uprising was successfully suppressed, Lenin knew that the time called for some concessions. To make a Communist regime succeed, he needed peaceful cooperation between industrial workers and the peasants.

The NEP was an experiment in a "mixed economy"; it was neither capitalism nor socialism. The profit motive was used as an incentive to create economic recovery, but the Bolsheviks felt that it was merely a temporary measure before true socialism would be the only economic philosophy in the Soviet Union. To spur the peasants to greater production and also to acceptance of the new regime, the policy of confiscating the entire harvest was discontinued and peasants were allowed to keep a portion of the crop to sell in a free market.

Private industry was encouraged and even foreign investment and management was permitted. One foreigner, a young American named Armand Hammer, had just graduated from medical school at Columbia University and came to the Soviet Union in 1921 to give medical assistance during a nationwide typhus epidemic. Hammer's father was a founding member of the American Communist party, but the young physician was not himself a Communist. On the contrary, he had already, while barely out of his teens, made a fortune taking over and running his father's pharmaceutical business. When he arrived in the Soviet Union, Hammer found that starvation, not typhus, was the biggest problem. He later wrote in his 1987 autobiography *Hammer*, "There came to me the single proposition which most dramatically changed my life. . . ." He made a deal, trading grain from America for furs and other goods from the Soviet Union.

Lenin approached the young American and asked him to choose an industry and operate it. At first, Hammer operated a concession for manufacturing asbestos in the Urals.

•

Then, in 1925, he asked to manufacture pencils, and for many years students had the name Hammer embossed on their writing implements. If Russians knew the name of no other American, they would always remember that of Armand Hammer. Hammer's trading and later diplomatic relationship with the Soviet Union continued until his death at the age of ninety-two in 1990.

While private enterprise was permitted in a number of economic areas, the Soviet government retained control of major segments of the economy. The Bolsheviks controlled foreign trade, heavy industry, farming, utilities, and banking. The coexistence of private enterprise and socialism was successful. By 1927 production reached prewar levels.

But Lenin had suffered a series of debilitating strokes during 1922 and 1923, and his control over the country's economy began to slip. He died from a stroke on January 21, 1924. The new leader, Joseph Stalin, although he pledged to continue Lenin's principles, had a different agenda.

Stalin's first so-called Five-Year Plan began in 1928. It was a wildly ambitious plan for completely reshaping the economy. Impossible goals were set to launch industrialization and the collectivization of agriculture. People were moved about like pawns on a chessboard, with little concern for their personal lives. Millions were taken off farms, uprooted from land they and their forebears had lived on for centuries and put to work in mines and factories hundreds or thousands of miles away. The wealth of the nation was spent on a transformation from agriculture and light manufacturing to heavy industry.

To accomplish Stalin's goals, the Russian people had to suffer even more than in the past. Their low standard of living fell sharply lower. In the cities, there was strict rationing. The government reduced the purchasing power of the ruble. By 1930, if life was bleak in the cities, it was bleak and precarious in the country. Stalin appropriated the twenty-five million small farms throughout the nation and forced the farmers onto collectives.

The government once again expropriated the entire crop, paying virtually nothing to the farmers of the collectives. Ridiculously low prices for food helped finance the industrialization of the USSR. Food was sold to industrial workers in the cities at artificially low prices, and on the farms, with so little food left, millions starved. Many farmers killed their animals in the field rather than turn them over to the government, or let crops rot in the fields rather than harvest them. The kulaks, peasants whose farms were profitable enough so they could hire some extra labor, were particularly resistant. Stalin eliminated between fifteen million and thirty million kulaks and other peasants by starvation, deportation to the Gulag, and murder.

When the first Five-Year Plan ended in 1933, many of the impossible goals had been met. The Soviet Union had become one of the world's leading producers of heavy machinery, metals, fuel, and chemicals. The cost in human life was staggering.

The second Five-Year Plan was equally brutal and equally successful. By the beginning of World War II, the USSR was second only to the United States in industrial production. This success was kept hidden from the rest of the world. When Hitler attacked the Soviet Union in 1941, he was unaware that his unprepared enemy had such a great capacity for the production of war matériel.

For four years the Soviet nation battled Hitler's armies. The cost in life and the nation's wealth was enormous. Whole industries were moved hundreds of miles to keep them from falling into the hands of advancing German troops. The level of production throughout the nation dropped precipitously. As the Soviet Army battled back and reclaimed the land, war production was stepped up. With all the country's resources concentrated on making war, and with severe rationing and terrible deprivation, the Soviet Army eventually took the offensive, driving out the invaders, sweeping through eastern Europe into Germany, and to victory along with its allies.

During the postwar recovery period, all of the resources of the Soviet Union were bent to rebuilding the shattered economy. Again, Stalin called on his people for personal sacrifice, to suffer for the good of the country. Wartime military discipline was maintained, even though peace had come. A workweek of forty-eight hours was standard. Currency reform at the end of 1947 destroyed the purchasing power of wartime currency and so wiped out wartime hoarders and speculators. Pressure was put on the farmers to deliver good harvests while, as usual, receiving little for themselves. The harvests in the final years of the 1940s were generally poor.

To increase the value of the home economy, Stalin seized machinery, livestock, and various raw materials from countries that were overrun by the Soviet Army during the war, shipping everything back to the USSR—particularly to Moscow and other major population centers in western Russia. The economy grew in strength, but the standard of living rose only slightly, remaining extremely poor.

After Stalin's death in 1953, the economy grew at an even faster rate—double the rate of growth of the economy of the United States—according to American economist Robert Heilbroner. The emphasis moved away from heavy industry toward agriculture, housing, and consumer goods. By 1960, workers' hours had been cut to little more than forty per week, and minimum wages and pensions had been increased substantially. Workers were also now permitted

•

to change jobs and even industries without the approval of their bosses.

There were major increases in capital investment in the farms. The way the collectives operated also changed. First, collectives were joined with other nearby collectives, making fewer but much larger farm organizations. The poorest collectives were restructured as state farms. Machine-tractor stations were abolished and their equipment sold to the collectives. As an incentive for the peasants to increase production, prices were raised and the pricing structure simplified.

But during Khrushchev's leadership and the early years of Brezhnev's rule, the Soviet economy was never as successful as it appeared to be. The great achievements of putting a man into space and other space exploration, as well as building a major nuclear arsenal, required dedication and constant supervision. Other areas of the Soviet economy were perilously ignored.

The Soviet economy seemed to be in a period of strong growth during the 1960s and into the 1970s, but the picture of a better standard of living for Soviet citizens was belied by a fall in average life expectancy, a fall that began in the 1960s. The USSR was the first modern industrialized country in history to suffer such a drop.

At the core of the economic problems that have plagued the Soviet Union is the nature of the economy as it developed under Stalin. This centralized command-economy developed in the way it did for one reason—to make the economic system responsive to and dependent on political goals.

Originally, the political goals were few. The command planning, as outlined in the first of successive Five-Year Plans, was able to set the parameters for the entire economy, down to the last nut and bolt. The key political goal

•

was the end of individual farming and the growth of heavy industry.

As the world's technology grew, as everything became more complex, the task of planning the Soviet economy down to the last nut and bolt grew to a gargantuan task and then to a completely impossible task. The job of planning the development, production, shipping, and distribution of what has grown to literally hundreds of thousands of different products simply outgrew the ability of the government to deal with it.

Since the task was impossible, it led to the entrenchment of what was the most difficult problem in the litany of difficult problems for the Soviet economy: the sense that no matter what you do things will not get any better. And things did not get better.

According to Gavriil Popov, Soviet economist and political scientist, former editor of *Voprosy Ekonomiki* monthly, people's deputy and later mayor of Moscow: "The real problem . . . lies not in the leadership, nor in the merits or shortcomings of this or that research institute, nor in the structure of governmental bodies, nor in the method of rule; it lies rather in an economy driven not by economic laws and considerations, but by a strictly political-administrative engine."

Maybe the most problematic part of the command-economy system was establishing "success indicators" for various industries. These goals were stated in quantities by the central planning bureau—so many kilos of nails, so many lengths of cloth, and so on, until every item had a quota assigned to it and specifications for items were often minute enough to be unworkable and so ignored. In an egregious speculation, if the quota for nails was expressed in numbers, the factory would produce many millions of the tiniest nails, without regard to usability. If the amount desired was expressed in weight, nails would be thick and heavy—and also useless. The concept was portrayed in the Soviet satirical magazine *Krokodil* by a cartoon of a plant supervisor showing off his entire quota for the year—one huge nail dangling from a crane. Goals for cloth were set by length, rather than quality. To generate length quickly, textile factories would produce a weave so loose that it was practically impossible to manufacture the fabric into usable clothing. Because of this, T-shirts manufactured in the Soviet Union were famous for having a life of one wearing.

A factory that makes shoes and has a quota of one hundred thousand pairs assigned to it must make one hundred thousand pairs. Under the command-economy system, it does not matter much if these shoes are so poorly made that they are unwearable, as long as the quota is met. And so, of course, human nature, or perhaps Russian nature, being what it is, the shoes *are* unwearable. If another shoe manufacturer comes along and makes shoes that are comfortable, he will sell his shoes and put the state enterprise out of business, and all of its employees out of work. This could not be permitted in a land of "full employment." Since the central planning bureau set the price of these shoes below what it cost to manufacture them, the shoes wound up pinching feet and causing corns in Moscow, St. Petersburg, and throughout the country. The central planning bureau also set most salaries so low that people could only afford to buy shoes that hurt their feet. (Keeping the wages low contributed to the general malaise and to the continuing low quality of products. Workers would say, "They pretend to pay us, we pretend to work.")

What had been forgotten in the equation was that many people will do anything to keep their feet from hurting. Some people will kill for a good pair of shoes. What started small, with just a few pair of good shoes, grew to a point

•

where it (along with other factors) spawned a major factor in the Soviet economy—the black market.

For years, in a country beset by shortages, anything could be gotten on the black market—for a price. The price was often high, and when the average salary was about two hundred rubles a month, beyond the means of most. There was also a social stigma attached to the black market, and dealing with the black market was illegal. These factors kept the number of transactions down. But as the trickle of stories about official corruption became a waterfall, as the people learned how the favored within the Communist party lived lavishly, the social stigma evaporated. With the coming of *glasnost,* the fear of punishment for something as trivial as dealing with the black market all but vanished. People whose feet hurt began to work extra jobs to make the money to buy shoes on the black market.

The black market handled more than shoes, but it was usually luxury and imported products that were available. Soon, others began to get in on the "free" market. A shipment of sausages headed for state stores would somehow disappear and be rerouted. This would create a shortage in the stores marked "Produkti," where the prices were controlled. Sausages were, however, available on the black market—for a price.

Government officials in the distribution chain had two reasons to divert products from the state stores to the black market. The first was the pure profit motive. The second, which came later, was to sabotage Gorbachev and his anticorruption policies. Gorbachev inherited the burgeoning black market, the corruption everywhere, and the sabotage. But one program that was at the heart of his reforming zeal caused difficult economic problems—the antialcoholism campaign. From the time of the czars, the government had the franchise on vodka. Before the revolution, this brought the government fully one-quarter of its income. Vodka was a big money-maker for the Bolsheviks as well. Gorbachev's temperance drive that began in 1985 cost the Soviet treasury a fortune without putting much of a dent in the problem of alcoholism. The slack in availability has been taken up by the black market and a rapidly growing home distillery industry.

Moonshine vodka, called *samogen*, has increasingly been distilled in apartments in the cities as well as in the countryside because there is a serious shortage of vodka in the government stores, where the shelves remain empty most of the time. "Last month we raided an apartment that produced 1,500 liters a month," said Moscow deputy chief of police Lev Belyansky in 1991. The policeman called for legalization of the home brew as the shortage of legal and affordable vodka has created an "explosive situation." The search for hard drink has created a situation similar to the Prohibition era in the United States, and bootlegging taxi drivers early in 1991 had a shoot-out at a Moscow taxi depot that left one dead. A reporter for the youth newspaper *Komsomolskaya Pravda* watched as a clerk at Moscow's plush state food store, Yeliseyevsky, where the counters are empty of vodka, guided thirsty shoppers to a back room where they could buy 10-ruble bottles of vodka for just 20 rubles. The customers got a bargain and the clerk netted a profit of 310 rubles (more than the average monthly wage) in only fifteen minutes.

At a conference of former American secretaries of state on October 12, 1990, at the University of Georgia in Athens, Georgia, the secretaries were asked about the Soviet Union's move to a market economy. Edmund Muskie, secretary of state under President Carter, had recently been to the Soviet Union. He said: "It will be enormously difficult.

•

We must help them financially and find the means to do that."

Secretary William Rogers, a Nixon appointee, said: "It will be difficult for them, but they're going to have to help themselves. We, at this time, can't afford to help them."

John F. Kennedy's secretary of state, Dean Rusk, who also served under Lyndon Johnson, said: "I've just returned from the Soviet Union. They have faith in a market economy, but they don't know what a market economy is. There's a long road ahead for them."

George Shultz, secretary of state for Ronald Reagan, said: "The problems are great, but I'm optimistic. In the early seventies when they needed grain, they didn't just negotiate a deal with us. They went around and quietly negotiated an advantageous [for them] contract here and another one there, making sure the prices they got were low. When world markets awoke to the level of their purchases and prices rose, they had their contracts at the lower prices they had negotiated. So don't tell me they don't know markets. They have some very smart people, very educated people, and enormous resources. They need to build a delivery infrastructure, but they can do it. And they have operating markets over there—black markets. Personally, I think they ought to turn over things to those markets—make them legitimate."

Some markets have achieved legitimacy. With the endemic food shortages, so-called "free" markets of small farmers with garden-grown vegetables have sprung up all over cities where state stores have no produce. The prices are higher than in the state stores, but they have products to sell.

While the few halting steps taken to convert the economy to a market-driven model under *perestroika* have made little impact, there have been some successes among the cooperative ventures being attempted in the Soviet Union. One such venture, a Moscow manufacturing facility, has turned an unsuccessful light manufacturing plant into a profitable one, in which the employees have seen their dedication to work result in pay increases of 65 percent. It was the idea of Yuri Korolyov, a forty-nine-year-old electrical engineer assigned to run the plant in 1986. Once laws had been passed permitting so-called cooperative ventures, Korolyov applied to the government for permission to turn the plant into an employee-owned cooperative.

The attitude of the 1,600 workers in the plant changed considerably once they had a stake in the plant's machinery and output. They began to perform maintenance on the machinery, which was neglected before, and take pride in the products they produced—such as motors for washing machines, timers for microwave ovens, and controls for small electric machines. Revenue went from thirty million rubles in 1986 to forty-four million rubles in 1989, and posting a four-million-ruble profit in 1989, rather than the yearly loss that had become expected.

But success is the exception rather than the rule. No matter which way Gorbachev turned after he took office as president in March 1990, the economy kept getting worse.

The distinguished Soviet economist Nikolai Shmelev, writing in *Novy Mir,* described the state of the economy:

> It is essential to realize that the cause of our difficulties is not only due to the heavy burden of military expenditures and to the highly expensive global responsibilities assumed by our country. . . . Persistent, long-term efforts to defy the objective laws of economic life and to suppress the age-long natural incentives to work have led to results directly opposite to those we had anticipated. We

•

now have an economy that is out of balance and
plagued with shortages, an economy that rejects
scientific and technological progress, one that is
unplanned and—if we want to be totally
honest—unplannable. . . .

Massive apathy, indifference, theft, and
disrespect for honest labor, together with
aggressive envy toward those who earn more—even
by honest methods—have led to the virtual
physical degradation of a significant part of the
people as a result of alcoholism and idleness. There
is a lack of belief in the officially announced
objectives and purposes, in the very possibilities of
a more rational organization of social and
economic life.

Clearly, all this cannot be swiftly
overcome—that will take years, perhaps several
generations.

In early September 1990, Stanislav Shatalin introduced
his plan to change the Soviet economy. Variously called the
Shatalin Plan and the 500-Day Plan, it was meant to be a
cold shower to a sleepy economy. Shatalin, an elfin, fifty-
six-year-old intellectual, had been snatched from the groves
of academe by Gorbachev to become senior economic advisor to the president. He had been censured three times by
the Communist party for his aberrant ideas. "In the Kremlin," he shrugged, "I am a Social Democrat working in the
headquarters of the Bolsheviks."

The Shatalin Plan would have taken control of the economy away from the central Soviet government in Moscow
and allowed each republic to control its own economy.
Much of what was owned by the state would be sold to
private enterprise. In its first phase, the state would auction
off some property and reduce the budget deficit from ap-

proximately 12 percent of gross national product to less than 1 percent. Subsidies to industry (about 3 percent of gross national product) would be ended, and farmers could get a share of land controlled by their collectives. Half of all smaller businesses would be sold, and wages would be indexed to support the purchasing power of workers' incomes.

At the end of five hundred days, most business would be denationalized and most prices deregulated. A private banking system would be run by a central money authority similar to the Federal Reserve in the United States.

Shatalin conceded that in the transition, millions would become unemployed, but he expected that they would be able to find work in an expanded service economy. The plan was to run on a strict timetable, with everything to be accomplished in less than two years.

Gorbachev favored the plan, but was afraid that it was too ambitious, particularly in its timetable. While he liked the plan in principle, it must have made embarrassing reading for him. In a unique English translation brought out of the USSR within a week of its publication, the 145-page document frequently mentioned the "errors" and "lack of decision" on the part of the Soviet government and ridiculed Gorbachev for his "indecisiveness." The document also boldly stated that ". . . it is obvious only a market economy can be the logical choice for an economic system of civilized man," discarding with a sneer more than seventy years of history and berating Gorbachev's avowed love of socialism.

Yeltsin embraced the plan enthusiastically. Finally, Gorbachev decided to back a less radical plan being developed, and promised to present this alternative plan shortly.

During the interim, before the alternative plan was released, the American Public Broadcasting System television show *Adam Smith's Money World* interviewed

•

Gorbachev on the economy at sessions of the Supreme Soviet:

SMITH: What about the pace of the reforms—will they take a long time to take effect?

GORBACHEV: A few months ago we thought we had a lot of time to work things out, but now there is very little. Time itself is determining the logic of perestroika, and it is time to move forward rapidly.

SMITH: Will there be any retreat ever, do you think, from the movement to market economy?

GORBACHEV: No, I think that as far as our choice to change to a market economy is concerned, society as a whole supports it. But how to change? That is what we have been discussing in recent days. It is the most important problem, the main topic for today. Nonetheless, the market will be the path that we will follow—in the context of the realities of our society, in regard to its various movements, problems and traditions—all of its peculiarities.

SMITH: Do you worry that in taking this step you will create gaps between the rich and the poor?

GORBACHEV: This is, by the way, a very good question. I could take, for instance, the point of view of our economists, as well as Americans, Japanese and French economists, who think that we should change to a market economy on our own terms. And, of course, in doing this, we are considering not only world experience but our own peculiarities as well. But most important, obviously, we wish to consider the very powerful and positive aspects of socialism, the experience of which I believe in, as they can be united with the private interests of human beings. By the way, even American economists warn that we should not copy their experience. They sincerely think that as far as there are positive aspects to our economy, to our society, that we should bring them into any transition to a market mechanism. This is very important, and I think that this is how it should be done.

SMITH: If you were looking at the Soviet Union 50 years from now, looking back, what is the most important thing?

GORBACHEV: I think that the decisions we will make in the last few months of this year are probably the most important ones we will ever make. I said this yesterday in front of the deputies. These are the most important decisions. And the way in which we made these decisions can lead us to a new type of society, life, a new form of economy, a new political process, even at the multinational ethnic regions of our country. Today we stand before the most salient decisions in the history of our nation. Not just for the years of perestroika.

SMITH: How can you convince the people and make them welcome this development and reassure them?

GORBACHEV: Well, this is a big issue. I think more than anything, people will be convinced by life itself. If they don't even see in their own lives that it is necessary to change the form of economic relations, and that it is necessary to return the land, the factories and industry to the people as owners, as managers of their own property, of the means of production, the use of the land, if people don't understand this, then there will be no change to a market economy. Our task is to create a situation through various decisions, laws, decrees which gives the individual the right to make the choice for himself. It would be strange if we were to invite people to try a new form of life which was supposed to help them realize their own potential and that in this new life, to force them, like people were forced onto the collective farms—it would be contradictory.

•

Gorbachev, speaking to deputies about Yeltsin's charge of his indecisiveness, had this to say: "People say I'm not decisive enough. Do you know what decisiveness is? It's supporting one's course. It's not deciding who to strike. We've had that experience already. I myself worked like that for nine years. I've had enough of it. I'm from that world, from the old mechanisms. If I hadn't had to go through all that, I would never have seen the need for perestroika. This program [Shatalin's plan] isn't perfect. And, listen, don't look at it as something where every step is etched out. We'd be stuck with it then. It's just there to point out the right direction. No, it's not going to be easy, but it's necessary. And, you know, maybe in this variant we have a conversion of theories of bourgeois philosophers and—well, it is something taking place now—when we combine our socialized society. Socialism with private interests. If we succeed in this, it will be a real revolution."

On October 16, 1990, Mikhail Gorbachev presented a compromise plan for economic reform to the Supreme Soviet. The plan would end the economic monopoly of the state, but it set no time limit for accomplishing this. The Soviet president proposed a more gradual transition, while Shatalin and those supporting the 500-Day Plan felt that a rapid transition was necessary to avoid the resistance of the bureaucracy.

Shatalin said he was "not very happy" with the new plan and thought it would not lead to a real market economy. Predictably, Boris Yeltsin denounced the plan, saying it would let the central bureaucracy hold on to power indefinitely. He thought it was doomed to failure. Gorbachev had no problem getting the support of the Supreme Soviet for the plan, but getting the republics to go along was another matter.

Gorbachev's market plan would have gradually phased

out price controls and, by the end of 1992, called for controls only on such necessities as bread, meat, dairy products, medicine, and transportation. Republics would be allowed to tighten controls or free prices or impose rationing.

Factories, farms, and housing owned by the state would be sold, and the state would no longer impose its management on farms. Collectives could decide for themselves whether to stay together, or separate, and republics could allow any member of a collective to claim and farm a piece of land on his own. There would be freedom of economic activity as a right and protection for small businessmen from the state. Foreign investors could invest in and own businesses in the Soviet Union.

The budgets of the military and the KGB would be reduced, foreign aid would be cut, and international projects would be put on a commercial footing. The state would keep control of transportation, defense, energy, communications, customs, monetary policy, and price regulations on a select list of products. Both the central government and the republics would have the right to levy taxes, and the state would gradually change the ruble to a convertible currency.

Wages would be indexed to account for inflation and each family would be guaranteed a minimum income, while the state would retain control of the export of important natural resources.

There would be a central bank modeled after the U.S. Federal Reserve system. Other banks would be commercial, and there would be funds made available to help businesses in trouble. Credit and other help would be made available to consumers for buying such major items as homes and automobiles.

By the end of June 1991, Gorbachev had made further

adjustments to his proposed economic policy. He indicated that he would not follow completely the recommendations from either the right or the left, but would go forward with a centrist policy, using some of the old-line Communist policy and some of the more liberal, market-oriented plan, following his usual policy of seeking the place in the center.

He said that he would not entirely support the radical economic plan developed by liberal economist Grigory Yavlinsky and a group of Harvard University economists to convert the Soviet economy into a market economy more acceptable to the West. Neither would Gorbachev completely support the "anticrisis" economic reform developed by more conservative Soviet economists for Prime Minister Valentin Pavlov.

According to Gorbachev at a session of the Supreme Soviet on June 21, 1991, he had put together elements of the Yavlinsky plan with elements of the Pavlov plan and, adding suggestions from the International Monetary Fund and the European Bank for Reconstruction and Development, created a program which he would present to the meeting of leaders of world industrial powers in London that July.

Responding to criticism that he was repeating his mistake with the Shatalin Plan, Gorbachev replied: "We had to cover this stage. Society was ill-prepared, no answers were available, we had to find the common mainstream of movement. We are now reaching a stage when direct action will be taken." But events overtook Gorbachev's direct action.

CHAPTER NINE

•

THE LAST COMMUNIST

•

WHILE the Russian and Soviet empires have always been ruled by a strong individual at the top, under Soviet law the Communist party was the boss. The Party and the Soviet government were parallel structures, but it was the Party that ran things. And the Party was run by the general secretary with the help and acquiescence of the two-hundred-member Central Committee and the twenty-member Politburo.

The powers of the general secretary were never written down—not defined and not restricted. Strongmen like Stalin could ride roughshod over the system. Once in office, the general secretary's term was ordinarily for life. Of the Soviet Union Communist party general secretaries, only Khrushchev was forced to step down.

But in the late 1980s, the Communist party lost the confidence of the people. By the end of the 1980s, Gorbachev's policy of *glasnost* left the people unafraid to voice their opinions. The people wanted free elections, not the kind where there was only one party to vote for.

Gorbachev saw the handwriting on the wall. He began

a process to transfer political power from the Party to the government. On March 11, 1990, as Gorbachev celebrated the fifth anniversary of his ascent to power, he proposed basic changes in the Communist party to decentralize and democratize the Party machinery. He proposed that his post, the top job of general secretary, be eliminated and replaced with a shared-authority system of chairman and deputies, among other decentralizing proposals. He also proposed that the emphasis be placed on individual Party members, rather than the leadership. These proposals were made as he prepared to switch from being general secretary of the Communist party to president of the Soviet Union—changing his emphasis from the Party to the government.

Gorbachev's proposals for Party overhaul were too little and too late. In popular elections that were for the first time open to candidates who were not Communist party members, dissident candidates were consistently favored to defeat Party members. Party membership, which had heretofore been necessary for political office-holding, was now a definite minus, and some candidates of the Party were downplaying or not mentioning their Party membership.

In the process, Gorbachev sought to preserve his own power—through a powerful presidency. An unrestricted powerful presidency was the last thing the Congress of People's Deputies, meeting to alter the Soviet Constitution, wanted. "I got really angry at the way he pushed through the law on the presidency," said a young Muscovite, Vasily Shakhnovsky, who was trying to develop a prodemocracy group within the Communist party.

Another young Muscovite, people's deputy and member of the loyal opposition Sergei Stankevich, felt that Gorbachev had let himself be misled by Party apparatchiks. "During the first stage of *perestroika*, it was reasonable for

•

him to be in the center of the road," said Stankevich, who is also a member of the Moscow City Council and whose youthful good looks made him stand out in the Soviet Parliament. "But the potential of this . . . policy is exhausted . . . and the society is developing much more quickly."

But the Parliament was a relatively conservative group that feared anarchy more than a strong president. Out of this came a presidency that for the first time in the Soviet Union defined its limits of power.

The first person elected to this new executive presidency was the general secretary. He had the support of the people, but by default, since the people, while not satisfied with the job Gorbachev had done, had not coalesced around any other prospective leader. According to polls taken just before the election, in January 1990, 44 percent of the Soviet citizens surveyed, when asked if they supported Gorbachev's political line, said they supported him fully. A further 37 percent said they basically supported him. So, 81 percent, a large majority, supported Gorbachev at the beginning of 1990. Only 16.5 percent expressed support for Boris Yeltsin.

What had been worked out in terms of the presidency was free general elections, every five years, beginning with what was to be the end of Gorbachev's first term in 1995. Candidates were to be citizens between the ages of thirty-five and sixty-five, and no elected president could serve more than two terms.

The new Constitution called for the president to be impeached for violating the law or the Constitution, upon a two-thirds vote of the 2,500 members of the Congress of People's Deputies, which would meet twice a year.

The president's vetoes of legislation could be defeated by a two-thirds vote of the Supreme Soviet, a full-time, permanently sitting legislature. The Supreme Soviet could vote to limit the president's power to make decrees or declare a state of emergency. It could also vote "no confidence" in the Council of Ministers (the cabinet) surrounding the president, which would force the council to step down. A new council could then be submitted by the president.

A line of succession was named, should the president be impeached or die in office, with the chairman of the Supreme Soviet (then, Anatoly Lukyanov) next in line and then the chairman of the Council of Ministers. A package of constitutional changes, given final approval by the Congress of People's Deputies on December 26, 1990, made the cabinet ministries directly subordinate to the president, rather than the prime minister. Also included were enormous discretionary powers of the president to suspend civil liberties, use troops and impose direct rule in trouble spots. Later in 1990, the position of vice-president was created, and Gorbachev was able to pick a vice-president who could succeed to the presidency ahead of the chairman of the Supreme Soviet but only after a battle in the Congress.

In addition to these momentous changes in the Constitution, Article Six, which had said that the Communist party was the nucleus of the Soviet political system, was changed to allow participation by other political parties.

The day after Gorbachev called for the overhaul of the Party, he received a call from the Congress of Estonia to set that country free from the Soviet Union. And in Estonia's sister Baltic republic, Lithuania, there was more than a call for freedom—there was a demand. The Lithuanian Parliament elected the first non-Communist premier of a Soviet republic, Vytautas Landsbergis, a music professor and head of the Lithuanian independence movement, and the Parliament voted to secede from the Soviet Union.

Although George Bush urged Gorbachev to accept the

•

Lithuanian secession, the Soviet leader expressed alarm at the Lithuanian Parliament's move. A deputy from the third Baltic republic, Latvia, had a dire prediction: "It's one of the traditions of the Soviet Union—the use of force," said Yuri Boyers. But Communist party hard-liner Yegor Ligachev said, "We will not use force. We must resolve this by political means. Tanks will not help in this matter."

The following day, while a specially convened session of the Congress of People's Deputies was meeting to consider the new powers Gorbachev had requested as president, Gorbachev rejected Lithuania's declaration of independence, calling it "illegitimate and invalid." He also refused to discuss independence with any of the other republics. Lithuanian delegates to the Congress would not vote on the new presidency, saying that they had no right to change the structure of the Soviet government while they were trying to withdraw from it.

The Congress of People's Deputies voted overwhelmingly for a powerful executive presidency by a vote of 1,817 for, 133 against, and 61 abstentions, on March 13, 1990. While Vitaly Korotich, editor of *Ogonyok* and a people's deputy, believed that too much power had been given to the presidency, he said, "I believe that Gorbachev, who destroyed totalitarianism in this country, will not be the man who will try to be a dictator himself."

On March 15, 1990, Gorbachev, like British king Henry VIII placing the crown on his own head, inaugurated himself as president of the USSR. He was the only person in the Soviet Union with the authority to perform such an act. He had memorized the oath and he swore on an amended Soviet Constitution that historically changed the nature of government.

While it was decreed that the person who held the office of this new Soviet presidency would be voted in directly by a ballot of the people, the first to hold the office was elected by the Congress of People's Deputies. He was the only candidate and was approved by 1,329 votes for, 495 against, 54 invalid ballots, and 122 protest ballots not cast.

Accepting the presidency, Gorbachev said, in part:

> I am aware that I am accepting my duties at a difficult time for the nation. I agreed to run for the presidency because I am convinced of the future of our fatherland and also because *perestroika* has become the meaning of my entire life.
>
> *Perestroika*, I believe, is the only possible way for this country to peacefully proceed to a fundamentally different society, from an authoritarian bureaucratic system to a humane and democratic socialism.
>
> We have been hampered by ingrained dogmatic views, the habit of taking a passive attitude, sitting idle and only doing what the boss tells us. All these handicaps are still making themselves felt. I would even say that despite all the economic and social difficulties and other thorny problems, inflexible mentality remains the biggest stumbling block to change.
>
> It is obvious, however, that *perestroika* should be radicalized. And I shall use my presidential powers above all toward this end.
>
> Nothing less than a breakthrough is needed. Otherwise, negative trends will mount even faster than before. I think we need decisive moves to radicalize economic reform.
>
> The laws cannot work all by themselves and grassroots initiative and enterprises will die unless we foster the appropriate economic environment. We must get down to creating a full-blooded domestic market.
>
> From now on the Soviet Communist party will

participate in elections on an equal footing with
other political organizations, working by
democratic means for the right to form union and
republican governments and local bodies of power.

The cold war has been done away with, but
military confrontation has not been overcome. This
is why, while giving indisputable priority to
political ways of insuring security, the president
must also, necessarily, guide the national defense
policy along the principles of reasonable sufficiency
and on the basis of the new military doctrine,
showing concern for the armed forces. A different
approach is unacceptable. As president, I would
like to assure you that this is how I shall act.

A month after Gorbachev's inauguration, his popularity
had slipped, in the same survey, from 81 percent to 65
percent. With the inability of the Gorbachev administration to stock the shelves of state stores (according to many
because of a program of sabotage by the bureaucrats) in the
capital or elsewhere throughout the country, the president's
approval rating moved steadily downward.

On March 19, 1990, results of local elections throughout
the Soviet Union showed how far apart the people and the
Communist party had grown. In the city councils of the
three largest cities of the Soviet Union—Moscow, Leningrad, and Kiev—opposition factions won majorities over
the Communists. In the republics, particularly Estonia,
Latvia, and the Ukraine, insurgents fighting for greater
autonomy or outright independence from the Soviet Union
won important seats in republic parliaments.

Gorbachev refused to yield to the wayward republics's
desire for independence, decreeing that Lithuanians were
not permitted to own or store weapons and securing the
borders to limit entry and exit from the Baltic state. By

•

March 24, more than a hundred Soviet tanks and 1,500 troops armed with automatic weapons entered the republic's capital, Vilnius, to put the pressure on the Lithuanian Parliament to abandon its declaration of independence.

The Soviet government proposed to Lithuania on April 20 that there be a freeze on any declarations of independence for two years as a basis for negotiation of the question. Lithuania was caught in an economic squeeze by the Kremlin, which had shut off oil supplies as well as metals, wood, tires, and sugar to the maverick republic.

While opinion in the United States and Western Europe favored freedom for the Baltic republics, their stake in friendly relations with the Soviet Union had become high, and consequently their money was on Gorbachev. George Bush and other Western leaders were conspicuously silent on the struggle between Lithuania and Moscow.

President Landsbergis looked to strike a deal with the Kremlin that would put a two-year freeze on independence for the republic, but, he said, he would not accept a deal that included Lithuania acceding to Moscow's sovereignty over the Baltic republic.

Meanwhile, Gorbachev obviously intended that other republics should learn from the Baltic example. Lithuanian leadership was pushing the Soviet president too hard, and the central government had to push back—but with the desire to slow down the processes. There were too many problems for the Soviet leader to focus on just one.

Gorbachev's difficulties were not just hundreds of miles away from the Kremlin on the shores of the Baltic. They were also on his front doorstep. The March elections had installed insurgents to run the Moscow City Council, and these insurgents had voted one of their own, free-market economist Gavriil Popov, to head the council as Moscow's mayor. In expectation of local permissiveness on anti-Party demonstrations, Gorbachev used his newly acquired powers to decree that the City Council would have no powers to permit or prohibit street demonstrations in Moscow; but, since the seat of the central government was there, that power would now be held by Gorbachev's cabinet, the Council of Ministers.

Gorbachev's popularity continued to wane dramatically, even as he tried to grasp the reins of power more firmly. What would have secured both popularity and power—improvement in the economy—seemed to be beyond his (or anyone else's) ability to effect.

Soviet economic experts visiting Washington said that the Soviet economy was in much worse shape than had been estimated by Washington—or Moscow. Economist and people's deputy Vladimir Tikhonov said at an April 23, 1990, conference sponsored by the American Enterprise Institute that the quantity of produce lost in the Soviet Union through waste and inefficiency greatly exceeded official estimates. "One cannot trust the figures given by the state committee," he added. Oleg Bogomolov, another economist who is an elected deputy in the Soviet Congress, disputed CIA figures on both the Soviet gross national product (too high, he said) and Soviet military spending (too low).

But in Moscow, President Gorbachev ruled out radical change—"shock therapy"—for the Soviet economy. Gorbachev had been tottering on the brink of ending government price controls and so beginning a rapid transition to a market economy. But stepping backward from his pledge only days earlier to introduce a market economy to the Soviet Union, Gorbachev spoke to workers in Sverdlovsk at the Uralmash heavy industry works on April 25, 1990. "We will not transfer to the free market out of despair, but in a well thought out manner," he said. "We have to think of the material security of the people. . . . We will not use methods of shock therapy."

Seeking support and trying to gauge the mood of the people, Gorbachev admitted to mistakes, saying "not everything has been smooth," but assuring them that Kremlin economic policies in the near future would try to cause "minimum losses." He told the crowd, "We need a convertible ruble and we need to open the country to foreign competition." He finished his talk by gently asking the workers, "We would like to get your opinion on what we have to do to correct the economic situation."

Gorbachev's three leading economic advisors, Nikolai Petrakov, Alexander Yakovlev, and Stanislav Shatalin, all exponents of a free-market system, agreed that the people would not accept the higher prices that would come with ending price controls. According to Petrakov, "All the opinion polls show . . . people accept rationing coupons and standing in line—especially during work time—but not price increases." Yakovlev said, "The shock therapy that people are talking so much about will not happen." And Stanislav Shatalin, the author of the 500-Day Plan that Gorbachev first accepted and then rejected later in the year, said in April 1990 that a banking system and fiscal and monetary policies must first be created before a market system could be embarked upon. "Without all of this," Shatalin said, "to introduce a market today would only be suicide."

Gorbachev had an answer of a kind from the people on communism's most celebratory day—May Day. At the May 1 annual parade in Red Square, marchers protested and jeered Gorbachev and *perestroika*. In an unofficial section of the parade, permitted by Gorbachev, placards were raised to the Soviet president, chatting on the balcony on top of Lenin's Tomb with the maverick mayor of Moscow,

•

Gavriil Popov, declaring DOWN WITH THE CULT OF LENIN and DOWN WITH THE RED FASCIST EMPIRE. Aging Kremlin officials watched with amazement, never before having seen such protest at a May Day celebration.

Early in May 1990, Gorbachev spoke on television to the people about a request he was making of the Parliament for an increase in the price of bread. He explained that bread cost more to produce than was being charged; that farmers were feeding bread—rather than grain—to their stock because the bread was cheaper; that children were using bread in place of balls to play games. Bread was selling for about twenty-two kopeks (there are one hundred kopeks in a ruble) a loaf, and Gorbachev proposed an increase in price to seventy-five kopeks, which, he said, the average Soviet citizen (then earning three hundred rubles a month) could afford.

Response from the people was immediate. Sales of flour, butter, bread, and other staples rose astronomically as people began hoarding food against a future rise in prices. The Moscow City Council voted to restrict sales of food and to require proof of residency in the capital to buy at state stores. Some Moscow residents—like Ada, forty-one, who had lived in Moscow for fifteen years, but whose residence on her passport still read her birthplace in Sverdlovsk— feared they would starve.

Two days before his departure on a summit trip to Canada and the United States, Gorbachev once again appeared on television and spoke to the people, asking them to remain calm and stop the panic buying that stripped store shelves bare in the capital and elsewhere through the country. Gorbachev asked for a "joint effort and mutual trust" to get through a tense, difficult and, frankly speaking, "dangerous" time.

The day before Gorbachev's departure, a trade deal was

•

concluded between the United States and the USSR, making American technology more available in the Soviet Union and lowering tariffs on such Soviet products as vodka, furs, and textiles for entry into U.S. markets. It was the first trade pact between the two countries since their alliance in World War II.

Gorbachev spent his last day before leaving for Canada privately appealing to deputies at the Congress of Deputies of the Russian Republic to refuse to elect Boris Yeltsin as president of the Soviet Union's largest republic. The congress was meeting in Moscow to choose its president, and Yeltsin was reportedly close to victory, with the Gorbachev- and Communist party-backed Alexander Vlasov trailing. But on the same day, deputies returning to their hotels for a lunch break passed through corridors of people in the streets, chanting "Yeltsin! Yeltsin! Yeltsin!"

On May 29, 1990, Boris Yeltsin was parliamentarily elected president of the Russian Republic, with a total of 535 votes, 4 more than the majority needed for election. Vlasov received 467 votes. Arriving in Canada at the beginning of his journey to the summit in the United States, Gorbachev was asked about Yeltsin's victory. He said he was happy to hear that Boris Nikolayevich had promised to "work fruitfully with the president of the Soviet Union," and added, "If, however, he is indeed playing a political game, then we may be in for a difficult time. So we will wait and see. Life is richer than any teacher."

Gorbachev's trip to Canada and then the United States was a personal triumph for both Mikhail Sergeyevich and Raisa Maximovna. The couple were greeted everywhere like visiting movie stars. They were praised extravagantly by the heads of Western governments and by leaders of the arts. It was a pleasant respite from the daily crises in the

•

Kremlin, but it counted for little at home, where people wanted bread, not circuses.

Meanwhile, Gorbachev needed to prepare for the Twenty-eighth Party Congress that began meetings on July 2, 1990, at the vast and modern Kremlin Palace of Congresses in Moscow. The Party's hold on the government had been severely weakened by Gorbachev's reforms, and throughout the Soviet Union people were saying (and feeling) that the Communist party was irrelevant.

The latest joke in Moscow went: "Why didn't I see you at the last Party Congress?" said one Party member to another.

"Ah, if I had known it was going to be the *last* . . ."

But the high-level bureaucrats, all Party members, were not willing to simply hand over the reins of power. The new rules only said there would now be *competition* for political positions and the Communist party, including its still–general secretary Mikhail Sergeyevich, was not willing to concede power to other factions.

Gorbachev made the opening address to the Party congress and sought to pull its dissident elements together, but he got a cool reception. Delegate Vladimir Bludov rose to demand that the entire leadership resign immediately, since it had failed to "fulfill the food program." Gorbachev appealed to the Party members to back his economic reforms, yet he made no concessions to the hard-line conservatives. He also pleaded with more democratic insurgents to stay with the Party.

He struck hard at the situation he had inherited from previous Soviet leaders:

> It was an extremely grim legacy that we inherited. Let us jointly recall and consider the facts.

Take the neglect in the countryside, in farming
and in the processing industry. Did it arise
yesterday, after 1985? Yet it affects the food
situation to this day as well as farmers' lives and
positions.

The grim environmental situation: more than
100 cities in a disaster zone, with 1,000 industrial
establishments brought to a standstill as a result;
the drama of Lake Baikal, the Aral Sea, Lake
Ladoga and the Sea of Azov; Chernobyl and other
accidents; the disasters involving railways and gas
pipelines. Are not all these the consequences of a
policy pursued for decades?

Then, Gorbachev accepted some of the blame for the
difficulties in which they found themselves:

There are many things we could have foreseen
and there are negatives processes, above all, in the
economic and social spheres, in inter-ethnic
relations, in the sphere of culture and ideology,
whose development we could have prevented.

The Political Bureau does not deny its
responsibility for these errors.

Then, Gorbachev struck the note he was to continue
striking, which led the democratic elements to believe he
was waffling on a market economy:

Deep-going change is under way in Eastern
Europe. When somebody says this is the "collapse
of socialism," we counter it with the question,
"What 'socialism'?" That which had been, in point
of fact, a variation of Stalin's authoritarian
bureaucratic system that we have ourselves
discarded?

Satisfying neither the liberals nor the hard-liners, Gorbachev nevertheless retained his Party leadership by heading off a series of votes on his stewardship. "If you want to bring down the Party, to divide the Party, just continue this way," Gorbachev chided the delegates. "But think seriously about it." He also got his own way when he won a vote on the structure of the Party leadership. The delegates voted to expand the Politburo, with the Party leaders of the fifteen Soviet republics assuring Gorbachev that power in this ruling body would not be concentrated in the hands of hard-liners such as Yegor Ligachev, who opposed Gorbachev's policies.

The following day Gorbachev was returned to leadership of the Communist party. There was literally no opposition. Ligachev, leader of the conservative faction, had let it be known that he was available for higher office, but he was not nominated. At the age of sixty-nine, his career had come to an end.

Within the Party and the government, Gorbachev was being given the opportunity to lead, but his victories among the Soviet Union's political representatives seemed hollow in the light of his continuously falling popularity among the people. In the waning months of the summer and into autumn, the economy continued to lurch from crisis to crisis, out of Gorbachev's control.

The atmosphere encouraged food hoarding, which was quickly followed by shortages in government stores of all basic goods. Food and other goods were available in the "free" markets, but the prices were high. Farmers were reluctant to send their crops to government warehouses at current prices when they knew that prices would soon be higher, so if they could, they brought their goods to the free markets, asking at least fives times what the government would pay. Throughout the Soviet Union, harvesting ma-

•

chinery that had for years been patched and patched and held together with spit and string began to break down. So did the delivery system, encouraged by the sabotage of government bureaucrats who worried about their jobs if a market economy became a reality. With the predictions of a cold winter, people began hoarding whatever they could find. Shelves in all the large cities were bare.

Thwarted by the Parliament in his attempt to raise prices to reasonable levels, Gorbachev appealed to the people to help bring in the harvest. He called on students and pensioners throughout the country to go to the farms and lend a hand to bring in what promised to be a record potato crop. A population now accustomed to daily crises could not be stirred to help. Finally, Gorbachev had to use soldiers and army vehicles to help bring in the harvest, but still potatoes rotted in the fields (or in government storehouses), and some farmers destroyed crops and animals rather than deliver them to the government.

Gorbachev was subjected to scathing criticism from Boris Yeltsin and others in the liberal wing of government when he reneged on the agreement to institute the Shatalin Plan for a five-hundred-day conversion to a market economy.

Conceding a crisis, Gorbachev promised in mid-November 1990 to a shake-up of the government and military in an attempt to get things moving out of a paralyzed political and economic situation. He refused, however, to consider sharing power in a coalition government with dissident groups. He had, since the Party congress in July, been setting up Soviet prime minister Nikolai Ryzhkov as the fall guy for the government's inability to deal with economic pressures. Now, Gorbachev announced a new emergency structure of the government, which eliminated Ryzhkov's

•

post and reduced the prime minister's cabinet to a "working apparatus of the new leadership."

The new structure was made up of the Federation Council (the leaders of the fifteen Soviet republics); a Security Council (which reported to the president and oversaw the army, the police and the KGB); and the president and his representatives. While the shake-up was intended to make the leadership more responsive to the people, the president had moved away from his liberal advisors and toward the more conservative elements in the government. When the time came to name a vice-president who would succeed him if he became incapacitated or were impeached, Gorbachev selected Gennady Yanayev (who would later betray him), a Party hack from the conservative wing. The outcry from liberals was loud and immediate. The new vice-president was likened among intellectual Muscovites to Dan Quayle, and the selection called "cynical."

The major shake-up came when Foreign Minister Eduard Shevardnadze, a Gorbachev friend from their early days toiling in the Party boondocks, resigned. It was high drama when Shevardnadze came before the Parliament and dropped his bombshell because, he said, he saw the government moving toward dictatorship. Gorbachev seemed genuinely stunned and betrayed, but Mikhail Gorbachev is known as a good natural actor.

As the new year came, life settled into daily political turmoil, the economic crisis still uneased and pressure on the government still strong from the runaway republics.

Although embattled on all sides, Gorbachev found time for some humor during parliamentary sessions. Speaking to reporters in the Kremlin lobby, Gorbachev told a joke about himself:

"They say that Mitterrand has one hundred lovers. One has AIDS, but he doesn't know which one," he said. "Bush

•

has one hundred bodyguards. One is a terrorist, but he doesn't know which one.

"Gorbachev has one hundred economic advisors. One is smart, but he doesn't know which one."

A few weeks later, there was shooting in Vilnius. Gorbachev retreated somewhat from the violence, but absolutely refused to hear of independence for the Baltic states or any other of the Soviet Union's unhappy republics.

When Gorbachev first took office, he knew that there were difficult times ahead, but nowhere on his agenda was there any policy to deal with growing nationalism in the republics. He had not even considered it a problem. Being attacked from all sides, the Soviet president brought his case to the people via television and waited for the event that would mark his first year in office—a national referendum on March 17, 1991.

On any election day in polling places throughout the former Soviet Union, there was always food available at low prices—sandwiches, tea, coffee and fruit. This increased the turnout and put the citizens in a proper frame of mind for voting for Party candidates and issues.

That voters in the USSR supported the Union (not, however, in the Baltic states) could have been no surprise to Gorbachev. But even he realized it was no ringing endorsement of his presidency.

On March 28, Gorbachev overreacted to a proposed Yeltsin rally in Moscow, bringing fifty thousand troops into the capital from outlying areas. This was the furthest swing to the right that Gorbachev would make. As if he thought he had gone too far, Gorbachev began to distance himself from those conservatives he had been courting and move toward a more liberal stance.

The agreement reached between Gorbachev, Boris Yeltsin and leaders of eight other Soviet republics at a dacha

•

just outside Moscow in late April 1991 showed a Gorbachev more in line with his past liberal policies. While Gorbachev had shown little interest in sharing power, he began to move his presidency in that direction. But it was too late.

CHAPTER TEN

•

THE EMPIRE CRUMBLES

•

WHEN Mikhail Gorbachev returned from the Crimea after the attempted coup fell apart, it was to a nation that had changed drastically in just three days. Gorbachev's leadership strategy had always been to co-opt the middle ground—the stand between those on the right (the Communist party hierarchy) and those on the left (the radical democrats and free marketeers). This way, he felt, he would be most in tune with the people and could control the political situation. But even before the attempted coup, Gorbachev's centrist position had become untenable. By merely standing still or making token changes, the country had spiraled faster and faster toward economic chaos.

In a soiled sweater and windbreaker at Vnukovo Airport he looked tired and shaken, a different man than the people usually saw. The only Soviet leader to continue in office after an attempted ousting, he had been betrayed by friends—and saved by a rival. While Gorbachev knew that some of his closest advisors and associates had betrayed him, what he hadn't faced was the extent to which his party and the source of his own power was involved. Gorbachev

251

seemed unaware of the growing evidence of the Party's complicity in the plot.

The next day, he was emotional at a press conference. He graphically described how he had been held and how his captors had tried to break him. And even when he knew the coup was coming apart, he feared for his life.

"The situation was critical. Those people were really people of an adventuristic frame of mind. They were risking a great deal. When they began to understand that their adventure was over, they, I think, could have been ready to do anything. So I was ready."

Gorbachev reaffirmed his faith in the Communist party. "I don't agree when you say that the Party as a whole is a reactionary force. I know hundreds of Party members, thousands of them, some are sitting here now, who are true democrats, committed to *perestroika* and to our struggle."

As Gorbachev's limousine swept him back to his office, it was clear he was unaware that the power had shifted from the Kremlin to the Parliament of Russia.

Later, Gorbachev and Yeltsin faced the assembled Russian Parliament. Gorbachev expected to be welcomed as a hero. Instead, he was there to be humiliated by his adversarial colleague. He began by speaking jokingly: "When we met, Yeltsin gave me a brief summary of my ministers' reaction to the coup, but I haven't read it yet."

Yeltsin, glowering, pointed his finger at Gorbachev: "Read it, read it out loud," he demanded. The audience applauded wildly. "They are the minutes of the Soviet cabinet session on the 19th, a meeting held when the Supreme Soviet faced armed attack."

He concluded his attack with, "Allow me to sign a decree, halting the activity of the Russian Communist party."

Yeltsin explained his behavior, saying, "Gorbachev cannot escape blame for the coup. Who chose those people? He did. He confirmed them. He was betrayed by the people closest to him."

Gorbachev loyalists defended him against Yeltsin's accusations. "They say democracy," said Gorbachev aid Chernyayev, "but President Gorbachev, he did his part, too. He was under pressure, but he never gave in. They [Yeltsin and the Russians] were all together. He was a prisoner on his own. They showed no understanding, either political or human."

Gorbachev pleaded with the Russian deputies to "be democratic. Show tolerance in everything. You must be democrats to the end. Only then will the people be with you."

It became apparent that the coup could not be dismissed as the plotting of just a few hard-liners. The fingerprints of the Communist party were everywhere. Soon after the coup folded, Moscow Party boss Yuri Prokofiev was one of the Party leaders accused of being involved in plotting the coup. He had been in the room when the Tass director had been given the documents announcing the coup. Now he returned to his office in the custody of a prosecutor. Prokofiev was defensive, and not just about his own role: he tried to portray the Party as victim. He was questioned about his involvement in plotting the coup, since from his very office the orders announcing the coup were issued to the head of Tass. He denied his involvement and claimed the coup was a "political farce" designed to destroy the Party.

Apparently frail, Anatoly Lukyanov was among the first questioned at an inquiry by Soviet members of Parliament. Gorbachev's former prime minister, Valentin Pavlov, fulfilled his last duties in the public prosecutor's office. He signed a series of arrest warrants, including his own.

Former KGB chief Vladimir Kryuchkov, a key figure in

•

the plot, said he had no regrets. Another key figure, Defense Minister Dimitri Yazov, said, "I am very sorry for everything that has happened. This is a disgrace for the armed forces. I am the person responsible for the armed forces and I take full responsibility."

At Communist party headquarters in Moscow, popular anger now turned on the whole of the institution that had ruled not just the Soviet empire but every aspect of everyday life. In St. Petersburg, too, the Communist party was seen as the force behind the coup.

The offices of the Party, now barred, were testimony to the low esteem in which people held communism. Inside the Central Committee building in Moscow was the office of the Party Secretariat. In their time, general secretaries like Gorbachev and Brezhnev presided over the Party organization from this room. During the coup, the Secretariat had been an active conspirator.

Across the Soviet Union, Party offices were raided and documents seized. In the sealed rooms of the Party offices across the Soviet Union, documents were missing or had been destroyed. Many were apparently shredded in last-minute panic as the coup crumbled. But many were discovered, including those sent from the Secretariat in Moscow. They proved to be the Party's undoing.

In the communications room in the Central Committee building in Kiev, investigators found evidence that the Central Committee in Moscow, from the very start of the coup, if not before, were sending out instructions using encoding equipment. These messages gave detailed guidance to local Party officials and factory managers on how they might support the emergency committee.

The privileges that went with Party membership were abruptly withdrawn. Powers that had swept officials past the bus queues now had to be handed back. Already weak-

•

ened, Gorbachev had been slow to distance himself from the Communist party, and its increasing complicity in the coup made his eventual demise inevitable.

Six days after the coup, Gorbachev spent the morning discussing whether he should resign as general secretary, administering the final blow to the Party. He was talking about something that no longer existed. Alexander Yakovlev commented, "It was like trying to offer tea to the corpse and arguing about the best way to do it."

But whether it meant anything or not, for Gorbachev it was a difficult decision. "For me, that was a big personal tragedy," he said. "I was near the final lap. I put all my energy into reforming the Party. I wanted to make it truly democratic. A party close to the people, and not a party of governing elite."

At the end of week, the people turned out in thousands for the funeral of the three young men killed on the Garden Ring Road. These were the dead in the people's revolution: Dmitry Konar, twenty-three, a veteran of the Afghanistan war and a maker of furniture; Ilya Krichevsky, twenty-eight, an architect; and Vladimir Usov, thirty-seven, a businessman. There was an official and a religious service. Politicians spoke and Russian Orthodox priests incanted prayers, even though one of the three martyrs, Krichevsky, was Jewish. Grief was widespread. Even the tough men of the KGB's Alpha Group, bareheaded at the funeral, wept openly.

Boris Yeltsin led the funeral procession. He had been quick to exploit Gorbachev's vulnerability over his faith in the Party. At the funeral Gorbachev appeared haggard. And yet he momentarily recaptured center stage from Yeltsin when he lay flowers on one of the coffins. "I bow down before these young people," he said. "They gave everything, even their lives."

Later that day, Gorbachev resigned as general secretary of the Communist party and dissolved the organization that had run the Soviet state since its creation.

The idols of communism began to come down. As the power of the Party was dissolved, crowds began to pull down its icons. Throughout the Soviet Union, statues of Lenin were toppled. In Moscow, in the square named for the founder of the Soviet secret police, Feliks Dzerzhinski, his statue that overlooked the infamous Lubyanka, headquarters of the KGB, was lifted off its pedestal by a crowd and discarded along with the images of other Communist heroes in a small park nearby.

Now, the empty pedestals on which these statues stood were topped with flags of the Russian Republic and scrawled with the graffiti of anti-Communist zeal. They became the monuments to what Russians hoped would be a better, freer age.

All of Soviet society had had its needs supplied for decades by the Party. Everything was connected with the Party. There was a popular poem that a young girl had written, "Winter has gone, summer has come. Thanks be to the Party." Now, in Moscow, middle-ranking Party workers tried to adjust to life without the Party. Most lost their jobs. They signed on at the local employment office, where for the first two months, they received full salary. Until then, unemployment for a Party official was simply unthinkable. The word for "unemployed" has no authorized Soviet meaning. For people who worked for many years in the system, there was a void which goes far beyond their losing their jobs.

After the Party was dissolved, Gorbachev still hoped to preserve the Union by ratifying the Union Treaty created in the weeks before the coup but still unsigned. For a time, it seemed Gorbachev's determination to maintain a union of republics, along with their existing political institutions, had the backing of Yeltsin's Russia.

During the following days Gorbachev persuaded the Congress of People's Deputies to accept the end of the old Soviet Union and align itself with a new form of union. According to the Union Treaty, the republics would be sovereign states, free to run their own affairs. The military and national security, however, would be run by a state council, which would include Gorbachev, and the leaders of ten republics, like Boris Yeltsin and Leonid Kravchuk of the Ukraine. The economy would be managed by a committee representing all of the republics.

It would be Gorbachev's last victory. The mix of independence on the one hand, and the remnants of a union on the other, posed a whole series of new problems. Even with the best intentions, the potential for conflict between republics was considerable.

Gorbachev had a brief honeymoon with Yeltsin. However, soon it appeared that Yeltsin wanted to establish Russian control over the new union. He installed his own ministries in Gosplan, the state planning agency, even though it was a Union ministry. The other republics accused him of exceeding his powers. Yeltsin withdrew the ministers, and excused his actions on the basis of having made a quick decision under pressure. He denied that Russia had any intention of assuming control over the other republics.

Nevertheless, Yeltsin's actions fueled fear in the republics that a Communist state might be replaced by a dominant and domineering Russia. In the victory celebrations over the coup, some leaders of the republics said that they were alarmed at the evidence of Russian nationalism. They resented that Moscow took all of the credit for fighting the coup. They were also concerned that so far only Russian

•

ministers had been appointed as officials of the federal union. Why, they asked, did Yeltsin insist on the prime minister being Russian?

An indication of how difficult it might be to contain the nationalist mood had been suggested when the Union flag above the Parliament in Kiev, the Ukraine, was replaced with a Ukrainian one. There was much rejoicing when the Hammer and Sickle was lowered. However, when the Ukrainian flag was raised, the crowd that had gathered for the event could see the old Union flag still fluttering behind it, like a red shadow. The celebratory mood of the crowd turned angry. The people moved on the Parliament, some pausing only to rip up or burn their Soviet Union passports. Even though the Ukrainian president had wanted to retain the Union flag until a referendum in December, he bowed to the people. Suddenly, the Ukraine, the second largest republic, declared its independence.

Yeltsin and his advisors were genuinely shocked by the Ukraine's decision. The prospect of this resource-rich area leaving the Soviet Union appalled the Russians. The Baltic states were one thing. But the Ukraine, the breadbasket of Russia, was quite another. In response, Yeltsin proclaimed that the Ukrainians were in violation of the Union Treaty.

The Russian president issued a statement saying that with this violation, borders might have to be redrawn. The euphoria over the defeat of the coup was dispelled by the specter of a violently disintegrating union. According to Yeltsin, the existing borders were merely symbolic, since previously the republics had all been part of the same USSR. Now, he said, with separate states, new demarcations would have to be carried out. The Ukrainians called the issue of borders "Russian imperialism."

If Yeltsin's statement on borders was intended to create a sense of crisis, it succeeded. An unofficial national guard formed in Kiev, and there was no doubt whom they regarded as a potential enemy. Yeltsin, the Ukrainians said, was an opportunist: he defended democracy, but as soon as the Ukraine declared its independence, he made a territorial claim to its land.

With tension rising, Yeltsin dispatched Russian vice-president Alexander Rutskoi to Kiev. Although Rutskoi announced that an agreement had been met, it was apparent that Russia had not lifted its threat to redraw the borders. The Ukrainians claimed that the new Union Treaty guaranteed their territorial borders as they had been defined by the Soviet Union. The Russians said that if a republic broke away, with no intention of signing the new Union Treaty, then borders were up for grabs.

Yeltsin flexed his muscles: the republics could have their independence, he said, but the process must be orderly, with economic ties retained.

The Baltic states had declared independence even before the coup. Now, with Byelorussia, the Ukraine, and Russia itself headed toward a separate federation, only Kazakhstan continued to back Gorbachev's attempts to maintain the Union.

There was fighting in Georgia and elsewhere. These instabilities terrified observers from the West. Even the more peaceful transitions to independence, in the Ukraine and elsewhere, held extra bad news for Gorbachev, placing fresh question marks over the stability of the military.

As the old Soviet Union broke up, Western concerns focused on its nuclear weapons. Instead of one control, three new republics had their fingers on the button. The West trusted Gorbachev, whose policies had broken the nuclear disarmament logjam and ended the Cold War. That cordiality remained evident at Gorbachev's last appearance

•

as an elected official on the international stage, the Middle East Peace Conference in Madrid in October of 1991.

A Soviet Union still existed when I returned there in October 1991. But the situation was highly unstable. At that time, you could feel the tension—and the excitement—in the streets. Change seemed to occur daily.

Gorbachev now was part of history—his place secure there, but there was little thought he would have any place in the new government. His power base was gone. But with this came a personal affection for Gorbachev on the part of many Russians—although few wanted to see him back in power.

Yeltsin, however, was not as popular as he had been. Now, it was *his* turn to be responsible for the lack of food and other goods in the stores and the generally deteriorating economic climate. Besides, Yeltsin's popularity with the people had been built upon his unpopularity with those in power. Now that he was in power, he was not as sympathetic a figure.

"The tanks will be back in the streets of Moscow," a friend in the Russian Parliament told me, "but this time they will be protecting Yeltsin from the people."

Another politician I knew who had been a deputy in the Supreme Soviet of the USSR felt that a right-wing nationalist takeover was coming if the kind of food shortages predicted for the coming winter actually materialized.

Vladimir Zhirinovsky, a reactionary who had managed to get a respectable number of votes in the Russian presidential election, was speaking for a militant new Russian nationalism. His solution to food shortages in Moscow would be to invade Poland and take what it had.

Others were not so bloodthirsty, but were equally aggressive. And there was in the streets much nostalgia for a

•

pre-*glasnost* Soviet Union. I asked science fiction writer Eremy Parnov what he was working on. "How can I work?" he replied. "Every day the prices rise, and what I receive in royalties becomes worth less. No publisher wants to publish anything until it is known how books will be published. It's crazy."

I was staying in the same rooms where I had stayed for the past four years. The rooms were always paid for by the theater. The price had been for the past three years 60 rubles per day. Now, the price was 650 rubles per day. A lunch with friends in my hotel that had cost 80 rubles in the past, now cost 500 rubles. And this was before Yeltsin's announced major price increases. There was a feeling of things out of control.

As winter closed in, Gorbachev continued to fight a losing battle to maintain a federation of former Soviet states over which he could preside. Gorbachev and Yeltsin invited the leaders of ten republics to the Kremlin. Only seven came. Their task was to hand over power to the republics without the entire structure of Soviet society collapsing. They failed. After seven hours of deliberation, the republic leaders had buried the Soviet Union. In its place they proposed an entirely new system—a commonwealth composed of fully independent states.

As the republics lined up to join the commonwealth, which would be led by Yeltsin's Russia, Gorbachev appealed on television against the move, calling it unconstitutional and predicting chaos. After independence, the republics were likely to look to their own interests first. Farms were likely to ignore contracts drawn up under the old centralized system. Already there were serious gas shortages in Ukrainian cities. Russia, suffering a fall in production, had reduced exports, including those to the Ukraine. In reaction, the Ukraine restricted food exports, putting Ukrainian needs first. Barter was often the only way to ensure supply of raw materials. Before reforms could be implemented, Gorbachev said, there could be economic disintegration.

Despite these dire prospects, just before the end of the year, eleven of the fifteen former Soviet republics signed an agreement to end the Soviet Union. Only the Baltic states and embattled Georgia stayed outside the new commonwealth. Four days later, Mikhail Gorbachev bowed to the inevitable. On December 25, he made his last television address from the Kremlin to the former Soviet peoples, resigning as president.

"Compatriots, due to the situation which has evolved as the result of the formation of the Commonwealth of Independent States I hereby discontinue my activities at the post of president of the USSR. This society has acquired freedom. It has been freed politically and spiritually and this is the most important achievement that we have yet to fully come to grips with. And we haven't because we haven't learned to use freedom yet."

In the months since the ill-fated coup, the world has witnessed the collapse of the Soviet Union and the emergence of independent states. Ironically, Gorbachev's *perestroika* proved to be the reform program which eliminated his position in the new commonwealth. Although Gorbachev retains a solid place in history, the future of the system is unknown. With the coming of the New Year, the Soviet flag was lowered.

Gorbachev's last public appearance was at a party for foreign news correspondents. He promised he would soon be back with plans for a new career in politics. Perhaps the most telling political epitaph was written by the man who has effectively succeeded him, Boris Yeltsin. "Gorbachev," he wrote, "started by climbing a mountain whose summit is not even visible. It is somewhere up in the clouds and no one knows how the ascent will end. Will we be swept away by an avalanche? Or will this Everest be conquered?"

INDEX

•

•

•

•